It Takes More than a Network

FOAL

It Takes More than a Network

The Iraqi Insurgency and Organizational Adaptation

Chad C. Serena

Stanford Security Studies

An Imprint of Stanford University Press

Stanford, California

Stanford University Press
Stanford, California

© 2014 by the Board of Trustees of the Leland Stanford Junior University.
All rights reserved.

The views expressed here are those solely of the author and do not reflect the views or opinions of the RAND Corporation or its sponsors.

No part of this book may be reproduced or transmitted in any form or by any means, electronic or mechanical, including photocopying and recording, or in any information storage or retrieval system without the prior written permission of Stanford University Press.

Printed in the United States of America on acid-free, archival-quality paper

Library of Congress Cataloging-in-Publication Data

Serena, Chad C., author
  It takes more than a network : the Iraqi insurgency and organizational adaptation / Chad C. Serena.
        pages cm.
  Includes bibliographical references and index.
  ISBN 978-0-8047-8903-5 (cloth : alk. paper))— ISBN 978-0-8047-9045-1 (pbk : alk. paper)
  1. Insurgency—Iraq.   2. Iraq War, 2003–2011.   3. Organizational change—
Iraq.   4. Organizational effectiveness—Iraq.   5. Insurgency—Afghanistan.   6. Afghan
War, 2001–.   I. Title.

  DS79.76.S457   2014
  956.7044'3—dc23   2013043449

ISBN 978-0-8047-9046-8 (electronic)

Typeset at Stanford University Press in 10/14 Minion

Special discounts for bulk quantities of Stanford Security Studies are available to corporations, professional associations, and other organizations. For details and discount information, contact the special sales department of Stanford University Press.
Tel: (650) 736-1782, Fax: (650) 736-1784

CONTENTS

Acknowledgments

I owe a debt of gratitude to a number of friends and colleagues for their support and assistance; without their stewardship, efforts, and counsel, this book would not have been possible.

At the University of Pittsburgh, I am indebted to Phil Williams for his continued willingness to advise and assist me. I would also like to thank Dennis Gormley, Donald Goldstein, and Michael Brenner for their friendship and support.

At the RAND Corporation, I would like to thank my friend and colleague Colin Clarke for taking the time to review my work in detail, for availing his expertise, and for providing steady counsel.

At the U.S. Army War College, I would like to thank Steve Metz for his friendship and guidance. It was at his suggestion that I further developed the central thesis of this book. He was also largely responsible for putting me into contact with many of the people that I interviewed or had discussions with while researching this book.

I would especially like to acknowledge the many named and unnamed veterans of the U.S. Army who selflessly took the time to inform me with their experience and expertise. In particular, I would like to thank General (Ret.) Peter W. Chiarelli, Lieutenant General Daniel Bolger, Lieutenant General David Perkins, Major General H. R. McMaster, Colonel James Crider, and Colonel (Ret.) Peter Mansoor. These discussions helped to refine my thoughts and provided the appropriate context for my understanding of the subject of this book.

At Stanford University Press, I would like to thank Geoffrey Burn and James Holt for their editorial support and advice. I would also like to acknowledge and thank my reviewers: their comments and contributions helped to make this a better book.

Most important, I would like to thank my family for always being there to provide me with support, especially my wife, Mia. Words cannot express how much she means to me.

Acronyms and Abbreviations

AAR	After Action Review
AQI	al Qaeda in Iraq
ASU	Active Service Unit
C4ISR	Command, Control, Communications, Computers, Intelligence, Surveillance, and Reconnaissance
COMINT	Communications Intelligence
DOD	Department of Defense
ETIM	Eastern Turkestan Islamic Movement
EFP	Explosively Formed Penetrators (and Projectiles)
EW	Electronic Warfare
FATA	Federally Administered Tribal Areas
FOB	Forward Operating Base
FRE	Former Regime Elements
HiG	Hizb-i-Islami Gulbuddin
HUMINT	Human Intelligence
IEA	Islamic Emirate of Afghanistan
IED	Improvised Explosive Device
IMU	Islamic Movement of Uzbekistan
INP	Iraqi National Police
IR	Infra-red
IRGC	Islamic Revolutionary Guard Corps
ISF	Iraqi Security Forces
ISI	Inter-Services Intelligence

IT	Information Technology
JAM	Jaish al Mahdi
JIEDDO	Joint Improvised Explosive Device Defeat Organization
LeT	Lashkar-e Taiba
MDMP	Military Decision Making Process
MSC	Mujahideen Shura Council
MTT	Mobile Training Team
NCTC	National Counterterrorism Center
NGO	Non-Governmental Organization
PDF	Portable Document Format
PIRA	Provisional Irish Republican Army
ROE	Rules of Engagement
RPG	Rocket Propelled Grenade
SGC	Special Group Criminals
SIGINT	Signals Intelligence
SOP	Standing Operating Procedure
STX	Squad Training Exercise
SVBIED	Suicide Vehicle Borne Improvised Explosive Device
TNSM	Tehreek-e-Nafaz-e-Shariat-e-Mohammadi
TTP	Tehreek-e Taliban (Pakistan)
UAV	Unmanned Aerial Vehicle

It Takes More than a Network

Introduction

Between 2003 and 2008, there were no fewer than ninety named insurgent organizations in Iraq engaged in a struggle against the U.S.-led Coalition and a nascent Iraqi government.[1] Some of these groups were indigenous to Iraq while others were composed almost solely of foreign fighters. Some of these groups existed prior to the invasion, and others formed only in the post-2003 period. In this five-year timeframe, these organizations—and doubtless equally as many unnamed other groups—executed no fewer than thirteen thousand attacks across the major cities and provinces of Iraq.[2] Many of these attacks were conducted against Coalition forces but many were also conducted against the Iraqi National Police (INP), the Iraqi Army, and Iraqi businessmen, educators, store owners, politicians, and civilians.

The actual size of the Iraqi insurgency is difficult to estimate.[3] But it is safe to say that its population easily numbered in the tens of thousands and may have even approached 100,000 active members at its zenith.[4] Estimating the size of the insurgency's support network is equally challenging. A 1963 Special Operations Research Office study of insurgent and guerrilla undergrounds (consisting of supporters providing supplies, shelter, finance, logistics, and so forth) in France, Yugoslavia, Algeria, Malaya, Greece, the Philippines, and Palestine revealed that in all cases undergrounds were much larger than the supported insurgency or guerrilla movement. The undergrounds in these conflicts ranged in size from being 2–1 (Palestine) larger to 27–1 (Greece) larger than the supported group.[5] Using this range as an estimative tool, if the Iraqi insurgency had 10,000 members, it may have had, potentially, 20,000 (minimum) to 270,000 (maximum) underground supporters. If the upper range of the insurgency's membership is used, then it may have had, potentially, 200,000 (minimum) to 2.7 million (maximum) underground supporters. These are quite large numbers in a country that currently has a population of roughly 30 million.

The Iraqi insurgency was unquestionably large and complex in terms of membership and composition. Adding to its complexity was its networked structure, disposition, and operations. Insurgent organizations operated on local, provincial, or regional levels. They were linked by shared membership, associations, familial ties, tribal affiliations, religion, ideology, needs, transaction structures, and the overarching goal of ridding Iraq of the U.S.-led Coalition and the government that the Coalition helped establish. These shared interests and the compelling goal of ousting what many viewed as a hostile occupying force were the unifying factors that both compelled the insurgency and gave it a measure of coherence. Few if any insurgent organizations had the capacity to conduct operations across the whole of Iraq, and none had the ability to coordinate operations countrywide on anything other than a very temporary basis. Nonetheless, the insurgency engulfed the Iraqi state: not as a structured whole but instead as a loose and shifting mosaic of small- and medium-size organizations sharing a mutual and broader interest. This phenomenon, although not sui generis or entirely new, had not been seen on this scale in previous insurgencies.

By late 2006 and early 2007, the insurgency had reached the peak of its activity. It had participating organizations in every Iraqi province. Foreign fighters traveled from the Greater Middle East, Asia, Europe, and Africa to fill its ranks. The Iraqi government had just been stood up, and the INP and Iraqi Army were fledgling organizations. Casualties crested for Iraqi civilians and for Coalition forces during this period. Opinions of the Iraq War were at their nadir internationally, and debate regarding the withdrawal of U.S. and Coalition forces had climaxed. Chaos and uncertainty reigned.

But within sixteen months the situation in Iraq nearly reversed itself. Granted, Iraq did not transform into a utopia, and as of this writing it still experiences persistent yet low levels of violence punctuated by the occasional mass casualty attack. Many of the indigenous organizations that composed the insurgency still survive but in alternative and less violent forms. Or, as is likely the case for a number of foreign individuals and groups, they have migrated to other conflict areas such as Afghanistan, Africa, or, more recently, Syria. Regardless, the Iraqi insurgency, as it had existed between 2003 through 2007, is no longer functional.

Partly, the insurgency's failure was the result of the successful, albeit slow developing and persistent, adaptations of Coalition forces in general and of the U.S. Army in particular. Credit for the ultimate dissolution of the Iraqi insurgency cannot be taken away from those who fought valiantly for the success of the new Iraqi state. I cannot and will not make that argument. But the actions and adaptations of Coalition forces tell only one side of the story of the insurgency's demise. Neither Coalition forces nor the insurgency operated in isolation. The insurgency too adapted. Initially its adaptations were successful and left Coalition forces reeling. But as the conflict wore on the insurgency's adaptations, indeed its capacity to adapt withered. Correspondingly, its ability to achieve its goals faded, and the insurgency dissolved. This book offers an explanation of why this happened.

THESIS AND RATIONALE FOR THE BOOK

An enormous, complex, networked insurgency, like the one in Iraq,[6] should have been highly adaptive. Indeed, for about three years, the Iraqi insurgency was quite adaptive. It routinely and successfully made organizational changes to further or achieve organizational goals. This was to be expected given the insurgency's complex composition and networked disposition: each of these characteristics individually and compounded endowed the insurgency with vast strengths. Its composition provided a range of differently skilled and experienced planners and operators. Its size provided mass, breadth, and durability. Perhaps most important, its structure helped fulfill its need for covertness,[7] yet enabled its symbiotic sharing of resources, knowledge, and personnel even or especially in chaotic milieus. Networks are oftentimes credited with a structural ability to learn and modify their behavior quickly, even in rapidly changing environments. They use this ability to adapt and to inculcate lessons and innovations into organizational processes and procedures to effect goal-directed or goal-oriented organizational change. In contradistinction to more formal or hierarchical organizational forms, networks usually maintain few durable structures that contribute to inertial organizational forces. They can and do change frequently upon receiving various and variable environmental stimuli. Insurgent networks are recognized as having advantages of organizational flexibility, adaptability, and creativity,[8] when compared with other possible organizational forms.

However, networks, particularly covert networks, also suffer from disadvantages. The same organizational structure that facilitates adaptation and flexibility is also less robust for other organizational practices and needs. Covert networks lack the organizational and analytical girth that accompanies more formal and open or hierarchical organizations. Data collection and analytical elements are not explicitly designated in this type of organization because of a need to maintain secrecy, a dearth of appropriate personnel, skills, or resources, or because of the structure of a network. Thus networks have difficulty comprehensively estimating environmental changes and assessing the effects of these changes on the network and on organizational effectiveness. Although covert networks are sensitive to changes in their environments because of inherent survival instincts and a correspondingly heightened sense of awareness, they do not maintain the structural capacity for significant analysis, the rigorous testing of competing hypotheses, or for comprehensively controlling their adaptive processes in concert with organizational goals. This is even more problematic for large, multinodal networked organizations separated by geographical distances and in competition with a large, trained, and heavily resourced opponent. A capacity for adapting rapidly does not imply a capacity for adapting correctly: an adaptation made might not have been the best available out of a range of possible options in support of organizational goals. Only if the changes made enhanced the organization's effectiveness in accomplishing its mission or achieving its goals were they of any value. Adaptation for the sake of adaptation, even or especially if only for organizational survival, is not necessarily impressive or significant in and of itself.

Unquestionably, the insurgency's success and its commensurate ability to adapt were abetted by its complex composition, networked disposition, and covert nature. But I argue that the insurgency was a failure in the long term because of these same organizational characteristics. *The thesis of this book is that the Iraqi insurgency failed to achieve longer-term organizational goals because many of its organizational strengths were also its organizational weaknesses: these characteristics abetted and then corrupted the insurgency's ability to adapt.* Its composition, disposition, and covert nature possessed it of many needed attributes but also limited its effectiveness and made the organization unwieldy and incapable of centralizing and decentralizing planning and operations effectively in support of its objectives. As the title of this book indicates, the Iraqi insurgency needed to be more than a network to adapt effectively for the achievement of its organizational goals.

I set out in this book to detail and explain how and why this was the case. I first examine the Iraqi insurgency's organizational adaptation between 2003 and late 2008. I then compare the findings of this examination with a similar exploration of the Afghan insurgency's organizational adaptation between 2001 and 2012. I compare the findings of the former against those of the latter to reveal important similarities and differences between two cases of diverse and complex covert networked insurgencies.[9]

This book provides a detailed examination of how the Iraqi insurgency adapted over time and sheds clues regarding the adaptive strengths and limitations of the diverse and complex covert network form in a competitive conflict environment. A comprehension of how the Iraqi insurgency—and comparatively, the Afghan insurgency—adapted provides a foundation for understanding the behavior of similar organizations operating in competitive conflict environments. Because insurgencies of this type are not going away and indeed may become more likely in the future, understanding how they adapt and the effects of their organizational composition and structure on the process of adaptation will not only aid in the appropriate application of resources in their defeat but may possibly help to limit their growth in the first place.[10]

METHODOLOGY AND ANALYTIC FRAMEWORK

I provide an exploratory and revelatory yet detailed case study examination of the Iraqi insurgency's organizational adaptation between the early-2003 and late-2008 period.[11] I treat the Iraqi insurgency as an instrumental case, one that reveals the adaptive strengths and weaknesses of a complex, covert, and networked organization operating in a conflict environment.[12] Although all organizations differ in terms of composition, disposition, goals, capabilities, and so forth, the Iraqi insurgency case is not so distinct from other insurgencies or indeed, the organization was not so different from other comparable groups as not to offer valuable insight into the characteristics and patterns of behavior of complex, covert, networked organizations in general.[13] Describing and explaining the interrelationship between these characteristics and patterns helps to explain and possibly even predict how similar organizations in similar operational environments will adapt.[14]

I conduct this analysis within a framework designed to describe the interrelated elements of organizational adaptation.[15] Using this framework allows for the examination of a range of factors within a single case and within the context of an overall process. Specifically, I examine how the insurgency adapted its organizational inputs, outputs, and learning cyclically and over time to achieve organizational goals.[16] Organizational adaptation refers to a complex and cyclical goal-oriented process of learning and change. To be adaptive, "an organization must take an action to support a particular organizational goal or mission, assess the performance of this action, and then adjust organizational inputs and outputs to better match the goals or mission of the organization based on this prior assessment."[17] Organizational inputs consist of but are not limited to: organizational context; group design and culture; materiel and technical resources; and external assistance. Organizational context consists of goals, rewards, information, training, and constraints. Group design and culture consists of composition, norms, and tasks. Materiel and technical resources consist of equipment, funds, and intelligence. External assistance consists of consulting, direct action, and cooperation. Organizational outputs consist of critical group processes: the application of skills and knowledge; task performance competency; and command, control, and communications. Organizational learning consists of knowledge collection, transfer, and integration. The process of adaptation is the cyclical modification of each of these preceding elements.

In the conduct of this analysis, I drew upon a range of sources produced during or immediately following the 2003–8 period of the insurgency that includes but is not limited to: theoretical and practical studies of networks and network behavior and the process of organizational adaptation; translated insurgent texts, doctrine, and interviews; periodical and newspaper reports on insurgent organizations and their evolution; scholarly studies of insurgent behavior and in particular their behavior in the Iraq conflict; and datasets describing instances and patterns of insurgent attacks across the major cities of the seven most violent provinces in Iraq.[18] I contextualize and help characterize this information with interviews of veterans of Operation Iraqi Freedom, many of whom deployed on multiple occasions to different provinces and cities in Iraq (and in Afghanistan). These semistructured interviews, conducted in 2008, provide a competitor's perspective on how the insurgency adapted over time.[19]

INTRODUCTION TO THE CHAPTERS

Chapter 1 provides the foundation for the analysis conducted in Chapters 2 and 3. First, it discusses the diverse and complex nature of the Iraqi insurgency. Second, it defines and describes the behavior of networks in general and of covert networks in particular. Third, it examines the structural strengths and weaknesses of covert networked organizations and discusses how these strengths and weaknesses affect and are affected by organizational adaptation.

Last, it provides a detailed rationale and framework for the analysis of the Iraqi insurgency's organizational adaptation conducted in Chapters 2 and 3.

Chapters 2 and 3 present and describe the Iraqi insurgency's adaptation from an organizational perspective. Chapter 2 focuses on organizational inputs, and Chapter 3 focuses on organizational outputs and learning. Each of these chapters details the insurgency's adaptive changes and the intertwined effects of these changes on the organization's ability to achieve its goals in the 2003 to 2008 period. These adaptations are summarized and assessed based on the network characteristics presented in Chapter 1 and are then used for comparative purposes in Chapter 4. Chapter 4 evaluates the Afghan insurgency using the same framework and similar resources employed in Chapters 2 and 3. The findings from this chapter are used to conduct a comparative analysis of insurgent organizational adaptation in Iraq and Afghanistan. Chapter 5 concludes the book. It provides a more detailed summary of my main argument and presents a number of implications for policy-makers and scholars. Chapter 5 concludes with recommendations for future study.

1 The Nature of the Iraqi Insurgency, Networks, and Organizational Adaptation

INTRODUCTION

The Iraqi insurgency's organizational adaptation was in many ways unique. Its distinctness stemmed from a number of characteristics including its size and diversity, the breadth and scope of its operations, and its organization. The insurgency was unquestionably complex, and its complexity, over time, both strengthened and weakened its capacity to adapt as an organization. Two fundamental factors affected the insurgency's capacity for organizational adaptation: its diverse composition and its disposition as a covert networked organization.

This chapter examines these factors and lays the foundation for the more detailed empirical analysis of organizational adaptation conducted in Chapters 2, 3, and 4. It first assesses the insurgency's composition. Then it examines the nature of covert networked organizations, or networks, and deduces the strengths and weaknesses of this organizational form. This chapter concludes by providing the framework used for the assessment of the insurgency's organizational adaptation conducted in subsequent chapters.

THE COMPOSITION OF THE IRAQI INSURGENCY

Organizations cannot be generically constructed. How an organization constructs itself is of paramount importance to its intermediate and long-term potential for success or failure in the achievement of organizational goals. This holds true for licit organizations such as industries, the military, or social and political groups as well as for illicit organizations such as criminal groups, terrorist organizations, or insurgencies. If an organization improperly arranges itself in light of its goals or its mission, it is likely to be both inefficient and ineffective and will eventually wither or fail to remain an ongoing concern. This is particularly true for insurgencies:[1] because of their size—they are typically larger than most other illicit organizations—and because of their need for varying levels of covertness—they cannot operate nearly as openly as licit organizations—they are particularly sensitive to the effects of organizational form and structure on their chances of survival and goal achievement.

Insurgent organizations configure themselves based on a number of factors including goals, sources of support, and the degree of member commitment to the goals of the organization.[2] Accordingly, their organizational complexion will be diverse and their forms will vary. But all successful insurgencies share a need for certain organizational qualities and skills: they must be flexible, and they must have the capacity to develop and merge assorted political and military capabilities in different combinations at different times, depending on specific organizational goals. In some cases, this necessitates maintaining both open and closed organizational structures.[3]

An organization's structure is closely correlated with its ability to adapt in different operational environments and against a range of competitors. Insurgent organizations tend to and must be adaptive across levels of warfare in order to achieve their goals:[4] adaptive speed is essential, and their structure must reflect this fact.[5] Rigidity in form and function is thus a recipe for disaster; but so too are excessive flexibility and structural plasticity. Because competitive environments change quickly and organizations must contend with innumerable operational variables, no organization is ideally formed or equipped—at least not in the Platonic sense—to seamlessly adapt and accomplish its goals.[6] However, the closer the organization comes to this ideal and the faster it can adapt organizational inputs and outputs to meet organizational goals, the more likely it is to successfully accomplish tasks and meet its objectives.

For the most part, like other modern insurgencies,[7] the Iraqi insurgency consisted of a mix of organizational forms and structures. Some elements of the insurgency were at their core hierarchical (for example, al Qaeda in Iraq, or AQI), while others were very flat, even spurious networks (such as localized community associations and ephemeral groups of bandits). Many organizations took on a hybridized form: organizations that were partly hierarchical and partly networked. Hybridizing an organization was one method used to take advantage of the centralizing strengths associated with hierarchical organizations. It also afforded the organization with a capacity for networked decentralization when the need arose.[8] Hybrid groups frequently mutated organizational forms, coalesced, divided, and borrowed or shared tactics based on tactical and operational requirements.[9]

In addition to being a collection of variously formed organizations, the Iraqi insurgency was also a mosaic, including in its ranks disparate local, national, and international individuals, groups, and organizations that had sometimes overlapping and at other times competing grievances, goals, interests, and modi operandi. The Iraqi insurgency consisted of individual and organized traditionalists, mercenaries, criminals, political organizations, tribes, gangs, smugglers, foreign fighters, and varying combinations of each. Some of these groups were formally created and enduring, while others were informal and temporary constructions.

For the most part, the organizations that composed the Iraqi insurgency shared the overarching goal of opposing the U.S.-led coalition and the newly formed Iraqi government by means of the competitive use of force.[10] In many instances, this drove explicit cooperation—when organizations or groups pooled resources or conducted joint operations—as well as tacit cooperation— when organizations or groups shared practices, techniques, and procedures through open forums and publications. They also shared organizational and operational needs for covertness,[11] sanctuary, and resources:[12] needs that were just as likely to cause competition as they were to drive cooperation. Goal variation as well as disagreements over means and methods of goal accomplishment quite often disrupted coincidental or coordinated forms of cooperation.[13] This divergence was spawned or motivated by manifold factors: backlashes for atrocities committed, overboiling grudges, political machinations, disagreements over leadership and organizational direction, ideological divisions, and nationalist versus internationalist leanings and interests.

Unlike its rather structured Maoist or militaristic counterparts from the twentieth century, the Iraqi insurgency was notable for its looseness and hence the complexity of its organization.[14] Because of its complexity, both in structure and nature, it is difficult to characterize the Iraqi insurgency in either common organizational terms or by terms of task orientation, doctrine, or shared interests. It was not one group but instead a confederation of individuals and organizations that sometimes worked together and at other times at quite different purposes.[15] Notably, and unlike other previous insurgencies, it never had a unified or unifying strategy.[16] Each group or suborganization formed to achieve organizational goals and to ensure organizational survival. Being a part of the insurgency was generally a secondary formative condition, if it was considered at all. The insurgency's structure, although difficult to define, is perhaps best described as a diverse and complex covert network, one composed of manifold other and variously structured and affiliated networks.

The insurgency's complexity and diversity was one of its greatest strengths while also being one of its greatest weaknesses. It was a strength when it led to unpredictable behavior and unfettered adaptation that confounded Coalition forces. It was a weakness when it led to conflict and poor coordination in the achievement of mutually held goals. How and when the insurgency's strengths and weaknesses materialized and how they led to adaptive successes and failures can be partly understood by examining the general nature of networks and of covert networks in particular.

NETWORKED ORGANIZATIONS

Networks like the Iraqi insurgency are distinguished by their organizational forms and functions. Unlike typical hierarchical organizations, networks are inherently flexible and can rapidly adapt to change—to take advantage of opportunities or to avoid threats to the organization. But networks also suffer from organizational weaknesses: they lack structural durability, can be unwieldy, and are subject to high levels of personnel turnover. These weaknesses are magnified for covert networks which, by their nature, are limited in their form and function by persistent security needs.

What Is a Network?

The term "network" can take on many different definitions depending on the organization that is being described.[17] Generally, networks consist of interlinked individuals or groups of individuals that oftentimes develop out of a preference for social interaction with similar others.[18] They can be fairly simple or complex, large or small, and are in the main inherently adaptive systems. In a network, each individual has an effect on the whole, and vice versa.[19] Networks are enabled or formed based upon shared values, norms, and trust,[20] and along shared interests in goal accomplishment.

Network Form

Networks consist of actors or nodes that share ties linking the parts of the network along recognizable paths.[21] Network ties serve to coordinate action,[22] oftentimes based on shared goals and decision-making premised on these shared goals. Patterns of coordinated interaction—produced either through communication or goal-oriented coordination—emerge and form paths. Although members of a network usually share associational characteristics, networks do not have boundaries like normal groups,[23] and they can be complemented by linkages to individuals existing outside of the more recognizable organization.[24] Network forms and interactions can be studied and understood as a whole. Examining patterns of relational structures within and among networks is possible without direct reference to the individuals composing the network.[25]

Network Function

How and how well a network functions is partly derived from the goals or objectives that spurred the network's genesis. Directed networks are formed to accomplish specific objectives and are consciously constructed based on organizational needs. Transaction networks form spontaneously and improve the efficiency of the markets within which they operate. Each can be highly structured, convenient, or loose,[26] depending on the environment surrounding the organization and depending on the function that the network is performing (a directed objective or a transaction supporting an objective). How well the network performs or how well information, ideas, and knowledge flow throughout the network in support of the network's goals is a function of the ties within the network.[27]

Covert Networks

Covert networks include in their ranks criminal, drug-trafficking, paramilitary, and other networks that must maintain a certain level of secrecy in the conduct of their operations. They are variously described as clandestine, illicit, secret, dark, and so forth, and they form the primary structure(s) that insurgents use in nonpermissive or high-conflict environments where there are manifold external (and sometimes internal) threats to organizational security.[28] They use clandestine arts or tradecraft in order to accomplish organizational goals, and they place a premium on survivability.[29] Structurally, covert networks adopt similar forms, employ a familiar operational logic,[30] and develop core and peripheral organizational elements.[31] These kinds of organizations do not expand randomly, and yet their growth does not follow mathematical principles. But they do grow, shrink, and divide purposefully—control is maintained by the core or the center of the organization even as the organization conducts decentralized operations.[32]

By nature, covert organizations must be very cognizant of their external environments and must structure themselves accordingly. Although these organizations consciously and circumstantially adopt various network forms for organizational goal achievement,[33] they are unlike other, more normal social networks in that they do not usually form ties outside of the existing network and even work to minimize ties within the network.[34] By necessity, covert networks will maintain a capacity for garnering information, intelligence, and operational expertise from extraorganizational sources but only on an ad hoc basis, so as to avoid detection or penetration by hostile actors or forces.

Insurgencies, as covert networks, are paradoxical by nature: they must maintain a balance between their covertness (to protect their operational elements) and their need to engage in more overt social and political activities whether for governance, public relations, or recruitment purposes.[35] Without security, insurgencies are unlikely to survive.[36] But absent an ability to engage in extraorganizational activities (to obtain information, resources, and so forth), insurgencies will fail to remain effective and may also not survive. In this regard, insurgent networks are unique: their competing needs for covert and overt behaviors and capabilities pits their organizational strengths and weaknesses against each other as they function and adapt to achieve organizational goals.

Network Strengths

Networks share a number of structural characteristics that offer operational advantages when compared with traditional or hierarchical organizational forms. Networks are smaller and flatter, disperse information rapidly, alter operations quickly, and, in the case of illicit networks, can disregard legal and normative constraints.[37] Networks can change form and perform differing tasks with minimal centralized direction as long as their members share or are guided by similarly held goals.[38] They can substitute equipment and technology, alter operational practices, or move their operational loci as necessary.[39] Diverse connections can be redirected as the network takes on new responsibilities or new actors.[40] Networks can also take advantage of opportunities that are negotiated between individuals in the network.[41] These strengths allow networks to defend themselves, manage risks, learn, and ultimately improve their operational effectiveness.

Structural Defense

Structurally, networks are endowed with manifold defensive mechanisms that make them generally resistant to penetration or compromise.[42] Networks that are established based on goals, trust, or other shared and reinforcing characteristics such as ethnicity or religious beliefs tend to have inherent defensive apparatuses born of these shared loyalties. Flexibility in form allows for numerous and layered organizational defenses.

First, networks can change their composition, form, and structure while maintaining their identity and performing necessary functions.[43] This is an important form of damage control that affords networks flexibility in managing risk while retaining functionality. Similarly, in distributed networks where power, capabilities, and functions are shared, the loss of any particular leader is unlikely to lead to a "power vacuum" as it might in more hierarchical organizational forms.[44] Networks that might fall prey to "kill or capture" methods employed against them will not cease to function because of the loss of a leader.[45]

Second, core network members tend to be unwilling to defect from the group. This allows networks to separate operations and management, develop core and peripheral elements, and ensure some level of compartmentalization, a key element of maintaining organizational and operational security.[46] Peripheral elements of the network can be augmented or replaced based on shared identities or ties and can be shed or dissolved in the event that they are no longer needed or represent a threat to the network's security. Having core and peripheral elements aids in protecting the identity of the network and in the durability of the network as interdicted parts can be replaced with new members.[47]

Lastly, networks can shield their activities and restrict information flows outside of the group. If a breach occurs or if the network is interdicted, networks can take advantage of "transactive memory" and other "latent resources" to recuperate quickly from any losses experienced.[48]

Freedom of Action

Organizations that plan and conduct their operations based on experience rather than rules and procedures tend to perform better than organizations that are regulation bound or standards oriented.[49] Networks tend not to be governed by rules and regulations as much as they are guided by form, function, and purpose.[50] Accordingly, networks do not necessarily act based upon standing operating procedures (SOPs), doctrine, or bureaucratic dictates but instead operate based on experience and a flexible knowledge of what works.[51] This kind of behavioral flexibility allows networks to use available information to make decisions and respond faster and more appropriately to environmental or organizational changes than more hierarchical and rule-bound organizations.

Knowledge Transfer

Networks of all types, but in particular fully connected networks, are well structured for knowledge transfer among their organizational members.[52] This is due to how the organization is constructed—along ties that directly and indirectly connect disparate parts of the network. Both strong and weak network ties facilitate knowledge transfer: weak ties help to link various types of networks—acquaintance networks with close-knit networks, for instance[53]—and strong ties are central to the transference of tacit or experiential knowledge among network members and aid in maintaining organizational stability.[54] The organizational characteristics that make networks efficient and effective mechanisms of goal achievement also serve to abet individual and organizational knowledge transfer.

Network Weaknesses

Despite their strengths, networks also share a number of organizational weaknesses that are in large part born of their structure. Because they can change quickly, networks many times lack the consistency generated by shared experiences and organizational bonding, they learn unevenly, generate limited organizational effects, and many times fall prey to internecine competition and conflict.[55] Additionally, a network in and of itself does not by its nature improve decision-making or increase membership access to information.[56] Although, in general, network structures can facilitate learning and decision-making through information sharing, networks that have to maintain heightened levels of secrecy and covertness tend to be stunted in their capacity for improving these processes.

Organizational Turnover and Lack of Redundancy

Organizations that change too quickly or too frequently often suffer from incomplete adaptations, or they adapt to environmental changes that are only temporary in nature.[57] Because networks are oftentimes specifically designed or formed for the accomplishment of limited goals or short-term tasks, turnover is endemic. Furthermore, because of their goal or task-oriented nature, networks tend to be lean on personnel. This lack of redundancy can affect the networked organization's ability to cope effectively with losses or possible defections. And although the ability to add or remove members and change structure is a strength attributed to networked organizations, high levels of personnel turnover inevitably lead to inhibited adaptability.[58] Turnover in an organization can occur because individuals leave,[59] or, in conflict environments, because individuals are captured or killed. Compounding this problem is the fact that when organizations are created or changed, guides to behavior, such as past experience or a shared understanding of rules, are lost.[60]

Uneven and Contradictory Learning

Different networks operating in different locales, even ones with similar goals and experiences, will interpret and respond to events and changes in their operational environments differently. These different perspectives can be useful insofar as they expand collective knowledge—that is, if the organization is structured to take advantage of disparate learning. But they can also be deleterious if they lead to the learning of conflicting or contradictory lessons.[61] This is problematic, particularly in a conflict environment. First, if an organization does not have the girth or capacity for sharing and standardizing some lessons, it might have to learn lessons repeatedly—a weakness that more formal and durable competing organizations can take advantage of. Second, uneven learning leads to diminished levels of shared awareness and stunts adaptability.[62] Last, successful organizations require an ability to make rapid, however temporary, changes as they learn.[63] Learning and effective change are inseparable. It follows that if an organization cannot effectively learn or if learning is uneven among individuals and groups, the organization will be unable to change or adapt to achieve its goals efficiently, or worse, effectively.

Limited Relationships

People in organizations rely on their ability to collaborate with others to gather information and solve problems.[64] Performing this function can be difficult or problematic for organizations that must maintain a level of covertness commensurate with hazardous environmental conditions.[65] Despite a latent structural capacity for increasing the size and reach of a networked organization, covert networks have difficulty linking knowledge and capacity with need because doing so might reveal the network's existence or key elements of the organization. This problem can compound and exacerbate other networked organizational weaknesses. Organizations that meet infrequently are also less durable and equally less likely to cooperate effectively.[66] Organizational behavior can quickly become erratic and unpredictable. Organizations that do not function in predictable, regular, or repetitive ways risk becoming disorganized and uncooperative.[67]

Covert networks suffer from recruitment limitations as well. Trust is a key element in their recruitment practices. But trust-based networks have structurally limited memberships. The talent that the network can recruit is thus limited to the ties that its limited membership can create.[68] In the event that the network must pursue talent or actors outside of its base of trust, there is a chance that the network will experience friction stemming from the conflicting goals, expectations, and attitudes of new members. When developing new relationships, covert networks have to expend precious resources to maintain acceptable levels of secrecy.[69] Limited relationships are both a structural characteristic of covert networks and a symptom of its need to maintain operational confidentiality.

Limited Effect

Networks that are formed for task accomplishment or goal achievement are likely to be limited in their ability to conduct other, particularly unrelated, or more complicated tasks. Since covert networks cannot risk meeting frequently or openly, they oftentimes are unable to conduct lengthy or intensive training. This limits the complexity of the tasks they can perform. As a result, their adaptive capacity will necessarily be slowed:[70] they will be capable of performing only certain types of operations with a required level of competence. This is problematic. When external environments change and achieving organizational goals requires an assortment of skills or membership with an array of talents, smaller and more task oriented organizations become disadvantaged.[71] As hierarchical organizations can stifle change in the process of achieving organizational goals, so too can a large group of individuals that are not well coordinated or are trying to achieve goals by using unfamiliar methods and means.[72]

Potential for Competition and Conflict

All organizations suffer from internal friction. Friction and even outright conflict can result from normal organizational processes including: task overload, resource depletion, individual and group attempts to accrue power within the organization, and deliberate withholdings of information.[73] Sometimes this friction can have positive results as antagonism can lead to creativity and competition. But in martial organizations where there are likely few rules governing member behavior or in networks where members might only be interacting because of mutually held goals, competition and friction can quickly escalate into violence and other destructive behaviors.[74] This in turn can lead to decreased levels of knowledge sharing, damaged relationships, and sometimes, organizational disintegration.[75]

Although common goals and tasks can unite organizational members and organizations, maintaining organizational coherence in a large network with varying or limited command and control structures, diffused authorities, and competing interests is very challenging.[76] Some degree of conflict is thus inevitable.[77] Conflict within and among organizations is even more likely in chaotic environments where violence is endemic and levels of trust vary and ebb.

THE DUALITY OF NETWORK STRENGTHS AND WEAKNESSES: EFFECTS ON ORGANIZATIONAL ADAPTATION

All organizational forms have structural strengths and weaknesses that are similar in nature and scope to those detailed above for networked organizations. And each of these strengths and weaknesses has an effect on how an organization adapts. Centralized organizational forms are well disposed for defined organizational objectives and can conduct operations with speed and efficiency. But they also suffer from brittleness, sclerosis, and the dulling effects of task routinization.[78] Decentralized organizational forms are well suited for diffuse objectives and are more adaptive and resilient. But they suffer from unpredictability and are difficult to control.[79] Whether an organizational characteristic presents as a strength or weakness depends on various internal and external factors: what is the organization trying to accomplish and how is it structured?; how are competitors structured and for what ends?; what are the prevailing environmental conditions and what is their effect on the organization as it tries to achieve its goals?

Organizational strengths and weaknesses can sometimes be two sides of the same coin.[80] This is particularly true for networked organizations, especially covert networked organizations, which are peculiarly sensitive to internal and external turbulence and whose strengths can quickly become weaknesses depending on the interaction between organizational structure, goals, and environmental change. The following networked organizational characteristics can dually be strengths or weaknesses, and each has an effect, albeit at different times and under different circumstances, on organizational adaptation.

Flexibility

The ability to change form and function is useful for responding to external conditions and when adjusting organizational inputs and outputs for goal achievement. But flexibility can also be a detriment if the organization makes inappropriate adaptations or changes its structure too frequently and thus disallows developmental economies to grow out of tacit knowledge and transactive memories.

Size

Having a small organization can contribute to adaptive speed and an enhanced ability to maintain covertness. A smaller organization, depending on the nature of its formation, is also likely to be more coherent and can maintain unity better than a larger or more populous organization. But a smaller organization is also likely to have limited reach, scope, effect, and durability (particularly if repeatedly interdicted). It will also be restricted in its capacity for expansion, because of limited membership, and it will have difficulty transforming in order to achieve increasingly complex goals.

Covertness

Covert networks can take advantage of structural defenses (see above) and do not have to follow rules that generally apply to other, more overt, organizations. But covert organizations must spend resources on maintaining secrecy, have difficulty interacting with other organizations, and have trouble marshaling resources in the event that what is readily available to the organization is insufficient for achieving organizational goals.

Information and Intelligence Gathering

A network that is operating with the support of a strong underground or that has the tacit support of a population can quickly and ably receive raw or processed information and intelligence from multiple perspectives and from across wide geographical swaths, with little risk of detection. Information and intelligence made available this way allows networks to commit resources elsewhere and reduces the assumptions they have to make regarding their environment. But if the organization loses favor with its base of support, it will also lose its eyes and ears and will quickly become much less effective. Additionally, if members of the supporting groups defect, the risk of interdiction will increase dramatically.

Information and Intelligence Transfer

Networks are well disposed to sharing information because they are many times unencumbered by formal rules or restrictions. They are equally well endowed with a capacity for transferring information on an as-needed basis absent bureaucratic controls. But because they typically lack a bureaucracy or institutionalized support, networks are devoid of the higher-order research and evaluation processes that many times exist in larger and more formal organizations. Additionally, networks that operate in hostile environments usually must maintain some level of secrecy; and, as J. Bowyer Bell argues, operating in a hostile environment impedes communications and coordination.[81] This presents a challenge. It is possible and indeed likely that lessons learned in one place and time are not easily transferred to other places and times—lessons learned can be incorrect, or they might not be interpreted correctly for application in different environments or circumstances. There also exists the possibility of the effects of a "telephone game" where information or content is distorted through attenuation as it passes through multiple actors or nodes in a network.

Diversity

Networked organizations are structured for goal accomplishment. The network's capacity to accomplish its goals is manifested in the skills and attributes of its members. A network must therefore be diverse enough to encompass all necessitated skills, or it must be capable of expanding as necessary. Diversity can be both a strength and a weakness. If a network is very diverse, it can accomplish many tasks and can tolerate a greater number of personnel losses. But it is also likely to be unpredictable and prone to conflict and interdiction. If a network is less diverse it will be less prone to interdiction and conflict, but it will also be less capable of carrying out changing or complex tasks. And if it is interdicted, it is less likely to survive.

An organization's structure and form must be suited to achieving organizational goals over time: it must take advantage of its strengths while minimizing its weaknesses in the face of competitors and under the duress of environmental change. Inherently, an organization must thus be able to adapt in order to be successful. Adaptation can be accelerated, slowed, improved, or worsened depending on how an organization is structured and depending on how this structure abets or inhibits an organization's effectiveness in achieving its goals. While diverse networked organizations have many strengths in this regard, they also share many weaknesses.

Defining and then describing how an organization adapts over time reveals clues as to how effective a chosen organizational form is for achieving its goals. Furthermore, it also helps determine the utility of the organization's structure as it relates to goal achievement. The following section presents a framework for assessing organizational adaptation.

A FRAMEWORK FOR ASSESSING ORGANIZATIONAL ADAPTATION[82]

Organizational adaptation is a complex and cyclical goal-oriented process of "learning and change."[83] To be adaptive, "an organization must take an action to support a particular organizational goal or mission, assess the performance of this action, and then adjust organizational inputs and outputs to better match the goals or mission of the organization based on this prior assessment."[84] Organizational inputs, outputs, learning, and adaptation form the cycle of the adaptive process. Organizational inputs consist of but are not limited to: organizational context (goals and rewards, information, training, and constraints); group design and culture (composition, norms, tasks); materiel and technical resources (equipment, funds, intelligence); and external assistance (consulting, direct action, cooperation). Organizational inputs feed organizational outputs, which consist of but are not limited to: critical group processes (application of skills and knowledge; task performance competency; command, control, and communications; and cognition and behavior). Organizational learning consists of but is not limited to knowledge collection, transfer, and integration. The final step in this cycle is adaptation—or the adjustments made by an organization to each of the preceding steps to achieve its goals or accomplish its missions and objectives.

Organizations, particularly those involved in martial competition or existing in chaotic and rapidly changing environments, must be able to adapt in order to remain a going concern or to achieve organizational goals. Organizations that are flexible, resilient, and willing to integrate new information and skills are a better fit for these types of environments than are hidebound or more rigidly structured groups. Responding to environmental changes requires that organizations contend with their competitors and be capable of matching organizational inputs and outputs with organizational goals.[85]

A capacity for adaptation—the ability to adjust organizational inputs and outputs to accomplish organizational goals—is partly a function of organizational design,[86] and partly a function of effectively incorporating information concerning the organization and its environment.[87] Smaller groups that are well connected can adapt quickly but might lack the organizational girth to accomplish large, multiple, or complicated tasks.[88] When small groups change membership frequently or make or suffer from compositional changes, they will steadily lose the ability to coordinate their activities and organizational processes.[89] Large organizations possess staying power and organizational depth but generally require substantial coordination for goal achievement and tend to adapt slowly, particularly in disorderly environments.[90] Both large and small organizations can benefit from member diversity, but both might also suffer from greater instances of interpersonal conflict.[91]

Effectively incorporating information, lessons, and innovations is requisite to an organizational adaptation cycle that is in synch with environmental changes. Environmental awareness is essential to understanding how environmental changes affect organizational goals, both positively and negatively. It is also linked to increasing operational effectiveness and to the development of organizational strategies.[92] Absent mechanisms for collecting, transferring, and integrating knowledge, such as SOPs or institutional databases, organizations might be incapable of learning the lessons born of experience, particularly if the organization suffers from high rates of personnel turnover.[93] When conducting missions under uncertain conditions, organizations that cannot process information quickly or lack information dissemination capabilities will suffer from decreased task performance capability.[94] More complex or interdependent tasks require greater levels of information processing or heightened preplanning. Without one or the other, organizations will have difficulty managing task completion or goal accomplishment. This can be problematic for smaller organizations that either lack resources or are neither capable of nor endowed for complex mission planning or conduct.

Organizational Inputs: Context—Goals and Rewards, Information, Training, and Constraints

Organizations are typically formed to achieve goals either in the short term—a singular or particular goal that is usually synonymous with the organization's mission—or in the long term—a series of goals that might change over time but are consistent with and contribute to the organization's mission. In the absence of a common set of organizational principles, standardized training, or commonly understood and accepted rules or constraints on behavior—all of which are likely conditions facing complex organizations formed and acting in conflict environments—goals serve as guides to organizational and individual task performance. Formal and informal reward systems aid in goal achievement by remunerating or punishing behaviors contributing to or detracting from goal achievement, respectively.[95] Clearly articulated goals help to maintain organizational discipline, contribute to the synchronization of disparate organizational activities, and generally abet coherent organizational behavior.[96] Sharing information throughout the organization, particularly in clandestine organizations where overt communications might not be practicable—who is doing/did what, where and when the activity is occurring or did occur, and how effective the activity will be/was in relation to achieving organizational goals—is requisite to the self-tailoring of individual and group behavior toward goal accomplishment.[97] In networked organizations, information flows both shape and are shaped by transactions among organizational members.[98] If information flows decrease for any reason, uncertainty—about the environment and the organization—will increase, organizational structures will likely break down, and the capacity for self-synchronization, the sine qua non of complex networked organizations, will diminish.

Organizational Inputs: Group Design and Culture— Composition, Norms, and Tasks

Composition refers to the individuals and their relationships within an organization. Norms refer to standardized or patterned behaviors that have an influence on how organizations perceive and conduct tasks. Culture is an accepted set of enduring organizational and behavioral traits that includes attitudes, values, and beliefs.[99] An organizational culture develops over time and is reflective of those attitudes, values, and beliefs commonly held by the organization's members. In this respect, culture acts as a modifier of organizational behavior insofar as it shapes, impedes, or accelerates certain group or individual activities and tasks.[100] Organizations whose membership and composition change rapidly or have only been in existence for short periods will accordingly have lower levels of culture and therefore fewer norms guiding their behavior and fewer restraints on how they conduct tasks.[101]

Matching elements of organizational design and culture to organizational goals through adaptation is necessary to ensuring goal accomplishment. Although networked organizations have an inherent capacity for organizational adaptation, their general lack of formalized structure and dearth of common culture can contribute to an inability to adapt effectively, particularly over long periods, toward organizational goals. Exceedingly complex and heterogeneous networks are likely to have incongruously designed organizational subgroups, varying normative boundaries on behavior, wildly differing cultures, and divergent capacities and competencies for task accomplishment. In some instances, where networks are fluid and information can be shared freely, this presents as a strength. But where network interaction and information sharing is circumscribed and where mobility among networks is limited, this can present as a weakness. When organizational composition, norms, and tasks are in conflict, either within organizational subgroups or among organizations, individuals and groups of individuals will have difficulty coordinating their behavior and adapting in concert to achieve organizational goals.

Organizational Inputs: Materiel and Technical Resources— Equipment, Funds, and Intelligence

The capacity to marshal resources is of critical import to organizational adaptation. Ensuring the optimal use of available resources contributes to overall organizational effectiveness. Without these resources, organizations will have difficulty planning, training, conducting tasks, improving task accomplishment, or assessing the effect of their operations.

For insurgent organizations, access to materiel and technical resources is vital to organizational success or failure,[102] and can significantly affect their ability to adapt.[103] Where available, either from a supportive population or government, materiel and technical resources not only improve an organization's ability to achieve organizational goals but also can accelerate its capacity for adaptation. Equipment can include any form of materiel of operational use (for example, vehicles, fuel, explosives, weapons, and so forth). Funds can include all forms of currency or tangible goods that can be used in trade. Intelligence is information that has been or can be analyzed in the planning, preparation, execution, and assessment of organizational missions or tasks.

Organizational Inputs: External Assistance— Consulting, Direct Action, and Cooperation

External assistance, manifesting from outside of a group or organization, helps organizations achieve goals by acting as a repository of information or as a source of additional support in the planning or conduct of a mission.[104] Consulting occurs when "an organization receives information or advice from external organizations that are either from within the organizational hierarchy, an extended network, or an external agency."[105] Direct action is tangible assistance that an organization receives in the conduct of a mission. Cooperation can include "any form of collaboration with partners from within or outside the organization."[106] Although external assistance can accelerate any organization's adaptability, it is of substantial import to networked organizations. Because of their generally smaller size and goal- or task-oriented nature, lack of formal analytical structures, and limited organizational breadth, networks can benefit greatly from peripheral support.[107]

Organizational Outputs: Critical Group Processes—Application of Skills and Knowledge; Task Performance Competency; Command, Control, and Communications; and Cognition and Behavior

Organizational outputs are critical group processes that are shaped and refined by the organizational inputs listed above. Task performance competency combines the application of organizational skills and knowledge, the use of command, control, and communications, and the harnessing of individual and group cognition and behavior in the pursuit of organizational goals. Task performance competency is "facilitated by smaller and flatter organizational structures, the ability to incorporate new information, and the ability to rapidly respond to changing circumstances."[108] An organization's capacity to apply its skills and knowledge and assess its performance is abetted by its ability to communicate during and after the conduct of missions. Insurgent groups use the Internet, visual signals, and cellular telephony, among other means of communications, to coordinate activities before, during, and after the conduct of a task.[109] To improve effectiveness,[110] organizations must take advantage of communications to command and control activities: a process of information sharing that abets self-organization.[111]

Cataloguing these critical group processes individually and collectively and providing feedback on their performance enables a better understanding of the utility of organizational inputs for output achievement and ultimately establishes a rationale for adjusting both.[112] Altering these processes in response to environmental changes or perceived organizational advantages or disadvantages is requisite to raising proficiency and competency, altering formal and informal network structures, and achieving effective organizational adaptation.[113]

Organizational Learning: Knowledge Collection, Transfer, and Integration

Organizational learning is necessary but not sufficient for organizational adaptation to occur.[114] Organizations require a baseline of knowledge—a collective and general understanding that organizational members share and apply in the conduct of their work[115]—to support goal achievement, and they must be capable of continuous adaptive learning to achieve organizational adaptation.[116] Michael Marquardt argues that adaptive learning occurs when an organization takes steps to achieve an organizational goal, analyzes the outcome in relation to the goal, and then adjusts the action based on the initial outcome.[117] Organizational learning can be assessed by judging the speed at which an organization learns (planning, implementing, and reflecting), its depth of learning (by assessing underlying assumptions and improving learning capacity), and its breadth of learning (the ability to transfer learning throughout the organization).[118] Organizational learning can also be evaluated according to its stages: cognitive; behavioral; and performance improvement.[119] The process of learning can occur formally, through instruction and training, or informally, through experience or interaction among organizational members or with other organizations involved in similar tasks or missions.[120] To learn, organizations and their members must go through a process of collecting, transferring, and integrating knowledge into the organization.

Knowledge Collection

Knowledge collection is the first step of the learning process. Conscious and dedicated efforts made for collecting and storing knowledge are directly linked to the rate at which knowledge is retained, leaves the organization, or is forgotten.[121] Knowledge must be collected on organizational inputs, outputs, and the learning process. It is vitally important that organizations collect knowledge on their external environment to ensure that adaptations made for achieving goals are tempered by conditions that may be beyond the organization's control or influence.[122]

Knowledge Transfer

Organizational learning is improved when information and knowledge—general knowledge and knowledge of organizational success and failure—is shared throughout the organization. Organizational learning can be slowed when organizations become defensive, fail to fully analyze their behaviors, or when they ignore or shun criticism.[123] Organizational knowledge transfer can be slowed when members of an organization are unaware that other members of the organization are possible sources of information or have necessary expertise.[124] Organizational learning is accelerated when organizations can quickly transfer knowledge and information. Knowledge and information transfers are improved, both in terms of speed and accuracy, when management layers are reduced and organizational members can share information more freely.[125] Organizations that have fewer managerial controls, are decentralized, and collaborate internally and externally are more likely to learn and effectively share knowledge.[126]

Equally important for knowledge transfer is an organization's ability to recognize the importance of new knowledge either as it contributes to goal achievement or as it refines or replaces old knowledge. Organizations must be willing and able to forget lessons when applicable. Retaining learned organizational practices and knowledge that is outdated or no longer fits with the external environment or internal structures should be rejected lest the organization become sclerotic and unwilling or unable to adapt.[127] This process can occur deliberately—when an organization makes efforts to incorporate new knowledge and dispenses with older practices and when organizational leaders and peers support the use of newly acquired knowledge[128]—or by happenstance, as when an organization loses membership. But if an organization unlearns too rapidly either by choice or by circumstance, it will necessarily have to relearn and update organizational knowledge repeatedly.[129] This can lead to resources being wasted and an increased inability to adapt organizational inputs and outputs appropriately.

Knowledge Integration

One challenge to knowledge integration is that certain types of knowledge cannot be transferred through instruction. While articulated or explicit knowledge can be shared among individuals and integrated into organizations, tacit knowledge cannot be easily shared if it can be shared at all.[130] How well an organization integrates knowledge is partly a function of existing knowledge and skills. If certain categories of knowledge are not easily understood and respective organizational members do not have the appropriate skill bases to relate to this knowledge, the organization may not be able to integrate either existing or new forms of information.[131] The smaller or more specialized the organization, the less likely it is going to be capable of integrating a range of new skills or knowledge.

An additional problem facing organizations trying to integrate new or even existing knowledge is that some information or skills can only be or are best integrated in person. Although videos, Internet postings, and instruction booklets may contain a trove of useful knowledge and information, the skills and mechanisms needed to apply this knowledge may not be obtainable without face-to-face interaction. In a study of various terrorist groups in Mindinao, the West Bank and Gaza Strip, and southwest Colombia, RAND researchers noted that technology and knowledge exchanges were typically conducted in person.[132] This can be problematic for groups that are trying to avoid detection, operate at a distance, or whose networked or cellular structures prevent close or frequent interaction.[133] Compounding this difficulty is the fact that organizations that are not well interconnected or do not interact frequently might integrate knowledge unevenly. This is a problem that occurs even within organizations that are well interconnected.[134]

CONCLUSION

This chapter discussed the Iraqi insurgency's composition, the nature of networked organizations, and the strengths and weaknesses associated with the networked form of organization. This assessment suggests that the Iraqi insurgency's diverse composition and its disposition as a networked organization had varying effects on its capacity for adaptation. In some instances its disposition and composition presented as strengths and enabled adaptation. In other instances they presented as weaknesses and had a deleterious effect on adaptation.

Distinguishing between these strengths and weaknesses and how each appeared in and through the Iraqi insurgency's conduct of operations and over time requires an examination of how the insurgency responded to changes in its operational environment. Specifically, this requires a detailed examination of how the Iraqi insurgency adapted, or how it adjusted organizational inputs and outputs to achieve organizational goals as its operational environment changed. Evaluating the Iraqi insurgency's organizational adaptation over time sheds clues as to the effects of its diverse composition on and the effectiveness of its networked structure for achieving organizational goals. This evaluation is conducted in detail in Chapters 2 and 3.

2 The Iraqi Insurgency—
Organizational Inputs

INTRODUCTION

In complex covert networks, organizational inputs can be highly variable and can be changed frequently in both the short and long term. Inputs can vary widely as the network adopts new members and as it makes changes to its composition. Levels of cooperation, coordination, and training can fluctuate frequently. So too can levels of access to equipment, funds, and intelligence. By design, very few organizational inputs will remain constant in a complex network as it responds to environmental changes and as it adapts to achieve its organizational goals.

In contradistinction to more enduring or formally structured and overt organizational forms, complex covert networks tend to be more sensitive to environmental fluctuations and can suffer great and even existential harm from organizational changes that do not abet the achievement of organizational goals. Although successive corrective changes can be made to compensate for errors, covert networks have few opportunities to get things wrong. The time and resources required to reflect on errors and implement corrective changes may not be available. Mistakes and failures can be costly, if not fatal.

Thus the ability to adapt rapidly can be an organizational strength: being responsive to environmental change can help an organization transform and survive. But this ability can also be an organizational weakness: the network can disrupt itself, sometimes irreparably, by changes that result in greater levels of organizational dysfunction or by adaptations that do not aid the organization in goal achievement.

This chapter examines the Iraqi insurgency's organizational inputs. Organizational inputs consist of but are not limited to: organizational context (goals and rewards, information, training, and constraints); group design and culture (composition, norms, tasks); materiel and technical resources (equipment, funds, intelligence); and external assistance (consulting, direct action, cooperation). Each of these inputs, individually and collectively, feeds and helps to shape and define the organizational outputs examined in Chapter 3.

CONTEXT

This section examines insurgent goals and rewards, information, training, and constraints.

Goals and Rewards

Depending on their role in the insurgency, each participant and suborganization had different goals and sought different rewards. Each set of goals and rewards initially fueled and later undermined the insurgency as it first waxed and later waned in power and capability. Some elements of the insurgency engaged in various anti-Coalition behaviors while later becoming involved in anti-insurgent action. Some Iraqis were involved in the insurgency and afterward in supporting the Coalition out of basic economic necessity,[1] while others joined in order to "prevent the establishment of a state dominated by Shiites and secular Kurds."[2] Some insurgent groups were criminal-commercial in nature, while others were ideologically driven. As a result of these various motivations the reward system for each group was different: nationalist pride; ideological, spiritual, and religious recompense; and money all were fundamental yet distinct motivators.

Regardless of the rewards sought, the principal unifying goal of most if not all individual insurgents and insurgent groups was driving Coalition forces from Iraq.[3] In fact, the insurgency's manifold organizations held few principal goals in common other than a desire to remove Coalition forces from Iraq. Initially, the insurgency's goals were more nihilistic and obstructionist than positive in nature—ensuring that the nascent Iraqi government could not function.[4] Generally, the Iraqi insurgency sought to create a schism between the Iraqi government and people that would eventually lead to the withdrawal of foreign forces.[5] Not until later in the conflict did some insurgent groups give any serious thought to what would happen in the aftermath of a successful insurgency. The underlying differences in goals and the strange bedfellows that the confluence and divergence of interests engendered made the insurgency magnificently complex but also contributed to its eventual loss of influence and subsequent operational collapse.

As organizational goals, creating chaos or destabilizing the government instead of creating a political road-map for alternative governance not only required little support from Iraqis but also demanded little if any real coordination among various insurgent organizations.[6] Creating chaos demands very little planning. Indeed, the less planning and coordination conducted, the more likely the appearance or manifestation of turmoil and pervasion of anarchical conditions. Lacking a positive or value-added agenda freed the insurgency to conduct activities that were anything but productive or beneficial to the future of Iraq, its governance, or its citizens.[7]

Although creating chaotic, crisis like conditions might have been an explicit or intended goal of al Qaeda, affiliated groups, and organized criminals, it likely was only a secondary or tertiary effect of other groups' operations as they tried to achieve more limited and tangible objectives. For instance, while insurgent organizations disrupted communications, services, transportation, and energy distribution at will to create chaos for the population and Coalition forces, this also set the conditions for rampant criminal activities submerged and hidden beneath waves of disorder. Coincidentally, criminal activity created even more chaos and thus multiplied the effect of the initial insurgent action. Although the insurgency worked deliberately to achieve its operational goals,[8] the effect of achieving these goals created a chaotic yet convenient environment for various ideological and criminal enterprisers and the architecture for a reward system generating power, influence, and money.

Crime rose dramatically after the 2003 invasion. As the conflict evolved into an insurgent/counterinsurgent struggle and as Iraq was brimming with chaos, the rewards accruing to criminals increased considerably. Criminals, organized and otherwise, were able to take advantage of chaotic conditions as the country began to rebuild itself and as foreign and Coalition money poured into governmental and business coffers through aid and contracts.[9] Criminals were thus capable of feeding off the insurgency even though their objectives and motivations were substantively different from those of many insurgents. By some estimates, the majority of violent attacks in Iraq were criminal in nature and were motivated by economic considerations.[10] Even if these estimates are high, criminal organizations in Iraq created substantial instability, sowed fear and loathing into the Iraqi population, and exacerbated the effect of the ideologically and politically motivated branches of the insurgency. The reward for criminal activities in Iraq was money, the settling of scores against competitors, and the expansion of an illicit market that criminals controlled through legitimate and illegitimate "commercial" activities.

Criminals, or perhaps more properly "commercial insurgents" or "profiteers,"[11] supplemented or supplanted the normal economic activity that was disrupted by the invasion and the breakdown of state security.[12] Criminal activity fused with insurgent activity as funds generated by criminals were used to finance insurgent operations. Initially, foreign and local insurgent organizations contracted for attacks on Coalition forces were paid very little. Simple assaults on Coalition convoys, sniper-style attacks on outposts, and mortar attacks received scant financial reward. But as the insurgency grew in strength and sophistication and as the insurgent network became more dangerous and complex, the remuneration for attacks increased significantly. Contracted insurgents could expect to receive between $500 and $2,000 U.S. dollars for each operation and substantially more for successfully downing helicopters or airplanes.[13] Ultimately, rampant unemployment, negative economic development, and a scarcity of hard currency helped link together criminals, insurgent organizations, and the local population, however divergent their views of the conflict.

Unlike the affected population and criminal groups, AQI and AQI-affiliated organizations had manifold goals almost exclusively regional or internationalist in character: to contextualize local conflicts as part of a broader struggle against "apostasy" and "the infidel";[14] to establish a pan-Islamic caliphate;[15] to overthrow "non-Islamic" regimes; to expel Westerners from Muslim countries;[16] to compel the withdrawal of U.S. forces from bases in the Middle East; to build a following based on action not strategy; and to bring about the complete collapse of the Iraqi state.[17] For the extreme arm of a relatively extremist al Qaeda—represented by the Abu Musab al Zarqawi network—Iraq was treated merely as a potential base for supporting al Qaeda's operations abroad. Zarqawi specifically sought to divide Sunni and Shi'a by igniting a civil war in Iraq that could be exported to the greater Middle East and eventually to the entire Muslim world.[18] Eventually, AQI's ideology and internationalist goals, which were largely inseparable and reflected an almost complete disregard for the Iraqi population and Iraqi elements of the insurgency, contributed to the disentanglement of pan-insurgent goals and an operational estrangement that precipitated the decline of the insurgency.

Cooperation among various insurgent groups was critical for realizing the insurgency's principal unifying goal: the removal of Coalition forces from Iraq. The Sunni elements of the insurgency, by far the largest component of the overall organization, were critical to achieving this goal. For their part, Sunni insurgents were principally concerned with securing a greater role for the Sunni population in the postwar Iraqi political order. This could be accomplished by either banding together with other insurgent groups to compel a withdrawal of Coalition forces—who set and enforced the conditions necessary for a Shi'a majority in the new Iraqi government—or by working with Coalition and government forces directly, thus securing more political power.

Initially, the Sunni insurgency opted to cooperate with AQI and other similarly motivated insurgent groups to force withdrawal. But by mid-2004, significant political and operational divisions emerged that splintered the insurgency between more legitimate Sunni groups that were establishing power through political channels and Sunni insurgent groups that were establishing power by fighting against Coalition forces and the Iraqi government. Both of these Sunni groups were further divided from like-minded Ba'thist, nationalist, tribal, and foreign organizations by differing agendas, modi operandi, and long-term organizational goals.

Discord among insurgent factions only deepened as foreign elements of the insurgency—particularly AQI—became ever more radical as the conflict progressed. AQI's brutality and many Iraqis' realization that it was as much an occupying force as the Coalition exacerbated the insurgent rift.[19] Recognizing an opportunity to achieve organizational political and social goals by shifting allegiances, Sunni elements of the insurgency turned on their former foreign allies. The forty or so tribal chieftains that led the Sunni rebellion against the insurgency—calling themselves the Anbar Awakening—did so for three principal reasons: monetary, material, political, and physical support from the coalition; resentment engendered by AQI's infringements upon and disruption of tribal culture; and AQI's "growing encroachment on their traditional pursuits of banditry and smuggling."[20] In 2008, nearly 100,000 Iraqis—many former insurgents—were being supported and financed by the Coalition.[21] Former Sunni insurgents took positions at police stations and labored as "loosely supervised gunmen" supporting the Awakening Councils in Sunni dominated tribal areas.[22]

Insurgent organizations' capacity for achieving organizational goals and rewards varied inversely as the insurgency's strength ebbed and flowed. Achieving goals and rewards was partly a function of organizational size and resources, but, perhaps more important, it was also a function of group identity and association.[23] These binding characteristics withered as each group began to compete for resources to achieve its goals and as each group struggled to secure rewards for its actions: the glue holding together disparate groups dissolved.

Information

Controlling the flow of information during a complex insurgency is of paramount importance. This is particularly true of organizations that operate tactically but have strategic ambitions. Information not only instructs and educates but also shapes perceptions. For networked organizations, effective information gathering and dissemination can enhance solidarity, expand the influence of the organization, advertise the organization's activities, and help improve internal organizational processes. The insurgency in Iraq effectively used information to portray itself strategically, to coordinate operations, and to influence audiences that could either inhibit or accelerate organizational goals.

Influencing and at times controlling the information environment in Iraq required the commitment of resources. Many large insurgent organizations created dedicated information offices that issued communiques and frequently developed and posted assorted website content.[24] The information that these offices generated was used to strengthen resolve among dedicated members, influence potential constituents or the public at large, and to "enhance internal cohesion and morale."[25] The insurgency also used information to challenge the Coalition's agenda and to discredit the Iraqi Security Forces (ISF).[26]

For the insurgency, the spoken word was perhaps the most important method of channeling information. The oral transference of information was, for all intents and purposes, undetectable and almost impossible for the Coalition to interdict. And it was incredibly effective for transmitting information through a population that had highly variable rates of literacy.[27] The fact that Iraq's official language is Arabic allowed indigenous insurgents and many foreign insurgent groups to communicate information in a language unfamiliar to most of the Coalition but entirely familiar to the local population.[28]

To reach broader audiences and to enhance coordination among various insurgent groups, information technology (IT) was used in low-cost and innovative ways. The insurgency was flush with technically adept individuals that established and maintained elaborate websites used for broadcasts denouncing Coalition forces. To attract support and rally allied individuals and organizations, insurgent groups distributed videos of their attacks as well as imagery of dead American service members via the Internet. The insurgency also used websites like Jihadweb and Al-Firdaws to provide recruits with detailed directions for how to enter Iraq and to build the architecture for command, control, and information sharing.[29]

Al Qaeda effectively used IT to accomplish information-dependent tasks that were previously conducted by other, slower and more cumbersome means. These activities included propaganda, recruitment, fundraising, and indoctrination, to name a few.[30] Much of the information used for spreading propaganda and demonstrating the insurgency's capabilities was gathered during tactical attacks and was broadcast for strategic purposes. Many insurgent groups had cameramen at the site of an attack to capture images or footage that was quickly uploaded onto the Internet.[31]

The insurgency's use of IT for strategic purposes did not always achieve its desired intent and many times had consequences far beyond the control of the insurgency. For instance, operational videos, plans, and guidebooks, when captured, proved a treasure trove to Coalition analysts.[32] Additionally, hostage videos and hostage beheadings broadcast to cause fear and to rally support for the insurgency among sympathetic audiences often created revulsion and horrified viewers who had little previous exposure to the insurgency's actions beyond what they read in newspapers, magazines, or on the Internet. Strategically, videos capturing the slaughter of Iraqi civilians and the beheading of foreign contractors and military personnel demonstrated the savagery of the more radical elements of the insurgency and allowed foreign politicians and military leaders to engender greater resolve by painting the entire insurgency with one large, and decidedly negative, brush. These videos created graphic images that unconstructively supplemented and informed international audiences' impressions of the insurgency.[33]

Perhaps most vexing to Coalition forces was the insurgency's ability to use low-level and ubiquitous technologies to supplement and coordinate mass social networks and information flows within the insurgency. A soldier deployed to various locations in Iraq explains: "We were in an area that was very rural and poor. They didn't have any money, food and water was scarce, and yet they had what would be the equivalent of the iPhone here. They were taking video and calling from one sheepherder to the next to let each other know that we just came by a position. I was surprised that when we found a cell phone and you looked at it, they had better video than you or I have on our phones."[34] This technique was also used within the Iraqi government. Sources were developed by infiltrators, and operators were recruited for their access to information. Once gleaned, this information would then be shared with other members of the insurgency. By utilizing low-level communications devices in combination with well-placed sources, the insurgency created feedback loops that provided critical operational information, facilitated organizational control over operations, and enabled directed clandestine and overt information gathering to be used against the Coalition or for internal purposes.

Insurgent control and/or influence over the information environment in Iraq was abetted by IT but relied mostly on unsophisticated networks consisting of personal contacts, well-placed sources, and the ability to gather and spread information at low cost. Facility with information flows and largely unfettered access to information gathering and dissemination technologies allowed the insurgency to adapt at the tactical and strategic levels rapidly and simultaneously and further enhanced the insurgency's capacity for training, conducting intelligence operations, and facilitating interorganizational cooperation.

Training

Initially, the level of training and tactical acumen within and across the insurgency varied wildly. Former Iraqi military, police, and intelligence operators and the quasi-professional elements of foreign groups were experienced and had diverse levels of combat, paramilitary, or terrorist tactics training. Many members of the general population, the tribes, and the militias had some degree of familiarity with small arms and other light weapons but little if any real training on their use in an operational sense or in coordination with other weapons and operators. According to then Major General Daniel Bolger, the insurgency was tough and adaptable, but "they are not supermen. They are generally poor shots, lack meaningful combat training, and work in atomized, ill-coordinated cells and teams."[35]

Although Iraq turned into a large experiential training ground for thousands of insurgents and terrorists, coordinated training never reached a level of standardization, even with the aid of outside agencies and state-sponsored groups that helped the insurgency to become tactically effective. But this was not all bad for the insurgency. While standardization would have enabled greater efficiency and would have enabled the streamlining or modification of organizational inputs and outputs, standardization would have also created the capacity for replication. In turn, replication would have led to predictability: a sure danger for any insurgent organization.

Instead of becoming predictable by following a standardized training and operations template, the insurgency, as it adapted to achieve tactical effectiveness, remained unpredictable. Some insurgent organizations displayed an evolved competency and were capable of mounting complex baited ambushes incorporating a wide variety of tactics and weapons in well-timed and sequenced attacks. Other insurgent organizations mounted unintentional and haphazard—and, on occasion, intentional—suicidal massed attacks on Coalition forces with disastrous results. The net effect of varying competence and tactical inefficiency within the insurgency was significant, continual, and uneven adaptation that kept the Coalition almost perpetually off balance. Unpredictability and heterogeneous capabilities were as much inadvertent strengths as they were structural weaknesses. Failure invited change as much as success summoned replication: both taught valuable lessons and both engendered confusion among Coalition forces.

Training an insurgent is not a high-cost or laborious endeavor. Technically, most insurgent attacks are fairly simple to plan for and execute, and the weapons used in an attack or operation do not require a great degree of knowledge or sophistication to employ. Insurgent attacks in Iraq, which reflected imported knowledge gleaned from planning and executing terrorist or even standardized military operations elsewhere, were crude when compared with the complex operations conducted by modern militaries. Even the feared and deadly multiform Improvised Explosive Device (IED) attack is relatively low-tech and simple to construct and employ.[36] Similarly, the suicide attack is simple to rehearse and employ and is cost effective. Because of their simplicity, suicide attacks were assigned to new recruits that had few other discernible skills to contribute to the insurgency.

Although insurgent groups were initially disorganized and had limited aims and little need for specialization, this changed in 2004 as more and more former Iraqi military personnel joined the ranks of the insurgency and provided it with training and specialized skills.[37] Instilling basic combat knowledge across the insurgency enabled individuals and organizations to be much more adaptive. Since the insurgency only rarely employed truly complex attacks combining a large number of forces and weapons systems, simple training sufficed for operational effectiveness and for instilling enough baseline knowledge to allow for group-level adaptation.[38]

To supplement higher-order attacks, insurgent organizations drew from published military manuals and successful innovations by other insurgent groups. The insurgency had access to volumes of foreign and domestic military training manuals, as well as terrorist handbooks, and actively sought lessons from other insurgent and terrorist groups—including Hezbollah and Palestinian organizations—that contributed resources to the conflict in Iraq.[39] Foreign fighters provided manuals and training expertise in the form of encyclopedic collections produced by al Qaeda, which included lessons from U.S. and British Special Forces operations around the globe and Jihadist missions in Kashmir, Bosnia, Mindanao, and Chechnya. Lessons from these manuals ranged from how to employ communications effectively to weapons procurement and employment.[40]

The insurgency also took advantage of experts and skilled trainers when possible. Training sessions were conducted by veteran members of the organization. They incorporated lessons from each member's experiences and were held when the group was able to meet.[41] To be fully effective, training requires its participants to engage in the behavior being trained.[42] Generally, this rarely occurred in areas outside of direct insurgent control and was highly circumscribed even in areas where the insurgency held sway. Large and open or even clandestine gatherings were discouraged in order to protect the operational security of the organization and the safety of its members. Thus, the most advanced and time-consuming insurgent training was developed by experienced members or state-sponsored organizations that were capable of collapsing important lessons and training procedures into a shortened but intense regimen. Expert cadres developed spontaneously or were sought out much like the Mobile Training Teams (MTTs) used by U.S. forces.

In at least one case, a state—Iran—directly, if mostly clandestinely, contributed to the training of the insurgency. Iranian-sponsored training occurred inside Iran and in areas where Iranian-backed militants were in power—chiefly in Lebanon.[43] The Iranian program illicitly moved, trained, and armed Iraqis and used Iraqi master-trainers to conduct training inside Iraq.[44] Iran used the Islamic Revolutionary Guard Corps (IRGC) and the Qods Force to train Iraqi militants within the sanctuary of Iranian borders.[45] Professional training and material support provided by Iran was exported to Iraq via a trained cadre of insurgents and in the form of infiltrated experts hidden among supportive populations.[46]

The insurgency adapted to circumstance by conducting discrete training supported by multiple hosts, suffused training with valuable lessons learned through trial and error, and by borrowing and incorporating lessons from other organizations and sources both internal and external to the conflict in Iraq. Although the insurgency was by and large incapable of conducting sustained training and exercises, it compensated for this deficiency by deliberately modifying critical organizational inputs to expand organizational competency and by generously allowing for wide-ranging experimentation. Furthermore, the insurgency purposefully manipulated its networked structure for training and learning. Networking not only benefited the insurgency's operations by allowing groups to take advantage of stealth and speed, it also benefited its training and preparation by placing a premium on learning, innovation, and information sharing.

By chance and design and through success and failure the insurgency developed and trained engagement techniques that took advantage of its networked structure and reduced many of the technological advantages enjoyed by Coalition forces.[47] The insurgency trained to conduct swarming attacks followed by the quick disengagement and dispersal of forces. Additionally, the insurgency developed, synthesized, and trained in methods for causing the most confusion and damage possible through the least detectable means. Multiple remote IED attacks against soft targets, assassinations, and suicide bombings displaying varying degrees of competence all took advantage of the strengths of the insurgency while simultaneously defeating the technological superiority of the Coalition. Training for and employing dispersed and networked attacks generated complexity, avenues for adaptation—extemporaneous and deliberate—and unpredictability.[48]

Constraints

Barriers to entry in the current international security environment are few, and the ability of illicit groups and individuals to operate across and within borders has expanded. Unlike the conventional and state-based or sanctioned threats to security that dominated the twentieth century and earlier security landscapes, contemporary adversaries are considerably more adaptive and freely capable of adjusting to changes in the operational environment.[49] Threat organizations of various forms and motivation are facilitated by a host of operational enablers; their capacity has expanded exponentially. Illicit travel, finance, and trade can be conducted without state support, and attacks can be conducted with "little regard for borders, laws, and government."[50]

Despite an expanded capacity for movement and communication and a relaxation of traditional state-based controls on organizational activity, illicit organizations, particularly networked organizations operating in a failing or failed state, still share a number of constraints on their behavior. For instance, these organizations—particularly insurgent organizations—must: remain more often than not hidden from licit organizations and forces;[51] have some sanctuary for operational planning and the housing of materiel; attract personnel—both skilled and unskilled—to conduct protracted and expanded operations; and, develop an indigenous intelligence network to supplant the absence of a robust gathering and analytical capacity common to state-based organizations.

For the Iraqi insurgency, generating and retaining active and passive support for the insurgency and its operations was of principal concern. This required developing and taking advantage of vast social networks across wide and varied constituencies both within and beyond Iraq's borders. Sanctuaries and safe havens, either cross-border or local, have the potential either to prolong an insurgency's activities indefinitely,[52] or to dry up as support shifts or wanes.[53] For example, AQI used buildings in the belts surrounding Iraqi towns as safe houses, training complexes, and weapons caches and to escape observation and interdiction.[54] Correspondingly, those providing asylum to the insurgency had to be protected from undue harm. This was progressively more difficult to accomplish as Coalition forces increasingly operated within and among the population, forcing the insurgency to commit attacks that resulted in collateral civilian damages.[55]

Attracting local support for recruitment drives was also important, since the bulk of insurgent fighters were drawn from the Iraqi population. Recruitment required taking advantage of the same social networks that enabled and shielded insurgent operations. Personal contact and familiarity were considerable and necessary recruitment facilitators.[56] Although the Internet proved invaluable for insurgent knowledge transfer and propaganda purposes, it was not a significant recruitment enabler: recruits rarely mentioned the Internet as a recruitment tool, and few had ready or reliable Internet access. Instead, many insurgents were recruited through social, religious, and familial networks inside and outside of Iraq.[57] The difficulties associated with recruiting insurgents into Iraq were compounded by bureaucratic inhibitors emplaced by AQI on the passage of insurgents through Iraq's borders.[58]

Local support was also critical for gathering information and conducting analysis fused with a thorough understanding of the operational environment. A networked insurgency, particularly one with substantial foreign elements, does not have an inherent capacity for higher-order intelligence collection and analysis and must supplement the capabilities of its operators in this endeavor. For its part, the Iraqi population acted as the eyes and ears of the insurgency and provided a level of analysis impossible to obtain without the detailed knowledge of local personalities and conditions. When support for the insurgency faded and when indigenous Iraqi organizations shifted allegiances, what remained of the insurgency lacked any meaningful capacity for supporting durable long-term initiatives or for developing a comprehensive estimate of operational conditions. Moreover, the support of the population was a zero-sum game: any loss by the insurgency—either passive or active—was necessarily a gain for Coalition forces.[59]

GROUP DESIGN AND CULTURE

This section assesses the insurgency's composition, norms, and tasks.

Composition

What made the Iraqi insurgency truly unique was its immensely diverse, decentralized hybrid-networked character. It displayed characteristics common to other illicit networks described by Phil Williams: it varied by the size, shape, membership, and purpose of its constituent organizations; it was local, global, and directed yet highly decentralized; it focused on a singular goal while orienting on many other goals; and it was pervasive and yet intangible.[60] A veteran of operations in Baghdad in 2003 and the 2006–7 timeframe concurs: "Things didn't always apply across the board…different enemy cells were doing different things…There was no standard, we pretty much had to be ready for everything."[61] And as then Brigadier General David Perkins argues in respect to the variability of the insurgency, "You don't necessarily have a homogeneous enemy and it evolves at different times and places throughout the country."[62]

Heterogeneity and decentralization ensured that insurgent organizations would not have to bend their organizations excessively to match skills with missions. Instead, they could and did cooperate with one another based on shared requirements, interests, and goals, particularly when operations called for specialized functions and capabilities. But decentralization had the effect of reinforcing a localism that manifested in the rejection of defined leadership, a dearth of cross-organizational cohesiveness and eventually, unsuccessful efforts to constructively reconcile disparate organizational goals.[63] Absent an intrinsic center of gravity, commonly accepted core, and a defined command structure, the insurgency defied comparison with its more conventional and hierarchical predecessors.[64]

At times and across differing organizations, the insurgency exhibited hierarchical traits and tendencies.[65] This was particularly true of those organizations composed of former regime elements (FREs) and those closely associated with al Qaeda. At other times, the insurgency exhibited networked traits. This applied to many tribal and localized insurgent groups. Other organizations were hybridized and shared elements of both organizational types (for example, Fedayeen Saddam).[66] The insurgency was thus a loose arrangement of peripherally connected organizations acting initially in goal-oriented concert but with varying levels of intensity and ambition. The discovery, infiltration, or disbandment of any particular organization did not have a major effect on the rest of the network.[67] No single organization within the insurgency was supreme, and none had firm or durable control over other significant parts of the network.

The insurgency's composition was initially based on one shared goal: compelling the withdrawal of Coalition forces from Iraq. Circumstance more so than design impelled organizational form, and the former was shaped by the counterterrorist and counterinsurgency operations of the insurgency's chief competitors—Coalition forces. Objectives and goals helped direct but were not determinative of organizational function or the varying levels of cooperation that emerged between and among groups and individuals. And as with any insurgency, objective environmental conditions also helped shape organizations.[68] Thus the operational behavior and nature of the insurgency was as multiform as its composition.

The insurgency's compositional heterogeneity was reflected in its organization and in the breadth of its participating groups. Most of these groups, albeit to varying degrees, were supported by or had linkages to a number of larger organizations, although neither control nor coordination was implied by this relationship or its structure. Larger organizations were subdivided into a series of brigades and other organizational forms although the relationships and command structures differed in each—if they existed at all. Depending on organizational requirements and operational necessities, some larger groups took the opportunity to plan and coordinate activities and, on occasion, cooperate with one another through organizational consolidation.[69] Guido Steinberg shows that by late 2006 there was a consolidation effort launched by various national Islamist and Jihadist camps in Iraq.[70] Also in 2006, Ansar al-Sunna and the Mujahideen Shura Council (MSC) held joint planning sessions.[71] And in November 2006, the Mujahideen Army claimed joint responsibility for an attack with Islamic State fighters.[72]

The composition of and relationships within the insurgency, even at the highest organizational levels, changed according to opportunity and need. For example, as AQI's power further waned in 2007 it formed formal organizational partnerships and alliances with several other insurgent organizations and drew still others "into its orbit."[73] Coordination of this sort represented a tacit acknowledgement that not even a centralized and well-endowed insurgent organization like AQI could dominate or control the direction of the insurgency in the face of a varied and differently ambitious membership. When necessity and objective conditions dictated, organizations would cooperate with one another to the extent that was possible and when potential benefits could be realized.

AQI, at one end of the organizational spectrum, had a very structured organization consisting of: a commanding officer, an information officer, an intelligence officer, political committee, executive officer (with a martyrdom coordinator for regional or city groups), an Islamic law committee, a finance officer, and a logistics officer.[74] AQI also maintained tightly organized tactical units but devolved control of operations to a local emir.[75] AQI supported its tactical organizations with an intricate and fairly comprehensive logistical network that was established, in part, prior to the Coalition invasion in 2003.[76] To maintain loyalty and cohesiveness throughout the organization without micromanaging and compromising atomized operations at the tactical level, AQI, like other elements and affiliates of al Qaeda, recruited, promoted, and conducted operations based on family, friendship, and nationality ties.[77] Its flat yet organized cellular structure allowed echeloning and communication without reducing operational freedom or excessively breaching operational security.

At the other end of the organizational spectrum from AQI were the organizations and individuals participating in the insurgency on an ad hoc, skill set-premised, or contractual basis. Because the bulk of insurgent activity was taken up by thousands of part-time insurgents performing functions that supported the aims of more permanent insurgent groups, their participation in the insurgency was capricious and their level of performance was erratic.

Participants in the insurgency came from near and abroad. A mostly uncoordinated and essentially volunteer cadre of foreign fighters helped fill the ranks of the insurgency throughout the conflict. Attracted by the cause and by the chance of gaining operational experience, individuals from Eurasia and Africa traveled great distances to participate in the insurgency. Regionally, many individuals with direct or even distant relations to Iraq's Sunni tribes helped expand the insurgency's rolls.

The utility of these volunteers varied. Those foreign insurgents that were directed to Iraq by other groups tended to be of a better caliber and were more capable than their unsponsored counterparts.[78] Conversely, foreign fighters with little military or guerrilla training many times ended up being commissioned for suicide bombings or other martyrdom missions.[79]

Although there were many foreign fighters in the insurgency, native Iraqis, Iraqi tribal members, and Iraqi militias provided the bulk of insurgent personnel and resources.[80] Both tribes and militias provided some semblance of order and control within insurgent groups, and both contributed to attacks on Coalition forces. Militias in particular damaged Coalition and government efforts by weakening "government influence... providing unofficial (and effective) security in localized areas using illegal methods."[81]

Heterogeneous functional needs contributed as much to the composition of the insurgency as circumstance and organizational ambitions. This necessitated unique competency and leadership skills. Even in smaller organizations with limited capabilities, coordinating a diverse membership with varied functional capacities requires skilled leadership and organizational legerdemain.[82] As Bard O'Neill argues, "Whatever the scope of the insurgency, the effective use of people will depend on the skill of insurgent leaders in identifying, integrating, and coordinating the different tasks and roles essential for success in combat operations, training, logistics, communications, transportation, and the medical, financial, informational, diplomatic, and supervisory areas."[83]

The scope of the insurgency and each member organization's predilections were signaled by the types of targets each organization chose and their rationale for doing so: looters, organized criminals, and politically inspired insurgents were each differently motivated.[84] Nonetheless, conflicting insurgent aims and functional rationales converged despite limited levels of coordination among groups. Discerning the responsible party or motivation for an attack by merely identifying the target was nearly impossible.

The insurgency's composition at times depended on the capacity or will of a member organization to take on certain functions. This made for strange partnering. For instance, AQI and other elements of the insurgency partnered with criminal groups when their expertise was needed. This occurred despite the costs imposed on broader organizational unity. AQI's use of criminal smugglers and eventual efforts to control numerous smuggling networks led to competition with Sunni tribal leaders and compelled some Sunnis to cooperate with Coalition forces.[85]

Organized crime in Iraq was a means for the accumulation of resources, and it helped sustain and precipitate conflict while contributing to alternative modes of governance.[86] Criminal elements were also used by insurgent groups for the purpose and conduct of extortion, theft, and kidnapping for ransom.[87] Conversely, elements of organized crime groups in Iraq established symbiotic relations with insurgent organizations in order to better take advantage of the economic side effects of mass disorder. Linkages between criminal activity and insurgent behavior increased as participants' membership spanned multiple organizations. Criminal behavior in general increased as the insurgency waxed.

A variously composed complex insurgency, like the one that developed in Iraq, possesses manifold strengths but also suffers from the limitations associated with decentralized and diverse organizations: disharmony and disunity.[88] Disunity manifested structurally and culturally in the Iraqi insurgency and was difficult to avoid given the insurgency's varied composition and the breadth of contrasting organizational goals. Cooperation was as likely as friction as the insurgency wore on and as organizations took divergent paths toward their goals. For instance, even though AQI—dominated by foreign fighters whom many Iraqis resented, particularly as AQI's enhanced violence became more indiscriminate—and indigenous groups did share the goal of compelling a Coalition withdrawal, many formerly affiliated groups parted ways over time as they found better methods for achieving their goals. One group in particular, the Anbar Revenge Brigade, determined that it made more sense to rid their areas of al Qaeda operatives. This was considered more rational for organizational goal achievement than continuing cooperation in a losing proposition.[89]

The insurgency's diverse composition and networked structure endowed incalculable resources to various participating groups. Enhanced information sharing, the availability of key individual and organizational skills, and the power of numbers absent central direction or control all contributed to the adaptive capacity of the insurgency. But while a diverse composition provided a bounty of skills and resources, it also necessitated reconciling diverse objectives and goals. When organizational differences could not be overcome—as was the case with the Iraqi insurgency from at least late 2006 onward—and different groups sought different means to achieve assorted organizational ends, the insurgency's compositional diversity transformed from an asset into a liability. As a result of this fracture, the adaptive capacity of the insurgency plummeted and various formerly cooperating organizations turned into fierce competitors.

Norms

Organizational norms differed significantly because so many distinct types of organizations composed the insurgency. For instance, suicide bombing, acts of terrorism, or other taboo methods of attack were embraced by foreign insurgents—particularly those affiliated with Abu Musab al Zarqawi—but were only marginally accepted by many Iraqis and Iraqi insurgent organizations. Like other variable organizational attributes examined in this study, differing sets of norms led to inconsistent transorganizational behaviors and responses. The eventual dissolution of the broader insurgency and tectonic shifts in support for different insurgent organizations could be at least partially attributed to the capricious organizational norms exhibited by a number of insurgent organizations in Iraq.

Different sets of norms led each insurgent organization to set different standards of conduct for its members. Standards of conduct were increasingly important for retaining local support as the conflict in Iraq progressed and as general support for the insurgency waned. Local Iraqi populations enabled most if not all insurgent organizations while bearing the brunt of insurgent activity. Critically, their support was a necessary component to any insurgent organization's success, especially in the long term. Although violence in Iraq was endemic and the insurgency went out of its way to advertise that the government and the Coalition could not provide adequate security, the insurgency had to balance its barbarity against losses of the population's support.[90]

Norms shaped organizational behavior, which in turn had either a positive or negative effect on the attitude of the local population. Thus, where norms were more conventional and tempered, organizational behavior was subdued and the support of the population was retained. Where norms were unconventional and flexible, organizational behavior was unencumbered and the population's support was lost. Even among the more extreme foreign elements of the insurgency there was some recognition of this fact.[91] Organizational norms had to adhere to some standard or they would eventually jeopardize organizational goals: the latter had to be in concert with the former, and vice versa, as each helped shape organizational behavior, and ultimately, effectiveness. This was certainly the case when AQI rejected moderation in favor of greater group cohesion and as a result suffered a significant drop in the support it received from the Iraqi population.[92]

Methods selected or accepted for achieving organizational goals in some ways reflect organizational norms and predilections: the looser the organization's norms and the more expedient the method, the more likely extreme methods—such as suicide bombings and terrorism—will be adopted. Myopic method selection can have a decidedly negative impact on an organization's ability to achieve its goals, despite contrarian intent, when long-term objectives are sacrificed for short-term gains and the support of the population is not appropriately respected or accounted for. This is especially true when indiscriminate acts of violence are employed, which overwhelmingly and negatively affect the local population.[93] Norms and standards are difficult to maintain in a complex insurgency, even when their maintenance is critical to the organization receiving the support it needs to achieve its goals. Controlling organizational behavior across a loosely defined network of individual organizations, each having a parochial set of norms, is nearly impossible.

Norms significantly defined how organizations in Iraq conducted operations and managed internal organizational affairs. Tribal-based insurgents developed operational security methods based upon cultural and social norms rather than upon the bureaucratic norms typical of the cells of FREs involved in the insurgency.[94] Other groups set up tribunals and established specific rule books for the treatment of prisoners based on a standardized set of norms.[95] Standards of practice and behavior were also shaped by organizational norms and through positive interactions with Coalition forces. The consequences for violating organizational norms, even when in contact with the enemy, were sometimes dire. As one soldier deployed on the initial invasion and to Baghdad from 2005 to 2006 explains: "My guy that got killed was an IED strike. The guy that was the trigger man was killed by the insurgency because he chose the wrong target. They looked at bumper numbers and [our] units always passed through with no issue...We caught a few guys and they knew exactly what we were doing. We had local guys asking us, 'Hey, are all these your vehicles? Do they all have this on there?' 'Yeah, why?' It took us about a couple of days to figure out what they were doing...We had won the support of those people but the guys that were relieving me had pissed them off in some way so they were taking out their anguish and frustration on them. We were nice to them and helped them out and they respected us for that while they disrespected the units that didn't do the right thing. At the same time, they still have an obligation as part of their insurgency to do a mission but they picked and chose their targets accordingly."[96]

Despite initial organizational goal confluence and a generalized set of commonly accepted insurgent practices of violence, organizational norms for native Iraqi insurgents were strikingly different than those for foreign insurgents. This is partly explained by the fact that violent resistance is an accepted cultural practice in Iraq, as it is in many places, and has been ingrained in tribal traditions, communal identity, and values woven "deep into the social fabric."[97] This social fabric is built upon kinship (for example, tribal, clan, and family), association (for example, FREs), and local and nationalist interests. Kinship is regarded as the most important of the three.[98] Many Iraqis did not support the insurgency actively but admired its efforts nonetheless.[99] They shared a common interest in the ousting of the Coalition—a perceived common threat—and a sense of solidarity with insurgent organizations. Outside of a potentially shared Arab descent and perhaps a common language, foreign-born insurgents shared very few if any characteristics with indigenous Iraqi insurgents or the local population. Therefore violence inflicted by foreign-based insurgent groups was not nearly as accepted as violence perpetrated by local Iraqi groups and individuals. Organizational legitimacy and support from the population waned as levels of barbarism increased.[100] This behavior was usually the province of foreign-led or foreign-dominated insurgent organizations.

Normatively and organizationally, al Qaeda did little to support its cause as the population grew tired of the violence engendered by the insurgency. As one insurgent formerly in cooperation with al Qaeda explained: "Anyone who has followed the impact of Al-Qaida in the Diyala province will generally find that wherever they go, they cripple daily life. We can summarize their actions in the Diyala province as follows: demolishing mosques (as what befell the Kanaan Mosque) and interrupting prayers; stealing the salaries of deserving retirees; preventing rations from reaching the people of Diyala for allegedly supporting the Iraqi Ministry of Trade; stealing livestock, especially from the families of martyrs from the mujahideen; killing women and children, and mutilating their bodies, as what befell our brothers from Asaeb al-Iraq al-Jihadiya and some of our mujahideen in Kanaan and Bahraz; shuttering hospitals and stealing many valuable pieces of medical equipment, destroying them or else exporting them to unknown locations."[101]

AQI intentionally perpetrated grotesque acts of violence to cow or provoke the local population. These acts included the indiscriminate use of car bombs and chemical weapons;[102] the outright fostering of chaos and instability through violence;[103] the use of Suicide Vehicle Borne IEDs (SVBIEDs) to maximize civilian casualties; and the assassination and desecration of tribal leaders.[104] AQI's lack of normative proscriptions limiting the use of indiscriminate violence and terrorism led to a split with other insurgent organizations and an almost total loss of support from local Iraqis. As Nir Rosen argues, "In the end, Iraq's Sunnis wanted a stable Iraq, but under their control. Nor were they interested in Zarqawi's puritan ideology. It was probably disgruntled Iraqi Sunnis who provided the tip that cost Zarqawi his life."[105]

A failure to reconcile organizational norms and to realize the effect that disparate norms had on the local population eventually contributed to the dissolution of the relationships between foreign and indigenous elements of the Iraqi insurgency and a near total collapse of support for any foreign-led or affiliated insurgent organizations in Iraq. Organizational norms permitting behavior wholly unacceptable to the supporting population virtually ensured organizational divisions and failure in the long run.

Tasks

Insurgent tasks are derived from organizational goals and are shaped by environmental changes or cues. There is no prearranged list of tasks attendant to a nascent insurgent organization—it has little, if any, inherent organizational memory and is mostly free from bureaucratic direction. This does not mean that organizational members do not have memories, were not involved in or did not seek to develop bureaucracies in past endeavors, or that they are not subject to the rules and guidelines imposed by group membership. No insurgent organization is truly de novo. But despite past associations and affiliations, insurgencies generally have significant freedom in designing and conducting organizational tasks. Accordingly, insurgent organizations in Iraq designed and conducted tasks to support their goals. These goals included a combination of defeating Coalition forces, advancing organizational interests in postinvasion Iraq, and accruing power, prestige, profit, security, and influence. The insurgency had few benchmarks for establishing task sets other than some recurring tasks involving attacks on Coalition forces, the Iraqi government, and unaligned civilians. Organizational experimentation based on changes in the operational environment became endemic. Predicting insurgent behavior thus became nearly an impossible undertaking.

Organizational tasks predicated on defeating Coalition forces varied as the conflict proceeded but followed a fairly straight line from less to more complex and more violent attacks. A soldier deployed to Iraq in 2003 and from 2005 to 2006 explains: "On my first trip, they would hit and run, they did not want to conduct ambushes. Second trip: they were conducting baited ambushes and suckering us into heavy attacks."[106] Violent actions were a fundamental aspect of most insurgent organizations' task sets. Violence was for the most part planned and was used in an instrumental fashion to achieve organizational goals.[107] Accordingly, small arms hit-and-run attacks were initially staples of most insurgent organization task lists. Insurgent organizations built upon these tasks by incorporating a mix of automatic weapons and rocket-propelled grenades (RPGs) into coordinated and quickly evolving "micro" attacks that were short in duration but involved a respectable amount of planning and the command and control of various maneuver elements.[108] Most of these types of tasks required only modest organizational resources but proved difficult to defend against. And they typically generated the intended response by Coalition forces: the overwhelming employment of force resulting in significant civilian casualties and collateral damage.[109]

Depending on a particular organization's interpretation of the operational environment, different tasks were practiced, planned, and employed. Terrorist-style attacks were used to draw repressive responses from Coalition forces while and when the cost borne by insurgents carrying out these tasks remained low.[110] Insurgent organizations also created tasks based on the strengths of the networks that they developed—a capacity for quick assemblage and dispersal—and on the perceived weaknesses of their targets—an inability to predict attacks or defend against them. To accomplish this, insurgent organizations combined less complicated tasks into coordinated attacks by "swarming" as opportunities and targets presented themselves. Swarming allowed insurgent organizations to conduct attacks thusly: "Move slowly, in cycles, and episodically, concentrating on highly vulnerable targets at the time of its choosing."[111]

As the conflict in Iraq progressed, the insurgency developed a fairly common set of tasks that evolved and was refined based on organizational goals: political and military operations (counter-Coalition, and countercollaboration against the ISF); countermobility (convoys and transport); counter-reconstruction (infrastructure and contractors); counterstability (civilians, religious sites, and diplomats); and, counterelection operations.[112]

Progressively, this task set became more complex and involved more than just violence against competing organizations and designated targets. Correspondingly, fewer organizations had the capacity to carry out necessary organizational tasks or to exploit changes in the operational environment to achieve their organizational goals. Tasks including targeted violence, political maneuvering, and the defense of key territories and populations—to name a few—were difficult if not impossible for many organizations to accomplish.

As task sets became more complex and as the operational environment changed significantly, many organizations withered, consolidated, or became marginalized as they could no longer achieve organizational goals effectively. As organizations expanded, were co-opted, or lost influence, sectarian violence erupted. In 2006 and later,[113] organizational divisions over goals, missions, and direction led to internecine violence and fragmentation, largely between foreign-dominated and indigenous organizations.

MATERIEL AND TECHNICAL RESOURCES

This section discusses insurgency's gathering and use of equipment, funds, and intelligence.

Equipment

The Coalition's failure to secure weapons and explosives caches throughout Iraq ensured that the equipment necessary to wage an insurgency was not in short supply. Military-grade explosives, weapons, ammunition, and other specialized equipment, if not available at abandoned military posts or centralized in unprotected armories, could be found lying on roadsides or, in the case of rifles and other small arms, in many Iraqi households. As a soldier deployed on the initial invasion describes, the insurgency quickly put this equipment to use: "At that point in the war it hadn't gotten as vicious as it turned out. You got pot shots and hand grenades but IEDs weren't born yet. They didn't really show up until the summer of 2003…Funny as it may be, there were artillery rounds all over the roads we had been travelling. We would see them every day but we never paid attention to them."[114]

Most of the weapons and explosives available in Iraq were easy to move, hide, and use in attacks.[115] Other items that the insurgency needed and used—wiring, washing machine timers, alarm clocks, vehicles, ball bearings, garage door openers, binoculars, cell phones, video cameras, and so forth—could be found in one form or another in all modern and even less modern societies. Furthermore, the expertise needed for assembling and employing this equipment as weaponry—if not possessed by or available from organizational members—was published on the Internet, contained in various how-to manuals like the *Anarchist's Cookbook*, or was published in various military manuals on booby-traps and improvised explosives. For the higher-order construction, maintenance, and employment of small arms and IEDs, the knowledge obtained from former government employees, former members of the military, and trained foreign terrorists and insurgents sufficed.

IEDs and small arms need not be sophisticated in order to be effective—to advance organizational goals—and do not intrinsically necessitate great skill in their manufacture or employment. Each alone, combined or utilized as part of a simple or complex tactical operation—ambush, complex ambush, assassination, and so forth—is effective for killing soldiers, government officials, and civilians and for causing significant environmental chaos, psychological stress, and damage to infrastructure and vehicles.

But sophistication in IED construction and emplacement does add to the difficulty of detecting and defusing or counteracting the effects of these devices. Increasing the sophistication of IEDs—particularly when combined with the employment of small arms—expanded the range of insurgent operations. Armed with sophisticated IEDs, tactical operators could attack more and varied targets while not exposing the insurgency and its members to greater physical risk or detection. As insurgent organizations benefited from the use of IEDs, as stand-alone devices or in conjunction with other methods of attack, the IED became an organizational specialty.[116]

Much of the skill needed to make more complex IEDs came from insurgents formerly employed by Saddam Hussein's government and military. This capacity was further augmented by the skills and knowledge infused into the insurgency by the many trained and experienced foreign fighters pouring into Iraq from 2003 onward.[117] Many of the skills needed to mount more complex operations with small arms and explosives came from these same people. As their skills proliferated and as more and more unskilled insurgents became skilled through experience and training, the insurgency's capacity for conducting attacks grew, and opportunities for successful organizational adaptation expanded.

Although advanced tactics and skills proliferated throughout the insurgency over time, at no point did the insurgency reach any sort of technological parity with Coalition forces, particularly not in terms of resources or in their application.[118] This posed numerous problems for Coalition forces: most of their equipment, training, and intelligence gathering activities were designed for detecting and neutralizing the operations of similarly endowed high-tech adversaries. When the insurgency did employ advanced technological contrivances and equipment, it did so freed from the constraints and restrictions posed by SOPs, doctrine, or convention and thus many times avoided the detection methods and tools employed by Coalition forces. Often, the equipment and technology wielded by the insurgency was developed through Coalition countries' research and development. As then Major General Daniel Bolger argues, "Our enemy is a parasite, and our own technological culture is the host. Al Qaeda in Iraq and the Jaysh al Mahdi have no R&D and a rudimentary procurement chain. It's all our own technologies turned back on us. But freed from any rules or law, the terrorists think up things that would not occur to us, like airliners ramming skyscrapers on 9/11."[119]

Paradoxically, the insurgency relied on capability multipliers—such as the Iraqi population and various membership skills—that defied technical collection methods and confounded the Coalition's ability to develop a clear intelligence picture or to predict future operational and tactical adaptations.[120] The insurgency had no compelling need to pursue or adopt anything more advanced than what was available in Iraq: tactical success was being achieved with creative applications of what equipment and tools were readily available. Any attempts to acquire or to use more advanced weaponry would have generated indicators observable by the Coalition and detrimental to organizational security.[121] For instance, when Explosively Formed Penetrators (EFPs) were imported or provided to the insurgency, the networks supplying these devices were in many instances uncovered and interdicted. This led to a loss in capacity not only in relation to EFPs but also to the skills and capabilities that the members of these networks provided.[122]

While low-tech small arms and relatively unsophisticated IEDs were employed in the majority of insurgent attacks, the insurgency did utilize higher-tech inter-netted communications to transmit information, images, and lessons gleaned from interactions with Coalition forces. The same communications network created and used by the Iraqi state and Coalition forces passively benefited the insurgency. The insurgency did not have to create or control the network. Instead, it only needed to exploit the network's capacity intermittently. The insurgency, when not able to operate freely or with a high degree of personal contact, effectively reduced the distance between groups and transmitted communications, operational successes, and knowledge electronically.[123]

The insurgency enhanced its survivability and the effectiveness of its operations by applying its knowledge and experience to the equipment and resources that were available in Iraq. This had two effects: the insurgency did not have to risk partaking in observable attempts either to purchase or to acquire munitions, weapons, and explosives; and the insurgency was freed from expending funds or relying on the state-based partnerships characteristic of previous insurgencies. The insurgency was able to plan and prepare for conducting attacks while maintaining operational security. Whether or not adaptations based on the availability of resources were made consciously or were merely the result of convenient environmental factors, the insurgency nonetheless was capable of expanding its operational capacity while maintaining a discrete operational signature.

Funds

The insurgency supported its operations with funds obtained through various licit and illicit activities. These activities changed as the marginal costs of their conduct increased or decreased over time and as differing opportunities availed themselves. For instance, in 2004 the insurgency utilized courier infiltrated funds and accessed cached deposits of local and foreign currencies.[124] In later years and during the infancy of the state's security apparatus, the insurgency created or co-opted smuggling operations, kidnapped for ransom, counterfeited currency, and charged fees for services normally provided by internal security and border control agencies.[125] These funds were used to help sustain insurgent organizations and individuals in these organizations, pay for the services of part-time or auxiliary combatants, purchase information from the public and from corrupt politicians and security services, and enable other supporting and tangential criminal activities. The Iraqi insurgency's finance system was vastly different in character, scope, and method than the systems of external state support utilized during the Cold War and thus presented a range of unique consequences that flummoxed efforts to counter insurgent funding streams.[126]

Illicit activities conducted for monetary gain or to support other operations, either by design or merely circumstantially, have the side effect of perpetuating environmental and social conditions anathema to law and order. For instance, crime, looting, kidnapping, and murder—to name but a few insurgent activities—engendered fear of insurgent organizations and a mistrust of the Iraqi government and Coalition forces.[127] This occurred regardless of the specific target of the criminal activity and irrespective of whether or not general chaos was a prevailing goal of the organizations committing these crimes. The net result of the insurgency's engagement in illicit funding activities was the development of an adaptive framework for monetary and in-kind resource gathering. This activity directly and indirectly supported organizational objectives with, consequently, the added benefit of disrupting the mission of Coalition forces.[128]

Periods of conflict and instability afford insurgent criminal enterprisers exaggerated access to excess and underutilized economic capacity: chiefly, an un- or underemployed population. Regardless of their official employment status, Iraqis seeking wages were used to gather or shield critical information, provide much needed skills from their previous professions (many times martial), and conduct contracted insurgent work.[129] As David Kilcullen argues, the insurgents in Iraq "were wealthier than the population, and routinely paid poverty-stricken locals to conduct attacks for cash."[130] The economic disparity between the insurgents and average Iraqis was substantial. Although a number of hired insurgent forces were quickly killed through what Ahmed Hashim aptly describes as "Combat Darwinism,"[131] the insurgency benefited from their use. Contracted insurgents expanded the size and scope of insurgent operations and flooded the operational environment with potential and actual combatants. Regardless of how this pool of resources was specifically used, the insurgency manifested its own economy of force by paying for the services of an untapped and previously unpaid or underpaid resource. If for nothing else, the contract services paid for by insurgent funds freed committed insurgent forces to conduct higher-order planning and for the organization of longer-term, complex operations.

Supplementary income was an important motivator for many who participated in the Iraqi insurgency, a fact known all too well to insurgent organizations. As Ahmed Hashim notes, many insurgents had to "hold down a legitimate day job."[132] Supporting the insurgency, if not a primary job or chosen profession, was a form of moonlighting and, although dangerous, paid relatively well and was preferable to being paid little or nothing at all. Creating an alternative marketplace for skills and services significantly weakened the legitimacy of the Iraqi government while it simultaneously increased the costs of Coalition operations. During a period of institutional failure and a breakdown of the normal, functioning society, this marketplace thrived and became self-sustaining. The revenue used to support insurgent activities was returned through criminal enterprising and created a cyclical market closed to organizations and individuals not in league with insurgent forces.

Siphoning excess labor capacity from an aggrieved and impoverished population provided the insurgency with a resource-gathering and provisioning flexibility not available to law-abiding organizations, particularly not in a post-conflict environment where state and private resources were limited. As Steve Metz contends, "Conflict gives insurgents access to money and resources out of proportion to what they would have in peacetime."[133] Contracting goods and services with licit and illicit funding streams during a time of conflict creates a shadowy marketplace. The insurgency is then able to act as a clearinghouse providing employment opportunities and service provision outside of the control of sanctioned or government forces and agencies. Paradoxically, this helps create a form of stability and legitimacy that an insurgency can parlay into other gains: the benefits of creating alternative forms of stability accrue almost solely to insurgent organizations and not to the state or even the population at large. But accepting insurgent largess was a dangerous gamble. At any time, those benefiting from the stability and employment provided by the insurgents' alternative marketplace could easily become its targets.

Frequently, resources gained by the insurgency licitly but used illicitly also funded behavior that in turn engendered support from the local population. Insurgents received sponsorship from supporters of the resistance, Salafist charities, individual donors, and from mosques around the world.[134] These donations formed a large pool of funding to draw upon that was almost impossible to distinguish from myriad other financial transactions carried out on a daily basis.

Donations and volunteered support came not only from foreign sources but also from the indigenous population. Active and passive volunteerism on the part of many average Iraqis supplemented the insurgency's licit funding streams by reducing the potentially prohibitive costs of contracting out major portions of insurgent activities. This passive support was rewarded with the provision of security and in some cases access to social services largely unavailable after the fall of the Hussein regime. Creating unconventional forms of stability and legitimacy enhanced the reputation of the insurgency and cast a pall over governmental and Coalition efforts.

In addition to self-financing and licit support, the insurgency supplemented fund gathering with highly organized criminal activities that took advantage of circumstances and cleavages peculiar to Iraq. In at least one case, the insurgency took active steps to protect a legitimate business in order to ensure a lucrative smuggling operation. Oil smuggling in an oil-rich country surrounded by other oil-rich countries would not seem, prima facie, to be a highly profitable exercise worthy of significant resource investment by the insurgency. But this perfectly characterizes the relationship between the insurgency and the Baiji refinery in northern Iraq. The insurgency also conducted organized crime and worked with extant organized criminal groups as necessity or convenience dictated. Likewise, organized criminal groups teamed with the insurgency—if not already an active part of the insurgency—to engage in a mutually beneficial kidnapping business.[135]

By taking advantage of the circumstances peculiar to Iraq in the wake of the 2003 invasion and by utilizing criminal enterprise and licit and illicit funding streams, the insurgency became financially self-sufficient. This relationship was cyclical and dependent in its causes. Crime was used to gain funding to support the insurgency, and the chaos caused by insurgent activities was used to mask and cover rampant criminal enterprising. Both gave cause for continued local and foreign volunteerism and for donations from abroad. By 2006, the insurgency had raised "tens of millions of dollars a year from oil smuggling, kidnapping, counterfeiting, connivance by corrupt Islamic charities and other crimes" that the Iraqi government and Coalition forces were, by and large, unable to stem.[136]

The accrual of benefits from this mutually symbiotic criminal-insurgent relationship ebbed and flowed between and among various illicit groups. Variable and manifold funding mechanisms enabled the insurgency to adapt to and take advantage of changing circumstances and to circumvent counterinsurgent efforts to target any single source of exchange. Once gained, these funds were used to perpetuate the insurgency and to take advantage of systemic employment problems through the utilization of a capable and talented but chronically underpaid population. Unlike its twentieth-century counterparts, the Iraqi insurgency was particularly and almost wholly entrepreneurial and was thereby capable of creating and realizing advantages on an as-needed basis.

Intelligence

The insurgency developed an immense intelligence-gathering operation that exploited existing social and technical architectures. This apparatus consisted of and was enabled by—but not limited to—informal command, control, communications, computers, intelligence, surveillance, and reconnaissance (C4ISR) networks; messengers; the Internet; smuggling rings; close interaction with the population; street scouts capable of signaling; runners; and cellular telephony. Additionally, the insurgency learned about and developed the capacity to undermine many of the Coalition's most sophisticated intelligence gathering and analysis measures, including highly guarded Communications Intelligence (COMINT) and Signals Intelligence (SIGINT) capabilities.[137] Formal and informal social networks were converted into information gathering, processing, and transmitting associations that defied conventional countermeasures. Variously, individuals, families, groups, and tribes acted as the "eyes and ears" of insurgent combatant cells. The insurgency's human network conducted active and passive intelligence collection and, perhaps more important, engaged in significant counterintelligence operations. These counterintelligence operations not only identified adversarial collection methods and techniques but also took advantage of (mostly) undirected and passive deception and denial: insurgent activities were concealed when the population refused to or did not voluntarily pass along information or data relevant to Coalition forces.

Having access to thousands of unidentifiable intelligence collectors, processors, and filters enabled a high degree of control of the information environment and an appreciable degree of adaptive capacity. The insurgency collected information and deceived, misinformed, and deprived Coalition forces with the same informal networks it used to inform its own operations and planning. The insurgency's "eyes and ears" could be switched from passive to active, as necessary, to help identify critical nodes of the Coalition network.[138] When these passive measures were insufficient for protecting and informing the organization or when active supplementation was appropriate, the insurgency targeted the Coalition's collection and interpretive resources: specifically, translators and Human Intelligence (HUMINT) operators. Controlling the information environment and key pieces of intelligence, maintaining the capacity to suppress environmental and population-based indicators, using agents that had penetrated the Coalition to feed disinformation, and targeting competing intelligence-collection assets not only supported insurgent operational adaptation but also degraded and confused key informational and intelligence inputs to Coalition forces' decision-making cycles.

By far the greatest strength of the insurgency's intelligence system was its ability to actively and passively scan, observe, probe, and interpret ambient environmental conditions and Coalition operations and activities through its own dedicated collectors and through the eyes of an adjunct Iraqi population. The ability to use the Iraqi population as an intelligence-gathering network was the sine qua non of the insurgency's—particularly its foreign element's—intelligence-collection apparatus.[139]

Changes in the operational environment are far easier to detect and interpret when an organization's collection system is a constituent part of the environment being observed and/or operated in. This is true for any organization operating in a contested environment. To supplement mostly passive, population-centric collection methods, the insurgency also conducted active probing and sensing attacks. A soldier deployed to Baghdad recounts, "There was always the threat of one VBIED being followed by another. One part of their [the insurgency's] process was to figure out how long it took us to respond to a VBIED. They would set off one VBIED and you would get there, set up a cordon, and prepare. They knew how long it took you to get there so you would have to prepare for another one."[140] And as one soldier explains, the insurgency regularly probed and observed Coalition military units to determine if perceived superficial changes—to uniforms, equipment, and so forth—indicated potential or actual operational and behavioral changes: "In a report, someone on the council noticed that the people had become scared of our patches. When a new unit came in without those patches, that is when they decided to test to see if they were the same type of guys. This happened in Fallujah, Shula, and Ghaziliyah…the insurgency is very observant and watches every move—who is pulling security and who isn't."[141]

When operational regularities, constraints, or procedures—such as Rules of Engagement (ROE)—were detected, they were exploited for maximum advantage in ways that were difficult if not impossible to counter. A soldier deployed twice to Iraq provides an instructive example: "The enemy understood that we had boundaries and would use the rivers to bind us geographically. They would fire their indirect fire across the river in order to disrupt our boundaries. It is impossible to hide anyone to do observation of this. As soon as you enter an area or a house, the locals start acting differently and the insurgents can pick this up. Any change in behavior tips off the insurgents that the Americans are in the area. You cannot blend [in]."[142] Even minor changes were noted and exploited when possible: "They paid attention to the small details. Sometimes it only took them a week and sometimes it took six weeks but they would overcome and adapt. They were patient and it allowed them to get the edge sometimes and it forced us to readjust our game plan."[143] The insurgency exploited the Coalition's liberal use of and reliance upon SOPs, tools for collecting information on the operational environment, and early weaknesses at gathering anthropological information in Iraq. The insurgency rather quickly learned that the U.S. Army in particular prefers to assess and target *things* instead of *people* and that the army had difficulty measuring, developing, and capturing the multidimensional attributes of a complex insurgency with tools developed for more conventional operations.[144] One soldier recalled that observing the insurgency with commonly used Unmanned Aerial Vehicles (UAVs) was many times ineffective: "We could throw up UAVs all day long but the insurgents know what a UAV is. They have satellite TV and when they hear a lawnmower in the sky they go to sleep. The insurgents can watch TV as well as we can."[145]

A secondary and more pernicious strength of the insurgency's intelligence-gathering operation was its ability to penetrate competing military and government organizations both directly—through corruption or targeted subversion—and indirectly—through close or inside observation. The insurgency coupled its inherent surveillance and reconnaissance capabilities with information passed to it from sources inside the Iraqi security services. This kind of information was used to plan and conduct a number of attacks.[146] As one al Qaeda member recounts in his diary: "[O]ur Jihadi Movement goals at the early stages were to recruit as many as possible of the government employees in order to have access, sources and supporters among them in order to gain more information about the Government security forces and the infidels' military and tactical movements in order to ease our movements and missions against them."[147] This, in combination with other intelligence-gathering operations, provided unparalleled depth to the insurgency's ability to conduct and assess its operations in light of how its opponents observed and assessed the effects of these operations. This facility gave the insurgency a Janus-like observational power that was not similarly enjoyed by Coalition forces. The insurgency, for quite some time, was capable of not only adjusting its organizational inputs and outputs to achieve goals but also of viewing, in great detail, how counterinsurgent forces did the same. The insurgency's multifaceted intelligence-gathering architecture allowed it to efficiently hone its operational capacities while concurrently weakening those of its competitors.

The insurgency also took advantage of the intelligence-gathering capacities of other insurgent and terrorist organizations engaged in operations—against U.S. and other forces—in different operational theaters. For instance, insurgents engaged in activities against Israel and Russia and in Afghanistan shared analyzed information via websites and in-person with their insurgent counterparts in Iraq—and vice versa. Vast although mostly hidden transnational information sharing networks enabled the collusion of intelligence collectors of various stripes. Intelligence was compiled in one area of conflict and was transmitted via various means to other areas in order to improve operational capabilities and to exploit weaknesses that otherwise might have gone either unknown or undetected.

Although the insurgency maintained a durable and robust intelligence-gathering network for quite some time, this network was by no means permanent and thus was never a "dedicated" asset. As provinces, cities, and neighborhoods slowly acceded to Coalition and governmental control and later actively supported Coalition operations, the insurgency's intelligence capabilities diminished at an exponential rate. What at one point was a great strength became a great weakness.

For the insurgency, absent other traditional—military or defense—intelligence collection and processing capabilities outside of the Iraqi population and the direct observational power of organizational members, intelligence collection was truly a zero sum game: any loss was the Coalition's gain. The Iraqi population was a low-cost and ready-made intelligence network that could enable either competitor in this conflict. The insurgency's adaptability was premised on intelligence gathering, which was further premised on both active and passive support from the population. Transitively, adaptability and success was to a large degree founded on support from the population. As support waned, organizational adaptability quickly morphed into rigidity, and the insurgency's intelligence apparatus was reduced to the capabilities provided by its formal members.

EXTERNAL ASSISTANCE

External Assistance consists of practices of consultation, direct action, and cooperation.

Consultation

One of the many interesting and unique characteristics of the Iraqi insurgency was an almost complete absence of consultation with foreign powers and organizations not directly participating in or contributing to the insurgency.[148] Although some countries did covertly or passively support the insurgency (such as Syria and Iran),[149] for the most part, the insurgency did not seek out cooperative or consultative relationships with states.

Because of its networked nature, the majority of organizations participating in the Iraqi insurgency did not need the support of states to effectively survive or conduct operations. Instead, they could rely on intraorganizational capacities and cooperation to provide resources and counseling. Likewise, when leadership was drawn from external sources it was still indigenously tied to participating organizations—unlike in many twentieth-century insurgencies where external cadres helped guide insurgent action and behavior. Guidance in the Iraqi insurgency flowed loosely and extemporaneously from within and across various organizations.

The very structure of networked organizations nearly obviates the need for consultation.[150] Indeed, by their very formation, these organizations exist for goal accomplishment and therefore do not necessarily require consultation with or from other groups. Information that would normally be received through external consultation was generated within the organization or was incorporated through the creation of mutually beneficial relationships with other like-minded groups.

Direct Action

Disentangling direct external support to the Iraqi insurgency is a difficult task. The core of the insurgency franchised many of its operations to supportive locals and erstwhile communal groups. Likewise, the insurgency was supported by the direct action of various unrelated tactical operators that undoubtedly had some relationship with local insurgent groups but were for all intents and purposes external or adjunct members of the broader movement. Many members conducting direct action in behalf of the insurgency belonged to several groups at one time; their uniting purpose was defeating the Coalition and a common interest in weakening the position of the Iraqi government.[151] Direct action for and with the insurgency then is perhaps best described as actions taken in behalf of the insurgency without explicit, and solitary, organizational membership or discretional guidance.

Many criminal groups, organized, spontaneous, and without clearly articulated ties to any insurgent organizations, conducted direct-action missions that contributed to the insurgency and the general state of chaos in Iraq. These actions included but were not limited to robberies, assassinations, thefts of resources, and smuggling efforts conducted by criminal organizations or other profit driven syndicates. This occurred despite the fact that these organizations might have had no corresponding or shared political or ideological interests in common with insurgent groups.[152]

Foreign and local fighters expanded the scope of the insurgency without any initial or even enduring organizational ties. After the Coalition invasion, more than 1 million Iraqi men *and* women with professional training in the use of the tools of the urban guerrilla melted into the Iraqi landscape; many later returned to actively support the insurgency.[153] Scores of women fighters emerged to conduct missions to avenge family members and support al Qaeda's suicide bombing efforts despite having no formal organizational affiliations. Foreign fighters and volunteers also swelled the ranks of the insurgency with a zealous suicidal intent that was mostly absent from the local population and indigenous fighters.[154] At first, foreign fighters came from Palestinian camps, Jordan, Lebanon, and Syria. Later, militants emigrated from Europe and the greater Middle East.[155] Most of these fighters were not veterans of other conflicts but instead were first-time volunteers.[156]

Direct action in behalf of the insurgency by "ordinary" Iraqis, foreign fighters, and various exploitive individuals complicated Coalition efforts to police the community without also tipping its hand to actual or potential insurgents. Furthermore, a suicidal foreign component significantly elevated the costs of providing defense to key infrastructure and bases of operation. Even if direct action did little to halt the overall momentum of the counterinsurgency, it certainly complicated Coalition efforts and provided the insurgency with another, if unintended and sometimes directionless, arm to sow confusion and disrupt Coalition operations.

Cooperation

Networks can form, coalesce, and decompose as needed in a nearly unobservable fashion when aided by social, familial, and network ties and abetted by omnipresent IT. In this regard, the networked insurgency in Iraq was no exception, despite the sometimes competing or contradictory interests of its membership. Individuals and organizations were folded into other insurgent organizations based on similar interests, goals, ties, and motivations. But for the most part, they were able to act as insurgents while hiding among the population. Then Major General Daniel Bolger argues that, in Iraq, "Our enemy survives by blending into the population. These modern information technologies allow our foe to move as freely and swiftly as fish swimming through the sea of the people, just as Mao Zedong always said."[157]

Many insurgent organizations cooperated with and hired other insurgents—in a practice not dissimilar to Coalition service contracting—and a core of dedicated insurgents planned and managed their operations (suicide bombings, emplacing IEDs, and so forth). Expanding existing networks and developing new networks and matrices based on organizational needs and membership ties formed the basis of cooperation for the insurgency. In describing matrix warfare, J. Noel Williams explains that "members can share common economic interests on one level and join together to accomplish a specific goal and then disengage and reshuffle to accomplish a different set of objectives. However, these combinations need not be sequential, but rather can be concurrent and multi-various, such that at any given moment, numerous combinations and associations are possible between the same members, but for different objectives."[158] Cooperation along these lines made any disambiguation of the insurgency's structure almost impossible to achieve. The insurgency was equal parts ephemeral and enduring: effectively employing traditional methods of network analysis to disentangle the insurgency would prove difficult.[159]

Iraq's social structure and individuals' multimodal communal ties accelerated cooperation among various groups as the Iraqi state crumbled. Covert networks, the structures of which existed or were created prior to the invasion, gained purpose and cohesion as the insurgency evolved. This occurred without an appreciable amount of effort directed toward their formation. These networks were premised on preexisting social structures rather than on psychological factors.[160] The addition of motivation and common goals activated these ties and created a superorganization nearly imperceptible to outside observers.

Some cooperative networks and coalitions formed out of the mass of unemployed Iraqis created by the invasion. These networks grew without warning and expanded and contracted despite an absence of perceptible or public leadership and obvious organizational structures governing their behavior. Capabilities, availability, financial reward, and a desire to act bonded these groups. Insurgent organizational complexity and novelty made fighting the insurgency a much more difficult task than originally anticipated.[161]

A sizable cooperative network also grew out of Iraq's tribal population. Tribes consist of khams (all male children who share the same great-great grandfather); biets, or houses (vast extended families with hundreds of members); fakhdhs (group of houses, or a clan); and ashiras (tribal organizations consisting of a group of clans). Tribes can include up to 1 million members. An even larger grouping of tribes is known as a confederation, or qabila.[162] Many tribal members had useful, residual military experience from when they were supported and were armed for defense during the Iran-Iraq War and after the

Persian Gulf War.[163] Alone, a single tribe could be a significant force, commanding the resources of thousands of potential fighters. In collaboration, the tribes
formed by far the largest and most pervasive cooperative constituent network
of the Iraqi insurgency.[164]

Despite a constituency of vast networks of people with varying skills and
levels of leadership, the Iraqi insurgency was a truly disjointed effort throughout most of 2003 and into 2004. Nascent organizations lacked coherence and
capability, and individual members moved in and out of groups frequently.
Competition within groups and among individuals subverted cooperation
among organizations. This occurred despite the fact that this unorganized mass
of insurgents and insurgent organizations was collectively imposing significant
losses on Coalition forces and disrupting the formation of a new Iraqi government. Early attempts at cooperation usually took the form of disastrous mass
attacks that caused Coalition casualties but came at pyrrhic costs. The power
of networked cooperation did not reveal itself until later in 2003 and early 2004
and then, only partially.

Cooperative efforts were blunted through mid-2004 by organizational disunity stemming from internal debates regarding differing organizational goals
and interests. General disagreement among organizations on political and
ideological goals and even tactical methods and targets was a common fea-
ture of the insurgency throughout most of 2004. Notwithstanding intragroup
disagreements and divisions and an almost complete disregard for what a successful insurgency would require of the victors, by late 2004 the insurgency did
manage to develop cooperative methods based upon tactical realities and organizational needs. As Ahmed Hashim noted at the time, "[T]he insurgency is
not a united movement directed by a leadership with a single ideological vision.
Indeed, the insurgents may have calculated that their success does not now require an elaborate political and socioeconomic vision of a 'free' Iraq; articulat-
ing the desire to be free of foreign occupation has sufficed to win popular support. Because they wish to avoid fratricidal conflict, these groups are cooperating with one another and coordinating attacks at the operational and tactical
levels despite profound political differences."[165] Intermittent success against the
Coalition throughout late 2004 and early 2005, based on cooperatively planned
and networked attacks, provoked even greater cooperation among organizations despite competing organizational objectives and goals.

Regardless of the initial ad hoc construction and motivation of the Iraqi
insurgency, the effort became increasingly better organized through success-

ful tactical and operational cooperation. With cooperation came sophistication and organizational articulation. Ensuing competition led to mergers, defections, or the dismemberment of less effective or less persuasive groups. By late 2005 and early 2006, the insurgency was structured around more permanent, albeit still shifting and evolving, networks premised on competency and a capacity for augmenting external operations. Correspondingly, recognizable and geographically bound groups emerged based upon shared interests, fitness for goal accomplishment, and local affiliation. Informal divisions of labor also evolved within and across a number of formerly competing groups. Among insurgent organizations, there was an "increase in sustained cooperation and coordination in training, resource-sharing and the conduct of joint operations."[166] There was also collaboration on specific missions based upon the shared interest of attacking the same targets. The insurgency was self-sustaining and actualizing; it had its own experiential gravity that was shared across groups and borders.[167] Organizational coordination developed and collective learning about insurgent and counterinsurgent methods ensued. This extended to native groups and to the foreign elements of the insurgency.

Cooperation in Iraq among foreigners, particularly al Qaeda, and Iraqi insurgent organizations was "borne [sic] of opportunism and a narrow mutual interest in targeting coalition forces."[168] Although al Qaeda had its own and perhaps separate operational interests in Iraq, it provided organizational expertise, resources, and consultation to native groups in exchange for sanctuary, mostly among Sunni tribes and populations in the al Anbar Province.[169] Then Colonel H. R. McMaster argues, "The insurgency received extensive support from the transnational network of al Qaeda and associated movements and organizations as well as the external regime of Saddam Hussein that resides primarily in Damascus and elsewhere. So, they were able to establish bases of support within the country. Al Anbar was a base of support [as was] North along the Tigris and Diyala rivers in the Diyala Province, South of Baghdad, and in the Lutifiyah area. All these were safe havens that allowed the enemy to mobilize resources and access support: weapons, finance, munitions, assemble car bombs, those sorts of things."[170] Cooperation among al Qaeda-inspired and -linked organizations—especially those formed or supported by Abu Musab al Zarqawi—was initially based on mutual interest and the potential sharing of resources. This benefited al Qaeda insofar as it was able to establish a hub in Iraq. This benefited Zarqawi and his affiliates by allowing them access to al Qaeda's recruiting, financial, and logistical support networks.[171] Sunni organizations also benefited from Zarqawi's largess and appeal. But generally, and despite notable successes against Coalition forces, Zarqawi's methods were not well tolerated and his organization lacked support from Iraqis, even though he was amply capable of attracting foreign fighters and resources.[172]

Although Zarqawi's organization provided vast resources and expanded organizational capacity to associated groups, its ruthlessness also sowed division among once and newly cooperating organizations. Notwithstanding mutual interests, Sunni groups allied with Zarqawi grew disaffected with him and the "arrogant" behavior of al Qaeda fighters.[173] Cooperation was increasingly difficult to achieve because organizational objectives and attitudes collided. Al Qaeda was international in scope and was highly ideological.[174] Its perception of the conflict was tinted by its internationalist goals. Cooperating Sunni groups' perceptions of the conflict significantly differed: they saw their participation in the insurgency not as part of a greater international effort but instead as part of a nationalized struggle for security, power, money, and sectarian goals.[175]

Increasing tensions among local and foreign insurgent groups led to a fierce and violent competition for the insurgency's mantle of leadership, the creation of consolidated organizations, and the eventual disintegration of cooperation between and among al Qaeda–created and -affiliated groups and most native Iraqi insurgent organizations.[176] According to Abdul Bakier, "Al-Qaeda didn't understand the Iraqi mentality and tried to lead the community by establishing the Islamic State of Iraq, instead of coexisting with the different Iraqi groups. The targeting of Shiites and their shrines aggravated the Sunnis [sic] Iraqis as much as it did the Shiites because it upset the precarious balance between the Sunnis and Shiites."[177] AQI also began targeting competing and dissenting organizations with bloody attacks on tribal leaders throughout al Anbar Province and Shi'a targets throughout Iraq,[178] in an effort to force consolidation or submission. AQI's machinations backfired and led to only two consensually joining members: the Army of the Victorious Sect (January 15, 2006) and the Army of Ahlus Sunnah wal Jammah (January 28, 2006).[179]

The effects of al Qaeda's eventual failure and inability to cooperate along the lines of shared goals, or even in the organization's own interest, extended throughout Iraq with the emergence of various tribes and local citizens groups opposing the organization.[180] Any long-term or even renewed cooperation among these groups, given their divergent goals, was unlikely.[181] Al Qaeda's behavior also made it abundantly clear that cooperation based on a lone intersecting organizational objective did not necessarily translate into the successful recognition of other organizational goals.

CONCLUSION

How the insurgency adapted and modified organizational inputs variably affected its effectiveness in achieving its goals over time. As the insurgency adapted its inputs it altered its ability to perceive and further adapt to changes in its environment. None of the insurgency's organizational inputs can be properly understood in isolation: each had an effect on the whole and inputs generally expanded or contracted in concert.

Initially, unified organizational goals aided organizational coherence and allowed disparate individuals and groups to conduct actions that were mutually reinforcing, however uncoordinated. Mass membership, the inculcation of trained foreign fighters, and simplified tasks compensated for a lack of experience. Access to abandoned equipment and materiel made up for a dearth of organizational property and resources. As the insurgency expanded its rolls, it also expanded its organizational inputs.

The insurgency continued to reap the benefits of an expanding and more diverse network in the 2003 to 2006 period. Its access to information, through the population and through intraorganizational cooperation, and its access to materiel and technical resources grew exponentially. By late 2006 the insurgency had reached its zenith in terms of its size, its ability to generate casualties and chaos, and its capacity for adaptation. But its growth and diversity came at a cost. Its ability to mask planning and operational activities and maintain organizational covertness diminished with its increased size. As it became more successful its member organizations experienced greater levels of intraorganizational friction as each tried to advance its own interests and achieve its own goals, at times in complete disharmony. Competition increased as goals and norms diverged. And as organizational competition increased, the insurgency's ability to adapt decreased.

By 2007 and 2008, internecine fighting over goals and the means to accomplish goals caused organizational defections and divisions, which led to decreased effectiveness in terms of the insurgency's ability to adapt. As it became less diverse the insurgency also lost a great deal of support from within and from outside of the organization: information flows, fund generation, and intelligence-gathering operations were severely circumscribed. Although the organizations that remained in the insurgency were highly motivated, trained, and experienced and shared similar goals and obeyed mutually held norms, they lacked resources, membership, and local support. Furthermore, many of these groups were trying to achieve goals through tasks that were too complex to be undertaken by an undersized network. Membership in the insurgency declined further as groups withered, disbanded, or were co-opted or destroyed by Coalition forces.

Describing and understanding how these organizational inputs were modified as the insurgency adapted is critical to revealing the utility and effectiveness of the networked form of organization for achieving organizational goals. But the process of organizational adaptation is not merely a function of changing organizational inputs; organizational outputs and organizational learning must also be considered. Each of these dimensions of the adaptive cycle will be examined in the following chapter.

3

The Iraqi Insurgency—Organizational Outputs, Learning, and Summary of the Adaptive Cycle

INTRODUCTION

Organizational outputs result from the application of singular, successive, or past adaptations to organizational inputs. Organizational outputs are inextricably intertwined with the organizational inputs discussed in the previous chapter. And both are shaped by levels and methods of organizational learning.

The process of adapting inputs, outputs, and learning is cyclical. As an organization adapts its inputs to achieve its goals, it must do so based on learning and with an eye toward how changes to its inputs will positively or negatively affect organizational outputs. For instance, adaptations in training have direct and indirect effects on task performance competency. And changes in goals or the information an organization receives or shares can shape how skills and knowledge are applied to the planning and conduct of operations.

Although organizational outputs are shaped by and reflect adaptations to organizational inputs, the former can nonetheless be adapted somewhat independently from the latter. Being intertwined does not imply interdependence. For instance, skills and knowledge can be applied differently to achieve organizational goals even if those inputs affecting this application are held constant. Or an organization may decide to adapt its use of available materials based upon competitor reactions to previous patterns of resource use. This can be accomplished irrespective of changes in training, composition, or norms.

Adapting organizational outputs requires less resource shifting than does adapting organizational inputs. And outputs tend to be more sensitive to environmental change than inputs and are likely to be adapted more frequently. Thus, depending on the organization's goals and the breadth of its membership or network, it may be easier to adapt organizational outputs rather than inputs for the purposes of necessity or expediency.[1]

Similarly, organizational learning can be adapted relatively independently from either inputs or outputs, but its effects on cyclical adaptation affect both, sometimes significantly. If an organization fails to collect knowledge, transfer knowledge among members, or integrate knowledge as part of its adaptive processes, it will also fail to respond correctly to environmental changes, learn from mistakes, or take advantage of successes.

This chapter examines the insurgency's adaptation of organizational outputs and learning. Organizational outputs consist of but are not limited to critical group processes (application of skills and knowledge; task performance competency; command, control, and communications; and cognition and behavior). Organizational learning consists of but is not limited to knowledge collection, transfer, and integration. This chapter concludes with a summary of the Iraqi insurgency's adaptation of organizational inputs, outputs, and learning.

ORGANIZATIONAL OUTPUTS

This section discusses the insurgency's adaptation of closely related critical group processes, including the application of skills and knowledge; task performance competency; command, control, and communications; and cognition and behavior.

Application of Skills and Knowledge

The insurgency's skill and knowledge was derived from previous martial training and education and, as the conflict progressed, built upon shared information and experiences gleaned from the conduct of operations. Experiences from the Soviet-Afghan War, the conflicts in Bosnia and Chechnya, the Iran-Iraq War, and the more recent war in Afghanistan, all contributed to insurgent knowledge and skills. Increasingly, these skills were enhanced through operational practice in Iraq.[2]

The insurgency's skills and knowledge manifested as unsophisticated yet creative responses to Coalition behavior. In reaction to Coalition actions, the insurgency was uncannily parsimonious and demonstrated a confounding capacity for combining disparate skills, knowledge, and resources in its attacks. Its use of IEDs is a good case in point: their design was variously simple or complex, depending on tactical requirements, the skills of the user, or materials available; they were used stand-alone or as a component of a deliberate ambush; and they were used to cause mass carnage—as in the case of large VBIEDs—or to target specific individuals, as in the case of magnetic or sticky IEDs. As a soldier deployed to Mosul in 2004 notes: "The insurgency's level of desperation and its lack of technology was striking. They used the least sophisticated method to arrive at the same end-state: blow up a U.S. vehicle. They would hide IEDs in dead animals, flower pots, etc. It was so simple yet so difficult to track. These people had, and we found, anarchist cookbooks, and stuff like that. You had to have a good memory of where things were along routes. It could be a new flower pot or it could be a new IED. If you put a dead animal on the road, we assume that someone hit the dog. Nobody thinks that someone put an IED in the dog. One, it would be ignored. Two, it was disgusting and nobody wanted to look at it."[3]

The insurgency was also capable of changing tactics and techniques adaptively to respond to Coalition behavior while still achieving a desired organizational effect. A soldier deployed to multiple locations in Iraq explains: "They might not have had the equipment but they made do with what they had and they reacted quickly to how we did things."[4] According to then Lieutenant Colonel James Crider, skills and knowledge were used to quickly modify equipment simply but effectively: "Most IEDs are not that sophisticated. Yes, some work with IR [Infra-Red] sensors and such and it does take some skill to learn how to make them well but none are cutting edge technology. Deadly IEDs are the deeply buried ones that are artillery shells or homemade explosives and explosively formed projectiles, which are copper slugs that cut through the armor on all of our vehicles."[5]

An ability to adapt skills and knowledge sets based on experience ensured that the insurgency could effectively counter its competitors rapidly and in concert with organizational goals. Maintaining simplicity enabled speed and also aided the propagation of skill and knowledge sets to other organizations. This was reflected in the tactical but not strategic adaptability of insurgent organizations in Iraq. Colonel Peter Mansoor describes the insurgency's capacity for adaptation: "I think that they had a greater capacity to adapt at the tactical level and at the technical level than they did at the strategic level. You take AQI for instance; if we put armor on our vehicles, then they built bigger bombs. If we put counter-EW [Electronic Warfare] devices on the vehicles, they used pressure plates. If we used metal detectors to find the pressure plates, they would go to command wire. That kind of adaptation occurred regularly with the insurgents and AQI terrorists in Iraq. What AQI couldn't do as well was adapt at the strategic level. For instance, once the tribes had begun to turn against AQI in Anbar Province, because of the way AQI treated the tribal chieftains and brutalized the people, AQI was not nimble enough to alter its strategy."[6]

It is important to note that the insurgency was quite adept at adapting organizational outputs to achieve simple organizational goals. Because of its structure, the insurgency was endowed with an ability to quickly modify its skill and knowledge sets. Individual organizations could make changes based upon their own experience or based upon their knowledge of the experiences of other insurgent organizations operating within or outside of Iraq. Lessons were drawn from insurgent operations in Colombia, Afghanistan, Ireland, the Palestinian territories, Chechnya, and Pakistan, among other places where conflict had occurred in the past or was then presently occurring. Effective small-group tactics, means of avoiding detection, and methods for repurposing military explosives were imported into Iraq or were shared among organizations both actively—as when foreign fighters deliberately imparted hands-on knowledge to Sunni tribal elements of the insurgency in al Anbar Province—or more passively, as when insurgent groups captured knowledge of "what worked" from postings on the Internet.

Furthermore, the insurgency could adapt at a pace that its competitors could not match. For instance, while the insurgency quickly and from the outset shared lessons on how to modify and creatively employ IEDs in response to changing Coalition tactics and techniques, the Pentagon did not establish the Joint Improvised Explosive Device Defeat Organization, or JIEDDO, until 2006. This is not to say that individual Coalition units were not developing and sharing means of confronting and defeating IEDs, but instead that U.S. forces did not or were not able to leverage their considerable resources to respond centrally to this threat for nearly three years after the start of the conflict.

Where the insurgency suffered was in adapting skill and knowledge sets in concert and in a way that affected many organizations across wide areas. Tactically oriented adaptations did not translate into strategic adaptation. While their ability to adapt at the individual and small-group level was useful and helped preserve organizational survival, it did little to advance mutually held or strategic organizational goals. That required broad cooperation among manifold organizations, something that rarely if ever happened during the 2003–8 period.

Task Performance Competency

To enhance task performance competency, insurgent organizations initially had to invent tasks and training regimens to accomplish their goals. Few native organizations had any experience in planning or conducting insurgent operations. Disparate organizations with inexperienced members suffered when they tried to cooperate with one another because: (1) they did not know external (and some internal) members very well; (2) they had little to no familiarity with one another; and (3) they at times had wildly differing tactical capabilities. Although the detachment and secrecy accompanying insurgent anonymity did aid organizational security, it also had "unintended and deleterious consequences."[7] When insurgents do not know each other very well or are not trained together, solidarity and capability suffer. Furthermore, many insurgent tasks required coordination and an implicit knowledge of participating members' tendencies and skills. These were unknowable in the early stages of the insurgency.

As the conflict progressed and as the insurgency gained competency and experiential skill, so too did its competitors. Its competitors' progress and adaptations manifested in the previously mentioned establishment of JIEDDO, the development of counterinsurgency concepts and doctrine, changes to the organization and employment of forces (the use of combat outposts and company intelligence support teams, for instance), the reshaping of training regimens at the U.S. Army's combat training centers, and the creation and employment of indigenous Iraqi police and military forces. Thus the insurgency had to expand and modify its task sets continuously to accomplish its goals. Insurgent competence in this regard increased for a number of reasons: (1) proficiency in task accomplishment (experience levels rose and many incompetent insurgents were killed off); (2) organizations with experienced and professional operators joined the insurgency; and (3) established tribal organizations expanded the operational reach and knowledge pool of the insurgency.[8] Progressively, the insurgency incorporated experience and knowledge into combinative tactical proficiencies. Simple tactics were blended into more complex tasks to achieve organizational goals. Competency was increased by focusing on the perfection of these fairly simple tactical tasks in planning and in training. A soldier deployed to Irbil, Kirkuk, and Mosul in 2003 explains: "We learned that the insurgents do the same things that we do. We had video tapes showing that the insurgents rehearse their attacks, film them, and then conduct learning sessions. It is like our squad STX [Squad Training Exercise] for Christ's sake."[9]

But the insurgency both benefited and suffered from small unit tactical proficiency: simple tasks, no matter how well performed, could support the accomplishment of only a limited set of organizational goals. These simple tasks could at some point be predicted and countered, particularly if intelligence indicated the time and place of a likely attack. Even as task performance competency increased, small insurgent units capable of completing a bevy of simple task skills were simply not capable of achieving more complex organizational goals despite significant adaptations to Coalition methods, tendencies, and tactics. Persistent and deliberate counterinsurgent operations against small insurgent groups reduced the effectiveness of the overall insurgency. By late 2007 unrelenting Coalition operations caused insurgent organizations to fragment and to conduct fewer well-organized attacks, over longer periods, and with less success. The smaller the group, whether competent or not, the less robust the effect of its attacks and the less likely that its attacks could be synchronized with larger or more comprehensive organizational goals.

Command, Control, and Communications

While only parts of the Iraqi insurgency were hierarchical in structure, hierarchical lines of control did exist.[10] What hierarchy that did exist, notably in AQI and other al Qaeda affiliated organizations, was mostly insulated from quotidian operations and instead busied itself with providing guidance to decentralized cells and combatant units. Organizational functions were given definition by leadership, but action elements (suborganizational and contracted cells or small groups) operated without strict managerial constraints. AQI and affiliated groups maintained some semblance of direct command and control of their organizations through recruitment mechanisms, organizational rules, and by procuring and managing organizational resources. For instance, the use of oaths of allegiance, separation pledges, and receipts for purchases all helped AQI manage its organization and operations. Tribal and former regime-led organizations similarly retained vestiges of control that extended from pre-existing power and command relationships. Other organizations even managed to maintain the command of operations farmed out to a seemingly limitless pool of insurgents through various communicative means and ad hoc chains of command. Operators were assigned missions, were hired on an as-needed basis, or operated independently as necessary or expedient.

As the insurgency expanded in size and scope—mostly by the addition of small cells or through the incorporation of sundry foreign and local volunteers—it required enhanced management structures—such as some insurgent groups' use of personnel databases—to ensure that organizational activity and behavior were tied to or at least reflected organizational goals. This was made possible in smaller more cellular organizations by communications technologies—when and where they existed—that linked subgroups to leadership. Although organizing in many small cells enhanced overall organizational security and expanded organizational capabilities in general, maintaining structural command and control with these disparate organizational echelons was difficult to accomplish, even with the aid of various communicative tools. This problem was compounded when larger organizations contracted support from operators and where more centralized control was divested to affiliated local commanders. While maintaining a large but loose network expanded organizational capability and was necessary for organizational security, it also made unified goal achievement a complicated and difficult endeavor. Despite the capabilities demonstrated by smaller organizations during the war, achieving organizational goals still required direction and coordination for coherence. As Anne Holohan argues, networks are in practice hierarchical *and* networked, and therefore leadership still plays a role.[11]

Internet communications provided the tools necessary for furtive correspondence between leadership and operators and for organizational command and control both before and after operations.[12] Although other electronic and nonelectronic communicative devices and methods—disposable cell phones, radios and radio stations,[13] text messaging, encrypted messaging, social networks, word of mouth, and so forth—were used by insurgent organizations, few provided the anonymity, security, applications, and speed of the Internet.[14] Critical information regarding successful techniques and other organizational information was transmitted via the Internet in the form of after-action reviews (AAR), videos of successful attacks, and instructional guidebooks.[15] This capability obviated innumerable meetings between core and peripheral organizational members that would otherwise have been necessary. The Internet greatly reduced information transmission time—and thus enhanced the timeliness of various command and control measures employed by insurgent organizations—and enabled extraorganizational connections at a low cost—the organization did not have to manage the infrastructure required for its employment.[16] The fragmentation and lack of coordination typically attributable to illicit networks was at least somewhat reduced by the use of the Internet, even though the organization was, for the most part, physically decentralized.[17]

The inter-netted command and control exercised by a hybrid organization like al Qaeda is an instructive example of how many hybrid insurgent organizations operated in Iraq: a smaller centralized group commanding cells of "surrogates" absent a perceptible leadership structure.[18] Al Qaeda also established specialized councils to deliberate and provide guidance to disparate affiliated and subordinate groups. In order to exercise command and control of the organization's functions and to ensure centralized management, al Qaeda leveraged the Internet to disseminate standardized tactics, unify organizational positions and goals, and to recruit new members and organizations.[19]

The insurgency's use of the Internet abetted the virtual centralization of organizational planning and coordination as well as the decentralization of operations by allowing core leadership, where it existed, to guide disparate individuals and groups. Command and control was executed through the issuance of guidance, instructions, or information tailored to coordinating behavior toward achieving organizational goals.[20] Absent the Internet, insurgent organizations would have had to meet more frequently, communicate more openly, or operate with even less direction or coordination, and thus would have faced an even greater risk of detection. Using inter-netted communications for command and control purposes allowed insurgent organizations to mostly avoid a trade-off between covertness and organizational effectiveness.[21]

Centralization was critical to organizational goal achievement. Decentralization was critical to survival. As then Colonel H. R. McMaster explains, an ability to centralize influenced organizational effectiveness and thus goal achievement: "Where they had a safe haven, they adopted a centralized organization. Where denied a safe haven they would have to decentralize, making them less effective. Being centralized would allow them to have a better structure for coordination and mobilization of resources and thus be more effective. Once denied a safe haven a key adaptation was to decentralize a) to survive and, b) to operate differently so as to still have some kind of effect against the population and against our forces."[22]

Cognition and Behavior

Insurgent cognition and behavior were shaped by training, experience, and individual and group capacity for interpreting the environment. Unlike the Coalition forces it faced, the insurgency lacked any significantly influential organizational culture. Even as the insurgency grew in size and strength, an insurgent culture was slow to develop because of the frequent and sometimes rapid structural changes besetting insurgent organizations. Furthermore, few insurgent organizations had any significant or enduring martial customs or institutional heritage.[23] Most insurgent operators and organizations were relatively free from the constraining influences of organizational culture, especially when compared with their Coalition competitors. Insurgent cognition and behavior were more closely tied to the learning that occurred during operations against the Coalition. It was further shaped by organizational attitudes and training received throughout the campaign. Individual and organizational cognition and a concomitant capacity for integrating and applying lessons in the face of environmental flux largely determined organizational behavior and subsequent adaptations based on this behavior.[24]

Because insurgent organizations many times lack or are free from organizational legacies and established cultural practices, they can be either more *or* less adaptive, depending on their level of training, their experiential knowledge, and their ability to interpret environmental changes in relation to organizational goals. As Jeffrey White argues, "[N]ot every aspect of insurgent behavior is adaptive—adaptation does not and cannot explain all insurgent behavior, and some insurgent traits and behaviors can be nonadaptive."[25] Freed from a baseline of organizational training, martial ethos, and an institutionalized set of problem-solving and goal accomplishment skills, insurgent organizations can respond to environmental cues either correctly and competently, or randomly and incoherently, depending on which cues are received and how they are processed in relation to organizational goals. An organization's fitness for its environment is not static; fitness is a measure of an organization's capacity for correctly responding to changes in the environment.[26] In this regard, the absence of organizational culture and historical legacy that can shape and influence decision-making can either be a constructive or harmful trait depending on whether or not these characteristics expand or restrict the organization's capacity to interpret and respond to the environment.

Any conflict environment can change quickly and can thus render an organization more or less potent depending on the changes that take place and the organization's capacity to respond to these changes.[27] Cognition and behavior were thus variable individual and organizational traits that could either positively or negatively influence organizational adaptation. Abilities to control, manipulate, or correctly understand the environment were key cognitive and behavioral capacities determinative of organizational fitness.

ORGANIZATIONAL LEARNING

This section examines insurgent knowledge collection, transfer, and integration.

Knowledge Collection

The insurgency took great care in collecting information about their operations in order to learn and improve their tactics through adaptation. This was done overtly during operations, covertly through concealed observation, and surreptitiously through penetration of Coalition organizations. A soldier deployed to Mosul in 2004 describes insurgent activity on coalition Forward Operating Bases (FOB): "Some of the things that they would come up with were from people working on the FOBs pacing things off or using cameras. They were sneaky about getting onto our FOBs for observation. They knew as well as we did that in a country where there is no personnel tracking and on a FOB where there are, on any given day, 300 people coming to the gate looking for work, it is very difficult to identify one individual that you kicked out."[28] Insurgent groups collected and compiled data—sometimes with cameramen alongside combatants—that included the date and time of an operation, identification of the insurgents involved, and a record of the insurgents' military deeds.[29] A soldier deployed to Irbil, Kirkuk, and Mosul in 2003 and later to Baghdad and Ramadi in 2005 explains that while much of this information was used for the purpose of insurgent propaganda, its most critical application was in determining best practices and for sharing operational information within and across organizations.[30]

Collected knowledge was used to create visual records that other insurgents could emulate, incorporate into training, or learn from as part of a descriptive vignette. In addition to capturing operational knowledge on video, in short films, or in testimonies, the insurgency created volumes of documentary data that recorded quantitative and qualitative aspects of insurgent operations to include: programmatic texts, inspirational texts, martyr biographies, poetry, operational reports, periodicals, radio broadcasts, biographies, books, recorded statements, songs, and analytical statements.[31] Sharing recorded and analyzed data gave other members of the insurgency a template for their own collection and analytical efforts. Precise collection efforts ensured that preparations for operations and successes and failures in knowledge application could be understood and incorporated throughout the insurgency. Collectively, this knowledge formed a corpus of data that, when distributed either by hand or via the

Internet, enabled timely and relevant organizational learning without the loss of security normally associated with a training event or large gathering.

The ability to learn from collected knowledge allowed the insurgency to adapt to environmental changes: tactics were adjusted; skills were updated; operations were improved; countermeasures were noted; and capabilities were renewed. Since most of the insurgency's suborganizations had vastly different experiences, levels of training, and operational skills and knowledge, collected knowledge expanded the insurgency's core competencies and contributed to a standardized set of tactics and techniques that could be modified or enhanced for particular operations. Without collected knowledge, the insurgency would have suffered even more egregiously from knowledge gaps, lagged learning, and retarded operational capacity, all of which occurred in the later stages of the insurgency. Although, by 2008, the base of insurgent knowledge was quite high, the fractioning of the insurgency led to fewer instances of knowledge collection (as well as transfer and integration).

Knowledge collection is critical for a covert networked organization. Since many of the subgroups of an insurgency—particularly the smaller elements consisting of fewer than a dozen members—do not openly or regularly meet, particularly with larger or parent organizations, and might never have the opportunity to discuss operations, successes, and failures, collected knowledge acts as a static (archived) and dynamic (alterable and can be added to) alternative source for learning. When accompanied by oral or written communiques, critiques, and analysis, knowledge can be converted into operational intelligence. Knowledge collected this way expands learning geometrically as each organization makes inferences from the evidence provided and adapts this knowledge for application to local circumstances. For instance, although two insurgent groups might not have had the chance to meet or operate together, they could—and did in Iraq—post and share videos of IED construction and employment, instruct each other on how to conduct training sessions, or provide information on how to conduct an ambush. This information could then be used as a training aid or in the construction of an attack. When this secondary application is also recorded, analyzed, and shared, the pool of operational intelligence expands further and becomes a broad dataset that details both friendly and enemy operations. This dataset can then be drawn upon for intra-, cross-, and external organizational adaptation.

Although knowledge collection alone cannot replace the utility of actual training events and collective AARs, it can supplement organizational learning by providing instructive examples of actual operations. The Iraqi insurgency's deliberate capture of critical operational details as part of the knowledge collection process, the translation of this knowledge into multiple languages, and the addition of narration to imagery and videos all allowed the insurgency to compare and contrast the efficiency and effectiveness of its methods and in respect to Coalition responses. In the absence of collected knowledge, disparate networked insurgent organizations were cognitively impaired: their minimalist size, attendant security considerations, and a lack of analytical power shrank the individual group's erudition set to data gleaned from direct experience and distant inference. Each segment of collected and analyzed operational knowledge expanded the knowledge pool that various insurgent groups could draw upon when planning and training for operations.

Knowledge Transfer

Insurgent planners and practitioners alike have to be able to share knowledge within the group and with other groups in order to make even semicoordinated organizational adaptations. Adaptation is at least partially premised on cyclical knowledge assessment, transfer, and integration. This process is accelerated when and where knowledge is transferred across groups and geographical spaces and is implemented in alternative environments by organizations where critical input and output factors (training, task performance competency, learning, and so forth) vary. Combinatorial iterations of transfer and assessment amplify the salience of this process. If an organization cannot fully assess its collective knowledge base and implement alternative options for action premised on this knowledge in the achievement of organizational goals, its adaptations at best will be random and at worst will compromise the organization's coherence and chances of survival. Assessment and adaptation are thus premised on knowledge transfer and successful innovations based upon this knowledge.

The tangible representation of transferred knowledge is the spread of innovations. Innovations appear as creative, mimicked, and yet uncoordinated responses to those changes in the environment that either degrade or enhance the likelihood of achieving organizational goals. When multiple organizations independently sense a change in the environment—a new counterinsurgent tactic, for instance—they respond and then share knowledge of success and failure in responding to this change. This results in additional and more informed innovations. A typical IED cell's knowledge transfer process is illustrative: "IED cells often exchange information and transfer skills among one another by sharing videos of their respective exploits for training purposes. The IED unit includes several people, from those who procure the raw materials (usually from ammunition dumps), to the bomb-builder, undoubtedly the most technically skilled individual in the cell, who also doubles as training instructor."[32]

The ability to transfer knowledge effectively reduces the number of assumptions that an organization has to make regarding the effectiveness of its actions and responses. It also enables greater coordination within and among organizations with similar organizational goals and requirements. Devoid a capacity to share knowledge within and across groups, an organization would have to complete several response iterations to collect a similar amount of relevant environmental and organizational information. Furthermore, the information collected could or would only be analyzed by a single organization's members. Therefore, any information collected by an individual organization would lack robustness and would be less applicable to the refinement of an organization's adaptive cycle. Hence, the ability to transfer knowledge mitigates a number of networked organizational weaknesses: measurement and assessment capacity; the ability to correctly sense, probe, and respond to the environment; the external validity of organizational findings; and the number of assumptions made when planning and conducting operations. Organizational innovation and continued adaptation are enhanced by knowledge transfer.

Knowledge transfer spurs innovation in at least two ways: overtly (direct communication via personal connections) and passively (stigmergic environmental signals).[33] John Robb argues that there is a pattern to this process involving a cycle of innovation, adoption, and propagation.[34] The networked structure of the Iraqi insurgency enabled the organizational independence necessary for making timely and experimental innovations. Additionally, these small and mostly autonomous groups were motivated by survival and goal achievement and were thus intrinsically interested in improving their capabilities. Michael Eisenstadt and Jeffrey White contend that small groups are more likely than larger groups to innovate and share their innovations with other groups. Correspondingly, sharing knowledge among groups allows smaller groups to "achieve broader tactical and operational effects than they could on their own."[35] The tools and relationships necessary for sharing these innovations were omnipresent in Iraq.

Personal, intraorganizational, and interorganizational knowledge transfer was abetted by a variety of procedures and enablers available to most if not all Iraqi insurgent organizations. The insurgency adopted media techniques from al Qaeda's various internationally affiliated groups to support daily press releases, distribute printed materials, and offer various videos for download in a number of languages.[36] It also leveraged digital imagery and video as well as data storage and transmission devices for the transference of knowledge, information, and instructions.

The insurgency was also adept at confounding attempts to shut down its knowledge transfer activities. Content from disbanded websites was archived and presented on new websites, free uploads and downloads were made available, and compressed film files were developed for mobile phone transfer and viewing.[37] The insurgency developed and spread knowledge regarding tactical techniques and procedures via instructional articles, manuals, video films, books, PowerPoint presentations, and Portable Document Format (PDF) newspapers.[38] Weaponry usage, assassination techniques, and poison and explosives manufacturing were among a few of the subjects discussed and disseminated in these publications. Websites were also used to announce policy positions, alliance formations, strategic shifts, breaking news, and to comment on Western media.[39] Although intergroup personal contacts were likely the easiest and most used knowledge transfer methods, according to David Kilcullen, terrorist and insurgent groups had (and have) access to doctrine, information, and procedures made available either in hardcopy or through the Internet.[40]

Iraq's locally oriented insurgent organizations also contributed to knowledge transfer within and across organizations and through population-based channels of communication. Friendly populations, family members, and affiliates all contributed to the collection and then transfer of knowledge to the broader insurgency. When the environment changed and if no insurgent organization or only one organization directly perceived this change, the population indirectly supplied evidence and descriptions of the change that took place. A soldier deployed to Irbil, Kirkuk, and Mosul explains that Coalition actions, even simple response techniques and methods, were likely shared: "The insurgents are adaptive. When they shot at us with AK-47s, we returned fire with 25 mm rounds that were explosive. They didn't like that action at all and they learned not to shoot at us. People were watching and I am sure that our response was spread around to other people."[41]

Most insurgent groups were indigenous to Iraq, did not leave the country for any reason, and in many cases had deep local knowledge and strong connections to the population even when operating outside of their home neighborhoods. Where knowledge collection and transfer might have been difficult because an organization's members were interdicted, killed, or captured, and where collection and dissemination methods were problematical or impossible to employ, friendly locals collectively acted as a knowledge repository and transfer mechanism.

Knowledge Integration

The insurgency collected operational and organizational information and actively integrated it into published manuals, pamphlets, and electronic media that were later used to modify organizational behavior and inputs to the organization's adaptive processes. This process occurred formally and informally as circumstance and speed permitted.

Integrating knowledge was important for organizational adaptation in a number of key respects: a group's structure, if sufficiently variable or frequently disrupted, could dislocate or retard organizational memory; inexperienced newcomers could be taught lessons that most organizational members took for granted; change to organizational inputs and outputs could be progressive instead of random; and integration ensured that if sections of the organization were compromised or disabled, the rest of the organization could effectively carry on with planning and operations.

Organizations that took advantage of integrating the knowledge collected by its members and by other organizations were capable of adapting more quickly and appropriately than organizations that failed to incorporate hard-won lessons. Knowledge integration is critical to organizations that suffer rapid personnel turnovers. This is particularly true for smaller networked organizations that rely on mutually learned lessons and capability sharing for organizational goal accomplishment. For example, although AQI and other insurgent groups were capable of refilling their membership quickly, their new members, lacking experience and the knowledge learned by previous fighters, were less disciplined and resorted to less deliberate and more random violence.[42]

A SUMMARY OF ORGANIZATIONAL INPUTS, OUTPUTS, AND LEARNING

The Iraqi insurgency grew rapidly between early 2003 and 2004, and it continued to expand well into 2006. During its growth period the insurgency's composition changed radically. At first, the insurgency consisted of a fairly small number of disaffected Iraqis, FREs, and assorted foreign fighters. Some of these individuals had organizational affiliations, and some merely acted alone or as part of small groups in an effort to strike or lash out at Coalition forces. But between late 2006 and late 2008, the insurgency began to dissolve precipitously. Organizations switched loyalties, individuals returned to society, and many foreign fighters left to join operations in Afghanistan and elsewhere. The insurgency's diverse composition and networked disposition led to an uneven capacity for overall organizational adaptation. It enabled its early and midterm successes but also ultimately contributed to its demise. What were at times strengths became weaknesses and vice versa: variously, the insurgency's composition and disposition affected its capacity to adapt organizational inputs and outputs and to learn. The following section provides a summary assessment of the Iraqi insurgency's adaptive capabilities and processes.

Organizational Inputs—Context

The insurgency's expansion and diversity led to difficulties in appropriately adapting contextual inputs to meet organizational requirements. Increasing complexity led to convoluted goals and rewards that further led to competition within, between, and among organizations. This was increasingly the case in the 2006 and later periods as the insurgency fractured and previously cooperative organizations came into conflict with one another. Sources and the quality of information expanded and then decreased as constraints on organizational behavior became difficult to enforce. Organizational and environmental uncertainty and competition increased and an inherent ability to adapt to achieve organizational goals decreased.

Organizational complexity led to differing and competing goals and rewards that detracted from shared goal achievement.

As the insurgency became more complex its composition became more convoluted. Convolution exacerbated organizational differences and friction flourished: competition among organizations was just as likely as cooperation. An overarching transorganizational goal abetted explicit and implicit cooperative practices, but it did not suppress an interest in achieving other divergent organizational goals. Although the complexity of the insurgency confounded the efforts of counterinsurgent forces, created a massive de facto resource and personnel pool for affiliated organizations, and enhanced the insurgency's capacity for operations, it also diminished the organization's ability to positively adapt inputs and outputs toward coherent and common goal achievement.

Organizational complexity enabled and disrupted information flows in consonance with levels of cooperation and competition.

Dedicated resources (information offices, spoken word recordings, print materials, Internet broadcasts and databases, digital photographic capabilities, and so forth) and entrenched feedback loops populated by well-placed sources and local informants enhanced the insurgency's capacity for influencing the information environment. Ubiquitous, low cost, and replaceable technologies employed and operated on state or Coalition transmission systems allowed insurgent organizations to rapidly respond to and counter Coalition operations and share valuable lessons learned and other operational information. But as the insurgency came into conflict—such as when AQI fell out of favor with the tribes of al Anbar Province—and as organizations diverged, its sources of information collection and transmission dissolved. Ultimately, this led to a decrease in the insurgency's ability to control, and in the later stages of the insurgency to influence or even understand, the operational environment.

Training was born of experimentation and shared experience but could not be conducted broadly for the achievement of more complex or panorganizational goals.

The manifestation and employment of uneven skill sets led to operational failures and "Combat Darwinism," but also led to vast organizational experimentation. Coincidentally, insurgent experimentation and wily tactical innovations—deliberate *and* unintentional—kept Coalition forces off balance. Training occurred on the job, capitalized on the experiences of organization members, was supported by external groups and state-sponsored professionals, and focused in the main on low-tech and simple but coordinated tactics. Varied but broadly implemented low-level training exercises and rehearsals—many of which were recorded for educational purposes—ensured that the insurgency adapted comprehensively to individual successes and failures. But an inability, because of a need to maintain covertness, or failure, because groups had competing goals, to train to achieve more complex organizational goals or to enable the close coordination of multiple groups for broader military *and* political purposes lessened the utility of what came to be fairly advanced tactical capabilities.

Variable and loose constraints on organizational behavior led to organizational division and separation from supporters.

Insurgent organizations faced few constraints on their behavior other than the need to maintain population support: active if possible and passive if not.

This support facilitated and concealed operations, drove local recruitment, and helped maintain influence if not control over the information environment. Acting with impunity or a lack of sufficient respect for this constraint imposed significant organizational costs: information and resources were lost and the ability to adapt based on these resources was reduced.

Organizational Inputs—Group Design and Culture

As noted in previous sections, the insurgency's composition presented as an organizational strength and weakness. Its complex composition and networked disposition led to the inculcation of various organizational cultures and norms. Sometimes these cultures and norms led to cooperation—such as AQI's pairing with the tribes in al Anbar Province. At other times, such as when AQI's brutality became unbearable, cultures and norms led to competition and infighting. Cooperation increased the insurgency's capacity to adapt, and competition, for the most part, stifled adaptability.

Organizational diversity led to influxes of people, ideas, and resources but also led to goal divergence and uncooperative behavior.

The Iraqi insurgency's complexity derived from the number, type, and heterogeneity of networked groups operating in Iraq. Insurgent groups operated from Basra in the south to Mosul and Kirkuk in the north and were populated by locals as well as by foreigners from almost all continents. Its diverse composition made it exceptional as compared with previous insurgencies. But the insurgency's composition also disrupted coordinated goal achievement, organizational coherence, and broad, long-term, cross-organizational cooperation. The insurgency's diversity provoked organizational divergence and made partnering difficult. A lack of central direction and leadership inhibited adaptation toward commonly shared goals.

Norm variation led to discord and diminished levels of cooperation and support.

Norms, which influence behavior, varied among groups. Iraqi group norms were significantly different from those of foreign insurgent organizations. Iraqi groups, generally, were more restrained in their behavior and actions while foreign groups were not. Within the insurgency, conflicting norms disrupted the accomplishment of long-term goals and the cohesion of cooperating organizations, as groups treated each other and local populations differently and in turn received varying levels of support over time.

*As the environment changed the insurgency was incapable of matching
its tasks to its goals, particularly in the long term.*

Tasks are derived from goals and are shaped by changing cues emanating from the operational environment. Insurgent organizational tasks evolved as membership competency increased. But as the operational environment changed and the capabilities required for success compounded, few insurgent organizations could reasonably adapt their tasks to goals and requirements. Most organizations did not have the capacity to accomplish multiple, coordinated, complex organizational tasks beyond tactical attacks and ambushes. The competency and organizational skill sets required to complete complex, multidimensional tasks generally did not exist, and thus many organizations were unable to adapt appropriately.

Organizational Inputs—Materiel and Technical Resources

The insurgency manifested an ability to quickly use available materiel and technical resources to achieve organizational goals. The insurgency's parsimonious garnering and use of resources to great effect was perhaps one of its most significant adaptive capacities. It seemingly used all available equipment for arming its forces, developing creative means of communication, generating vast and many times undetectable streams of funding, and facilitating an enormous intelligence-gathering and -processing apparatus without recourse to research and development agencies. Its greatest weakness was a lack of organizational girth—an inability to completely integrate intelligence with other resources and to leverage it for use in multiple organizations simultaneously for military and political goals.

*Equipment was used parsimoniously and effectively in the achievement
of organizational military goals.*

The insurgency had ready access to enormous amounts of military-grade equipment, explosives, small arms, ammunition, user manuals, and communications devices. In addition, the insurgency had access to other low-grade electronic equipment and industrial supplies used for booby-traps, IEDs, and observation. Insurgent organizations used all available equipment and tools, employed skillfully, to enhance their survivability, expand stand-off attack distances, and coordinate networked hit-and-run attacks.

Insurgent organizations created funding streams and adapted them to manage operations and organizational expansion.

Licit and illicit funding streams were used interchangeably to finance operations, enable recruitment, and contract support from the local population via supplementary income streams. Insurgent organizations paired with organized criminal groups and/or adopted their tactics, techniques, and procedures when possible. Insurgent organizations engaged in crime, looting, and kidnapping to raise funds, took donations from external organizations and charities, and colluded with corrupt organizations and individuals. The insurgency was largely and variably self-financing, and it thus confounded Coalition attempts to cause an operational collapse by cutting off or disabling any particular source of funding.

Intelligence gathering and processes spanned organizations and provided invaluable information for adapting organizational inputs and outputs.

The insurgency developed an expansive social and technical intelligence collection and sharing network and used it to actively, passively, directly, and persistently observe its operational environment. Dedicated organizational assets and sensitively placed sources conducted express intelligence gathering, while the Iraqi population provided general information on Coalition movements and on the effects of insurgent organizational activities. Intelligence that was gathered pervasively on the terrain, government deliberations, and Coalition actions was shared among insurgent organizations to inform and tailor the planning of, training for, and execution of operations. Although this apparatus broke down as organizational infighting increased and as the Iraqi population became disaffected, many insurgent organizations, even in the waning days of the insurgency, still maintained small, yet effective, intelligence gathering apparatuses.

Organizational Inputs—External Assistance

The insurgency took advantage of the external assistance provided by foreign fighters and assorted illicit groups that formed or operated in Iraq after 2003. Some organizations provided guidance and manpower, while still others conducted operations that collectively clouded the operational environment and made distinguishing insurgents from average Iraqis a nearly impossible task. But increasing levels of external assistance also led to competition, organizational fratricide, and significant goal divergence.

*Limited external consulting resulted in greater independence but
perhaps less coordination than could have been achieved otherwise.*

External consultation with organizations (particularly states and their functionaries) that did not have direct ties to individuals and groups in Iraq was limited. The variety of capabilities and resources brought to bear by manifold organizations participating in the insurgency obviated the need for state-based assistance and allowed for significant and relatively independent interorganizational consultation. Thus insurgent organizations were not subject to the controls and whims of external powers and were able to make decisions and engage in acts based on internal organizational interests. This was beneficial insofar as it allowed for independence and freedom of maneuver and association. But higher degrees of independence also impinged on coordination, coherence, and effectiveness.

*The chaos manufactured by the insurgency increased exponentially
when other illicit organizations conducted direct action in support of
the insurgency or in parallel to its activities.*

Individual actors, external but indigenous Iraqi organizations, criminal groups, and foreign organizations all contributed to the Iraqi insurgency even if the effects of their actions were only tangentially or indirectly tied to the goals of insurgent organizations. The prevailing chaos permitted various activities that expanded the effects of the insurgency (crime, looting, revenge killings, and so forth) and significantly disrupted Coalition efforts. Direct action on behalf of or benefiting insurgent organizations slowed the Coalition's adaptive cycle and allowed committed insurgent organizations the time and space to adjust organizational inputs and outputs with more discretion.

Cooperation was as likely as competition.

Insurgent groups (tribes, FREs, foreign groups, various militias, and criminal organizations) cooperated when their goals aligned and when mutual benefits could be realized. But while the diverse nature of the insurgency provided opportunities for cooperation, it also ensured organizational disunity as differing organizational goals and interests came into conflict. Disunity led to friction and ultimately disrupted cross-organizational capacities for adapting resources to organizational goals. Competition for goal achievement further caused a rationing of organizational capital.

Organizational Outputs—Critical Group Processes

Organizational outputs are critical group processes that are shaped and refined by the organizational inputs described in Chapter 2 and summarized above. Importantly, as organizational inputs were adapted for goal accomplishment, the success or failure of these adaptations had effect on the insurgency's capacity for carrying out critical group processes. The critical group processes described in this chapter fed into one another and expanded or contracted in concert.

Insurgent organizations quickly adapted skills and knowledge to the effective completion of simple tasks.

Insurgent skills and knowledge were initially derived from member talent and training but were later expanded by organizational experiences. Skills and knowledge were applied to train for and coordinate more complex task sets (for example, ambushes, raids, sequenced explosions) composed of fairly simple (such as small arms employment) but synchronized and, more important, repeatable organizational skills. This increased the rate of organizational adaptation and enhanced the iterative propagation of skills in harmony with organizational objectives.

Organizations, limited in size by a need for covertness, increased task performance competency but with decreasing marginal returns as the environment required more complex capabilities for goal accomplishment.

The pace of competition with Coalition forces required consistent and perpetual task modification to achieve organizational goals. Insurgent task competency increased over time. But because of limitations on organizational size and an inability to train frequently or coordinate with larger organizations, increases in task performance competency had less and less effect on the achievement of organizational goals. Military and combat capability was not translated into building mass support or for the purposes of providing acceptable forms of alternative governance. To achieve broader goals effectively, the insurgency required a progressive capacity to accomplish more complex tasks. This could not be achieved by smaller groups: interorganizational training and cooperation were significantly circumscribed by a need to maintain covertness and secrecy.

The Internet and other means of social networking and coordination
allowed for virtual command, control, and communications.

Hybrid organizations with small operational cells used the Internet and so-cial contacts to coordinate operations and adaptations within and across orga-nizations and to provide command and control, guidance, and direction. Cen-tralization, either physical or virtual, was required for greater comprehensive organizational effectiveness. When organizations were penetrated or were dis-lodged from physical locations, the Internet was used to centralize command and control virtually. This capability persisted even when organizations came into conflict in the later stages of the insurgency. The use of social networks for information transfer was sharply circumscribed as networks divested mem-bers, broke down, or no longer communicated.

An ability to sense the environment and adapt accordingly shaped and
was shaped by cognition and behavior.

Insurgent cognition and behavior were variably shaped by organizational and individual abilities to receive, interpret, and incorporate information on organizational and environmental change. These patterns broke down as or-ganizations lost their ability to sense the environment—because of a loss of support or a collapse in cooperation—or when organizational behavior was not adapted according to the reactions it engendered in other organizations or the Iraqi population.

Organizational Learning

The insurgency's ability to collect, transfer, and integrate knowledge ex-tracted from individuals and organizations and gleaned from operational ex-perience created an organizational and environmental awareness that allowed it to adapt its inputs and outputs to achieve goals. The insurgency developed and used diverse collection and transfer methods that took advantage of avail-able technologies and the transaction networks developed by its members and member organizations. When competition ensued and the insurgency began to lose the support of the Iraqi populace, its ability to collect, transfer, and integrate knowledge decreased. And despite the insurgency's high levels of ex-perience and knowledge at that point, it became less adaptive. Absent robust knowledge collection and transfer capabilities, it was unable to integrate new knowledge into its membership and operations quickly and effectively.

Knowledge collection enabled adaptation, but the insurgency's capacity
for collecting knowledge decreased as the network lost membership
through competition and defections.

Knowledge collection relied upon and was aided by the overt documentation and recording of operations, covert observation, and the surreptitious penetration of Coalition and governmental organizations. Knowledge was collected by manifold organizations and individuals and through various means to include video, imagery, spoken word, diaries, semiofficial records, and databases. It was distributed and integrated to adapt training and task performance. Its collection expanded the adaptive capacity of disparate organizations by creating a record and database of organizational knowledge tempered by organizational success and failure. Knowledge collection varied positively with interorganizational cooperation and with population support.

Concealed and rapid knowledge transfer allowed disparate
organizations to share ideas and experiences without direct contact.

Knowledge transfer is reflected in innovations and the spread of innovations. Transfer within the Iraqi insurgency was made possible by assorted media: video and audio recordings; print; and Internet web pages. Transferring knowledge reduces the number of assumptions that an organization has to make in planning. Weaknesses, such as the inability of smaller organizations to comprehensively assess the operational environment and the effects of its own activities, consistently and correctly respond to environmental changes, and externally validate conclusions and adaptive changes to organizational inputs and outputs, were reduced by the effective transfer of knowledge.

Knowledge was integrated through experience and experimentation, but
levels of integration suffered from high personnel losses and turnover.

Lessons and knowledge were integrated in informal doctrine and through exchanges of information between and among organizations and their members. Knowledge integration helped offset the organizational memory problems associated with networks that experienced high turnover or interdiction. As long as organizations continued to cooperate toward the accomplishment of shared goals, knowledge integration helped shape adjustments of inputs and outputs coherently across organizational boundaries. When competition was the norm, these patterns of knowledge integration were disrupted.

CONCLUSION

The adaptations the insurgency made to organizational inputs, outputs, and learning truly reflected the strengths and weaknesses of its complex composition and networked disposition. Its flexibility, size, covertness, and diversity were at times beneficial and at other times deleterious.

First, the insurgency's diverse composition allowed it become very effective at achieving simple organizational goals through the application of greater levels of skills and knowledge. Over time, experience and diverse membership significantly abetted the insurgency's skill in performing tasks to achieve goals. Insurgent organizations many times outpaced their Coalition competitors in terms of tactical adaptation, invention, and ingenuity. What the insurgency could not achieve, however, was a level of coordination necessary for translating disparate action into coherent and broader goal accomplishment. Tactical and rather isolated adaptations, even when effectively shared, did not necessarily aid in the achievement of strategic or interorganizational goals. A number of adaptive groups that are good at a set of fairly simple tasks do not necessarily make an effective whole. And effectiveness does not translate into effect: small pin-prick style operations, although disruptive in mass, did little to advance organizational goals.

Second, becoming more and more proficient at relatively simple tasks had a pernicious side effect: competitor organizations could begin to predict, preempt, or foil insurgent attacks. What covertness was maintained by secrecy was offset by increasingly predictable modi operandi. This was problematic given that interdiction resulted in capture, death, the loss of resources and, ultimately, the severance of organizations from one another. These effects were compounded and in turn led to smaller and less connected networks and a decrease in the insurgency's overall ability to adapt critical group processes, either efficiently or effectively.

Third, the insurgency's ability to centralize for effectiveness and coherence, and decentralize for security and survival, varied in tandem with its behavior. Organizational behavior varied based on the diversity of its composition. Behavioral variance, depending on its noxiousness or benefice, led to increased or decreased levels of support from other organizations and the Iraqi population.

Fourth, as the insurgency became larger and more diverse, organizational goals came into conflict and organizational friction became the norm. What command and control existed became disjointed, and coordination and cooperation suffered. Since the insurgency remained fairly large, it was also subject to more and more breaches of security, which led to further organizational discovery and fracturing.

Last, adaptations to organizational learning took advantage of the diversity of the insurgency's membership, its collective experience, and available means of transferring knowledge via concealable methods and means. But when this diversity led to fractures in the insurgency, the network correspondingly proved much less effective at collecting, transferring, and integrating knowledge, which is perhaps the sine qua non of organizational adaptation. Of course, smaller and aligned organizations could still share information and use shared knowledge to adapt their organizational inputs and outputs in line with organizational goals even during the insurgency's decline. But the breadth of information shared and depth to which it was analyzed dropped significantly as the insurgency fell into disorder.

While these findings in and of themselves are instructive and of utility insofar as they inform the thesis of this book, and as they expose the strengths and weaknesses of the Iraqi insurgency, they are not nearly as revealing as they could be without being compared with a similar case of covert networked organizational adaptation. Chapter 4 makes this comparison. It provides an examination of the Afghan insurgency's organizational adaptation and then compares the findings of this analysis against those presented in this chapter.

4 Seeing Afghanistan, Thinking Iraq— Evaluating and Comparing the Insurgency in Afghanistan

INTRODUCTION

Afghanistan has been suffering from some form of conflict since its invasion by Soviet forces in 1979 and has essentially been engaged in a civil war, insurgency, or counterinsurgency since that period.[1] The most recent conflict—beginning with the 2001 Coalition invasion of Afghanistan—was preceded by a struggle among warlords,[2] for control of what they historically considered to be their territories and, ostensibly, for the governance, however disjointed, of Afghanistan.[3] The Taliban emerged from this conflict in 1994, and although at the time more accepted in Pakistan than Afghanistan, it eventually wrested control of both the central government and a large portion of Afghan territory from the warring factions.[4]

But following the 2001 Coalition invasion of Afghanistan, the Taliban was again reduced to insurgent status. The remnants of its government and leadership as well as many of its supporters were scattered about Afghanistan and neighboring countries, with Pakistan being the predominant destination. Initially it was a small and rather homogenous Pashtun-dominated movement with membership numbering perhaps in the hundreds or low thousands. Over time, the Taliban insurgency began to grow and attracted fellow travelers into or near its orbit including vestiges of al Qaeda, Hizb-i-Islami Gulbuddin (HiG) led by Gulbuddin Hekmatyar, the Haqqani network led by Jalaluddin Haqqani, foreign fighters, criminal organizations, and various tribal and subtribal elements.[5] According to recent estimates,[6] the insurgency continues to grow and now counts tens of thousands of supporters and fighters as members.

But because of its history and numerous other more present faults, the insurgency has not achieved and does not maintain mass "popular" support.[7] Even within the insurgency, there is division. Yet, while being fractious, it has not fractured. It has managed to adapt to Coalition surges, impositions on its internal and external bases of support, captures and deaths of key leadership, and shifting internal alliances.[8] While wildly imperfect, the Afghan insurgency has steadily adapted frequently and correctly enough to make progress toward achieving some of its fundamental goals. Although this story is incomplete, it is instructive insofar as it sheds light on how an insurgency that is at least broadly similar in size and scope to the one that existed in Iraq has not only managed to survive for a longer period but has organizationally adapted to become even more effective over time. The central question of this chapter is then, comparatively, how does the Afghan insurgency manage to leverage the strengths and counter the weaknesses of its complex and covert networked organization better than did its counterpart in Iraq?

This chapter evaluates this evolution and the Afghan insurgency's adaptive cycle and uses the same analytical framework applied in the previous two chapters. It is meant to be comparative insofar as it reveals organizational and adaptive similarities and differences between the Iraqi and Afghan insurgencies. This comparison is useful for contrasting the adaptive strengths and weaknesses of the former against the latter. Although there are many differences between the two insurgencies—most important, that the Afghan insurgency is ongoing and thus any analysis of its ultimate effectiveness can only be speculative[9]—there are also many similarities: both faced or face an international coalition and governments installed and supported by these coalitions, respectively; both were or are large, complex, and diverse; neither was or is purely networked but shared or share many networked organizational properties; both existed or exist in roughly the same period and thus the technology, weapons, and other resources available to each is comparable; and each insurgency's composition and disposition was or is both a strength and weakness in respect to organizational adaptation and goal accomplishment. It must be noted that because the Taliban is by far and away the largest single component of the Afghan insurgency,[10] with estimates that it represents up to 80 percent of the insurgency's armed strength,[11] it will receive the bulk of analysis in the chapter.[12] This chapter concludes with a comparison of the previous chapter's findings against the strengths and weaknesses of the Afghan insurgency.

ORGANIZATIONAL INPUTS—CONTEXT

This section examines insurgent goals and rewards, information, training, and constraints.

Goals and Rewards

The goals, expected rewards, and related motivations of each of the Afghan insurgency's constituent groups vary. Some individuals and organizations have a general interest in opposing what many consider an apostate, corrupt, and failing regime, while others fight for fundamentalist and nationalist causes, material benefit or opportunism, parochial and familial purposes, revenge, xenophobia, as part of a defensive jihad, pleasure, or out of fear.[13] Naturally, many of these motivations and goals are overlapping or even competing and might change in step with varying conditions, pressures, and opportunities.

The saliency of particular motivations and thus individual and organizational involvement in the insurgency has waxed and waned over time. The Taliban, per its genesis and regeneration, seeks to retake control of the governance of Afghanistan.[14] Criminal organizations, illicit goods traffickers, and black marketers want an Afghanistan that is amenable to if not supportive of their business practices.[15] Foreign militants from Arab states, neighboring Tajikistan, Uzbekistan, and Pakistan, and as far away as Chechnya, Germany, and Turkey, have found common cause in Afghanistan and have traveled there to fight and to provide expertise.[16] Al Qaeda, with its internationalist goals, has been involved in the insurgency in one way or another since its most recent recrudescence in 2001.[17] It finds safe harbor along Afghanistan's eastern border, and it provides the insurgency with expertise, logistical support, weaponry, and funding. Elements of Afghanistan's Uzbek, Turk, Aimaqs, and Tartar populations support the periphery of the Pashtun-dominated insurgency,[18] perhaps with the expectation of better or more equitable future governance. Despite different motivations and expected rewards, nearly all of the insurgency's participants share the commonly held goals of removing Coalition forces and influence from Afghanistan and surrounding states and replacing the Karzai government that the Coalition helped introduce and continues to support. This shared goal has led to the manifestation of a diverse, increasingly widespread, and yet very localized metastasizing of the Afghan insurgency.[19]

The Taliban, the largest single constituent of the Afghan insurgency and the initial target of the Coalition invasion, recognized early on that it needed to modify its original puritanical ideological goals in order to attract and maintain a broader base of support. This has been one of its chief organizational adaptations, regardless of how self-serving, temporary, or chimerical this shift might in reality be. Changing its purported goals has led to an increased capacity for successfully meeting these goals, insofar as it is now perceived as less an imposing fundamentalist movement as it is a serious and reasonable alternative to the Karzai-led government.[20] Its progress toward achieving these goals is at least partially reflected in its growing capacity to attract passive followers, recruit fighters, and retain the support of various populations within and external to Afghanistan. And, transitively, its ability to accrete support is reflected in its capacity to realize its organizational goals, particularly as the central government's capacity to govern comparatively weakens and atrophies.[21] Modifying its goals from the almost purely ideological and religious to ones that relate more closely to governance and nationalism has allowed the Taliban and closely associated groups to appeal to a wider audience.[22] In the early days of the postinvasion insurgency, the Taliban relied strongly on prominent Pashtun tribes, madrassa students, and refugee camps for personnel and support.[23] But as the insurgency gained momentum and a degree of success, it was able to broaden its recruitment efforts to non-Pashtun tribes.[24] By 2006 and after a number of battlefield successes, the Taliban expanded its recruitment base from rural to urban populations, and it made attempts to reach out to a number of former mujahideen commanders.[25] It has leveraged and continues to exploit informal family, tribal, friendship, religious, and interest networks in a coordinated effort to find new recruits that it can further indoctrinate into the insurgency's cause.[26]

The Taliban has carefully woven its new narrative of governance and justice with military action against the Karzai government and the Coalition, the successful establishment and conduct of parallel governance outside the confines of Kabul, the dispensation of security and resolution of grievances at the provincial and village levels, and the provision of other goods and services that either the state has failed to provide or that are absorbed by corrupt political and business leaders. In doing so, it has gradually but appreciably garnered support and has created a real sense of legitimacy, however distorted, that is almost wholly absent in the present government.

But as the insurgency's base of support expands, so too does the possibility that it will at some point experience significant friction.[27] Because the Afghan insurgency is diverse and because its manifestation is very much localized, it is almost inevitable that the overarching goals that presently at least partially bind the insurgency in common cause will wither.[28] It is hard to say what might trigger this divergence, but it is certainly reasonable to expect that when the bulk of Coalition forces do finally leave Afghanistan, simmering grievances are likely to reemerge and overlapping interests are likely to dissipate.[29] The Taliban, al Qaeda, Hizb-i-Islami, the Haqqani network, as well as various tribes and former warlords and their supporters, and criminal organizations and their shadow networks, are just as likely if not more likely to engage in internecine fighting than they are to find common ground, particularly in respect to their views on the governance and control of Afghanistan's licit and illicit resources.[30] Differences related to ideology, kinship, ethnicity, culture, and nationality, particularly among the core leadership of each of these groups,[31] will almost certainly come to the fore.[32] A general resistance to Pashtun dominance will also likely reemerge among Afghanistan's minority populations. Additionally, the small, localized factions that compose a large portion of the insurgency's foot soldiers and engender its capacity for controlling large swaths of territory will surely return their focus to atomistic local issues and away from the broader issues of nation building and central governance.

Since the Coalition invasion in 2001 and shortly thereafter, the organizations composing the Afghan insurgency have, for the most part, suppressed their inclinations to fight one another and have found that a mutually symbiotic resistance to the Coalition and to the Karzai government is at least temporarily acceptable, if not beneficial, in light of possible alternatives. It could be that these groups have either found enduring common ground among their varying goals or that, more likely, their three-decades-plus collective experience in conflict has taught them a certain amount of strategic and tactical patience. But as Linschoten and Kuehn remind us, "The political vacuum that followed the ouster of the Taliban gave ample space for old and new conflicts to erupt."[33] It remains to be seen if additional conflict will erupt after the departure of Coalition forces, but Afghanistan's history suggests that once these external parties exit, conflict is as likely if not more likely a fate than is any enduring peace.[34]

Information

Control of the information environment in Afghanistan is contested, but the insurgency has managed to develop effective means for expeditiously communicating messages to both internal and external audiences through web-based, print, and various digital platforms. Information is shared efficiently and effectively for the purposes of conveying organizational agendas, countering Coalition communications, and even for coordinating quick-hitting swarming attacks on specific targets.[35] The insurgency has no less than four target audiences for its messages: its supporters, neutrals, Coalition leadership, and networks that can endow or are imparting resources to the insurgency.[36]

The focus of the Taliban's internal and external information campaigns is to promote nationalism, whether real or perceived, while avoiding other potentially fractious messages such as those based upon ethnicity or tribalism. This has been useful for attracting support as well as recruits and has demonstrated a sophisticated knowledge of local issues, perceptions, interests, and goals.[37] And despite being decentralized, the Taliban and associated organizations have been able to develop a number of formalized information-sharing outlets and publications, including *Al Samood*, *Tora Bora*, and others, that are linked to various regional and international media channels.[38] Other smaller groups, whether directly affiliated with Taliban or other elements of the insurgency, run their own communications and propaganda outlets.[39]

Despite its successes in information processing, sharing, and messaging, the insurgency sometimes suffers from its decentralized disposition and cannot or does not fully control organizational communications. Despite having members with technological savvy that are capable of exploiting electronic communications, the insurgency's decentralized structure makes it difficult to collate information or unify messages.[40] For instance, the Haqqani network issues statements through its own media platforms, and its members conduct interviews independently of the rest of the insurgency.[41] Additionally, because the insurgency is complex, it has difficulty controlling the messages it sends through its behavior and actions—violence committed by criminal, insurgent, and terrorist networks operating in parallel but externally to the Taliban is at times difficult to control.[42] Regardless of their actual association with the Taliban, the behaviors and actions of these groups are nonetheless attributed to the insurgency as a whole. And despite sharing similar aims and goals, even high amounts of information sharing and centrally coordinated messaging will not necessarily ensure command and control over these organizations. The insurgency's diversity almost predetermines its inability to maintain control over the whole of the information environment and the factors that contribute to the construction and maintenance of this environment.

Training

The frequency, level, and type of training the Afghan insurgency requires and receives has been relatively consistent over time and in concert with its organizational goals. In general, the insurgency's goals have necessitated only that the plurality of its members possess basic military skills that either were developed through years of conflict or could be relatively easily trained in-country or in nearby sanctuaries in Pakistan.[43] When required, more advanced or technical skills could also be trained or imparted on an as-needed basis.

Because the insurgency's leadership retains a degree of relative, if only indirect, control over the actions of smaller supporting groups, the skills required by different organizations for effective goal achievement are for the most part compartmentalized and simplified. Individual insurgents and smaller organizations need only to be trained for accomplishing what are relatively routine and repetitive insurgent tasks, such as planning ambushes, conducting surveillance and intelligence gathering, securing and/or controlling individuals, villages, and insurgent commerce, or constructing and then emplacing roadside bombs or IEDs. And because the insurgency's leadership issues directives, rules, and instructions that help coordinate if not orchestrate regional and even local behavior, individuals and organizations across Afghanistan do not have either to expend significant resources or to betray their covertness when pursuing training that cannot be readily imparted by locally available sources or through other easily obtainable means.[44]

The bulk of formalized and semiformalized insurgent training occurs either in Pakistan, along the border of Pakistan, or on-site by skilled foreign fighters, particularly those actively in league with al Qaeda or other prominent Pakistani or Pakistan-based jihadist militias or organizations.[45] Foreign fighters embedded in small, mobile insurgent organizations or units act as trainers—like MTTs—and advisers that serve to actively support operations and provide oversight and advice on their conduct.[46] Beyond conducting routine combat, military, and rudimentary IED or bomb-making training, foreign terrorists and insurgents also provide other expertise and resources for the conduct of more exotic or complicated operations requiring specialized tactics or technologies,[47] including complex ambushes or large-scale raids. But for the most part, the training required for achieving insurgent organizational goals is neither complicated nor particularly difficult to impart.

Notably, many elements of the Afghan insurgency have adapted their behavior so as to avoid chance or extemporaneous direct confrontations with Coalition forces. Members seem to have learned that this is many times a losing proposition; what appears to be a possible short-term victory turns out to be in the long run rather pyrrhic, as chance engagements shed telling clues to counterinsurgent forces in respect to organizational size, composition, weapons, communications, and tactics. When possible, smaller insurgent groups confronted by forces or situations that might require significant fighting simply disperse and reconstitute at a later time.[48] Although this behavior is deliberate its effects are likely coincidental insofar as they have reduced the need to train more complicated maneuver formations and techniques. This benefits the insurgency tremendously since, absent substantial experience and regular exposure to or contact with adversary forces, proficiency in these skills would require: (1) more sophisticated trainers; (2) a greater frequency of training; (3) the deliberate and persistent monitoring of counterinsurgent methods and techniques; (4) the investment of greater organizational resources to training, particularly in terms of time, ammunition, and personnel; and (5) some form of centralization and/or easily accessible—and likely stationary—camps to support and facilitate training. Ultimately, these skills would also be more difficult to transfer to other individuals and organizations as casualties mounted or as organizations experienced personnel turnover. Adaptation in that respect would certainly suffer if the insurgency had a need for developing or made earnest attempts to develop more sophisticated and widespread training regimens.

The level of control imposed upon associated and subordinate insurgent organizations in Afghanistan, however indirect this control might be, has ensured a semblance of coordination among organizations in the achievement of pan-organizational goals.[49] In turn, this coordination has had the effect of at least somewhat standardizing and minimizing training requirements throughout the insurgency. A form of specialization has emerged that has reduced organizational requirements to adapt. This has allowed individuals and organizations to maintain their covertness while still contributing effectively to the accomplishment of the insurgency's goals.

Constraints

From an organizational perspective, the Afghan insurgency is more coherent than its counterpart in Iraq. It maintains at least a modicum of centralized direction over the behavior of constituent organizations and individuals, has relatively defined leadership, and is not subject to major divisions or regular conflict among its members or member organizations. While this significantly benefits day-to-day operations and overall coordination, it does not obviate the challenges imposed by having to operate predominantly as a covert networked organization. The insurgency is far from being truly and formally structured, and insurgent behavior, even if punishable, cannot be controlled throughout all of Afghanistan's provinces. As Peter Thruelsen notes, the dynamics of the insurgency vary from one area to the next, and its organization should not be conceived of as a unified.[50] A lack of unification, although beneficial in many operational respects, has implications for organizational effectiveness in terms of coordination and behavioral control. It also raises the likelihood of potential defections, infighting, and reduced recruiting potential.

While sharing a common interest in ejecting the Coalition from Afghanistan and the region, the insurgency is still segregated along many lines, and most constituent organizations have their own distinct support structures and leadership.[51] For instance, at its top levels, the Taliban is guided by the Quetta Shura and provincial shadow governors.[52] At its lower levels it is aided by local leadership (funded by the Taliban), full-time fighters, and active supporters.[53] It is also supported actively and passively by part-time fighters and sympathizers.[54] Despite being fairly well organized and stratified, the Taliban is still very much a localized and decentralized insurgency.[55] And while this stratification presently aids its operations and maintenance of covertness, it is also likely to form the basis of future divergence and organizational splintering in the absence of a common threat.

Unlike the more diverse Iraqi insurgency where few if any groups had as their goal the governance of Iraq, the major player in the Afghan insurgency, the Taliban, is quite interested in future governance and thus must now and in the future appeal to a broad range of groups and interests.[56] It is constrained by this insofar as it must be more conciliatory than it otherwise might be and must tolerate power-sharing, less conservative ideologies,[57] and external influences that it might otherwise try to combat, weaken, or curb. Furthermore, its own organization is not entirely cohesive, and fragmentation within and among groups is a persistent danger.[58] The Taliban now, and even more so in the future, will have to contend with the regional and subregional networks that hold sway in areas where its presence is weak or nonexistent. For instance, while maintaining a national presence, HiG's influence is most strongly felt in Kunar, Nangarhar, and Nuristan provinces.[59] The Haqqani and Mansur networks are strong in the southeastern regions of Afghanistan.[60] Other Islamic networks—Sufi, Tablighi, and Deobandi, for example—also hold sway.[61] And all have some form of linkage to individuals and organizations in Pakistan.

Despite having to maintain varying but certain degrees of covertness, the Afghan insurgency has not been constrained in terms of its ability to generate or attract support, garner attention, or in its recruitment efforts. Nor has it been particularly constrained in regard to its operations, except, and principally, as it restrains and polices its own activities. When convenient and useful, it can still engage in spectacular and exceptionally well planned and coordinated attacks against Coalition forces or interests. Its relatively inclusive rhetoric and governance message—as well as a number of its actions, to include the establishment of parallel governance structures—has mitigated many of the centrifugal forces that plagued the Iraqi insurgency's achievement of its goals. A deep and general dissatisfaction with the central government in Kabul combined with the egregious corruption that characterizes the government's bureaucracy and security agents has also helped in this respect.[62]

ORGANIZATIONAL INPUTS—GROUP DESIGN AND CULTURE

This section examines the insurgency's composition, norms, and tasks.

Composition

The insurgency is composed of allied and sometimes competing individuals, tribes, warlords, terrorists, and a number of coherently led suborganizations.[63] It is segmented into what Thomas Ruttig defines as "seven armed structures": the Taliban; the Haqqani and Mansur networks; the Tora Bora Jihad Front; HiG; small Salafi groups; and former mujahideen groups.[64] It is also composed of numerous smaller networked organizations.[65] Its complexity and diversity, much like those of the Iraqi insurgency, are both a strength and weakness: it covertly leverages the behavior, skills, and influence of its component groups while it struggles to maintain organizational control. But unlike the Iraqi insurgency, the largest component of the Afghan insurgency, the Taliban, has positive goals—governance—and structures in place to enable organizational consonance with these goals.

The Taliban—or the Islamic Emirate of Afghanistan (IEA)—is by far the largest constituent Afghan insurgent organization and is ostensibly led by Mullah Mohammad Omar.[66] It is mostly Pashtun in ethnicity—Afghanistan's largest ethnic group—and maintains leadership councils, or *shuras,* that are based inside of Pakistan.[67] The Taliban emerged during fighting in Kandahar in 1994 with the goals of providing a stable state functioning under *sharia* law.[68] Although the Taliban was removed from governance following the 2001 Coalition invasion and forced to go into varying degrees of hiding in Afghanistan and Pakistan, it was able to organize a renewed insurgency, however small, disorganized, and uncoordinated it may have been, in early 2002.[69] Like most insurgent organizations, estimates of the Taliban's size have varied over time and are subject to uncertainty, the nature of how broadly the Taliban is defined as an organization, seasonal changes and local conditions,[70] and whether or not its name is being used as shorthand for the entirety of the insurgency. Thus, depending on how its membership is tabulated, the Taliban might have up to seventy thousand members but can probably only count on fifteen thousand full-time fighters, which are likely only a small percentage of the total force.[71]

The Taliban is organized vertically and operates a "shadow state." It is also horizontally networked along religious and tribal lines.[72] Different analysts and scholars discern different levels of cohesiveness and structure within the Taliban's organization.[73] Most describe its organizational structure as a decentralized network,[74] with many smaller and localized groups acting in support roles.[75] Some of these localized groups act as "franchisees" retaining independence but brandishing the Taliban name.[76] The Taliban is not as organized or structured as other well-known insurgent organizations or along the lines of classical Marxist movements,[77] but it nonetheless maintains identifiable structures and chains of leadership.

In terms of recruitment, the Taliban and other groups have been successful in expanding their operations. They have gone from populating their organizations with ethnically and historically aligned family and tribal members,[78] to drawing from a range of sources including Pakistan's Federally Administered Tribal Areas (FATA) and refugee camps as well as from Afghanistan's rural populations and unemployed urban populations.[79] As Peter Thruelsen argues, given the ethnicity of southern and eastern Afghanistan and western Pakistani tribal areas, the Taliban "can be said to have an unlimited base for recruitment."[80]

The Taliban maintains formalized structures such as its leadership council and provincial councils, which serve to "provide the movement with a visible, institutionalized leadership and predictable patterns of decision-making."[81] Operationally, the Taliban is organized into what Francisco Sanin and Antonio Giustozzi term as "fronts," which are formed through individual initiative but are supported with supplies and cash from the central organization.[82] These fronts are supported tactically and technically by mobile formations that maintain personnel with specialized skills not generally present in smaller organizations.[83] At the lowest local or village levels, the Taliban is supported by small and relatively independent cells, which are organized around the leader that recruited the cell's members. These cells are networked underneath a "district-level" Taliban leader, which in turn is networked underneath a "province-level" leader that might be further connected to a national-level leader.[84] They typically contain between ten and fifty part-time fighters and they tend to operate independently. But they sometimes operate interdependently or "reciprocally" with the Taliban hierarchy or with other cells, particularly when performing intelligence work, passing information, supporting media operations, or conducting training.[85] Similar to but distinct from fronts are guerrilla elements that are many times paid for providing support such as reconnaissance or transporting supplies or for fighting alongside full-time fighters.[86] These guerrillas fight "almost entirely in their home valley" and rarely conduct operations of their own volition.[87]

These relationships and the number of layers or cells in each network vary. The looseness of this structure allows the individual cells to pursue more local goals or to support district and provincial goals when necessary, but all the while in consonance with overall Taliban strategy.[88] It also reduces the organization's footprint in any given area and allows for concealment and dispersal when necessary. The Taliban deliberately tries to keep these suborganizations and components small, probably in an attempt to facilitate control and to minimize the aspirations of any particular leader or group. Indirectly, this also increases these suborganizations' capacity for adapting to local conditions while staying in tune with the strategy and goals of the governing organization. In this respect, the Taliban has, at least presently, simultaneously tempered potential points of friction, increased the insurgency's reach, and maintained covertness all while retaining mechanisms for organizational command, control, and coordination. This is particularly significant given the Taliban's size and prominence within the insurgency and in respect to its need to develop alliances, or at least amicable relationships, with many other less prominent insurgent organizations.

Norms

The insurgency, particularly the Taliban as its largest constituent, tries to appeal to the broader Afghan population,[89] while retaining organizational coherence,[90] and in doing so has had to circumscribe the potentially alienating behavior of its membership. The Taliban entices appropriate behavior by dispensing rewards and support. It punishes members who do not live up to organizational standards either by withholding monetary support or remuneration, applying public and physical violence, or by alienating the persons or organizations committing an offense.[91] As the Taliban continues to expand, it necessarily has to maintain or enforce greater levels of organizational discipline in order to appropriately manage the behavior of its members in respect to organizational norms.[92] Even minor offenses such as the double taxation of heroin production are rebuked by the organization's leadership.[93] In its attempt to maintain the norms that it has established, the Taliban expends quite a bit of its resources on policing individual and organizational behavior.[94]

For the most part, the Taliban and other Afghan insurgent organizations try to develop positive relationships with locals and with one another and thus in the main behave accordingly.[95] The Taliban, for one, has developed standards of behavior that its members are supposed to follow when engaging the local community.[96] Additionally, the Taliban issues *layeha*, or "codes of conduct," that, among other things, establish chains of command to help prevent organizational fragmentation and help garner the public's support.[97] Although suicide bombings were and are used in the conflict,[98] they have never been fully accepted by the Afghan people. And although effective, these methods are not broadly embraced by the Taliban[99]—in fact, the Taliban was initially compelled or at least chose to outsource the conduct of many of these bombings to non-Afghan insurgents or terrorists.[100] For related reasons, the Taliban has tried to avoid mass casualty bombings, when possible. When suicide and other attacks result in mass casualties or indiscriminate death, the Taliban typically denies responsibility for these acts,[101] or ascribes blame elsewhere.

Tasks

Over time, the insurgency has become much more adept at aligning organizationally required tasks with organizational goals. For instance, whereas when the insurgency first started gaining momentum after the 2001 invasion it routinely and rather haphazardly engaged Coalition forces and was for the most part indifferent to collateral damage, the insurgency now shows much more deference to the Afghan population and much more respect for the power and capabilities of Coalition forces. It has in essence realized that in order to accomplish its foremost and primary goal—the removal of foreign forces from Afghan soil (what it terms the defense of the Afghan people)—it must go out of its way to retain the support of the population. This realization is reflected both in word,[102] and deed, as mass casualty attacks have been limited and instructions have been issued stressing the protection of the Afghan people and their property.[103]

Although Taliban commanders and their associated networks have the autonomy afforded to a decentralized organization, they still follow broad guidance that helps shape if not coordinate their performance of various supporting tasks. In the conduct of their operations they generally seek to: hinder government outreach and undermine the central government's legitimacy; erode public support in Western capitals; undermine the morale of Afghanistan's security forces; demonstrate the reach and capacity of the insurgency with complex attacks; and target local leaders that evince progovernment sentiment.[104] Knowledge of these tasks and their performance, in turn, also helps to guide and inform the composition, size, and activity of regional and local organizations.[105]

ORGANIZATIONAL INPUTS—MATERIEL AND TECHNICAL RESOURCES

This section evaluates the insurgency's gathering and use of equipment, funds, and intelligence.

Equipment

Much as in Iraq, Afghanistan is awash in much of the equipment and materials required for the conduct of an insurgency. This is in no small part due to the fact that Afghanistan has been involved in conflict for more than three decades. During this period, Afghanistan's war economy allowed if not fostered the growth of a vast network of military and criminal entrepreneurship embedded in and capable of leveraging what has been termed a "regional conflict system" stretching from the Caucasus in the west to Kashmir in the east.[106] Skilled personnel and advanced equipment, where not available, could be found and moved into the country by these entrepreneurs. In addition, al Qaeda, Tehreek-e-Nafaz-e-Shariat-e-Mohammadi, the Islamic Movement of Uzbekistan (IMU), HiG, and the Eastern Turkestan Islamic Movement (ETIM), Pakistan's Inter-Services Intelligence (ISI), among others, all provided or continue to provide materiel and experienced personnel support.[107]

The Afghan insurgency relies on a vast ad hoc network of underground cells and covert transport capabilities to move supplies and materiel into and throughout the country.[108] Many of these cells leverage family and tribal linkages to communicate needs, for shelter, or for facilitating the movement of funds, people, and equipment into Afghanistan.[109] Communications, always subject to Coalition eavesdropping, are kept as simplistic and decentralized as possible to prevent monitoring and interdiction.[110] When necessary and where expedience is required, insurgents will communicate with radios, cell phones, or satellite phones,[111] but they mostly rely upon more rudimentary and socially supported means of communications, such as courier or word of mouth. Tribal linkages in Afghanistan and Pakistan, particularly among Pashtun populations, contribute information, weapons, money, and other needed material support to the Taliban either during the conduct of or in preparation for operations.[112]

The insurgency is especially economical in the procurement and use of equipment and associated personnel. IEDs, landmines, rifles, rocket launchers, explosives, artillery shells, and the personnel necessary to employ each effectively in support of organizational goals are all managed with significant parsimony. The Taliban in particular goes to great lengths to ensure responsible use in this respect: members of the Taliban are answerable for their equipment and its employment, and each is held accountable by his superiors.[113] Much as with the Iraqi insurgency, when the Afghan insurgency has been short on personnel, it has employed mercenaries to fire shots at Coalition forces or to emplace IEDs, particularly in areas where it had limited presence or control.[114] To ensure the retention of skilled or experienced personnel, the Taliban has paid its fighters an indemnity of U.S.$140 to $150 per month—a significant sum of money in Afghanistan.[115] And, as was seen in Iraq, the insurgency creatively and effectively uses technology to support operations, communications, propaganda efforts, and the maintenance of organizational and individual covertness. For example, the Taliban uses common devices for more sophisticated purposes, such as the use of a Sony PlayStation controller, perhaps as a detonation trigger,[116] and has modified available resources for the achievement of more precise effects, such as the employment of shaped and directed IEDs.[117]

By combining simple tasks and largely available equipment with limited operational objectives, the Afghan insurgency has effectively ensured that it uses materiel and personnel parsimoniously. Employing already existing supply networks based on trusted and enduring relationships helps to keep overall operational costs low and allows the insurgency, for the most part, to avoid the more sophisticated detection efforts that are employed by its adversaries.

Funds

The Afghan insurgency has diverse funding sources that generate large sums of money and in-kind materiel supplies through a system so encompassing and widespread that its interdiction would be a nearly impossible undertaking.

Funds are derived from various licit and illicit sources including but not limited to the drug trade, international aid, taxation, agricultural services, bartering, protection rackets, kidnapping, charitable donations, and the control of numerous border crossing points.[118] Cash as well as vehicles, advanced telephony, weapons, fuel, ammunition, food, and medical care are all received as means of payment.[119] The taxes—or *ushr*—that the Taliban collect "cover the bulk of their operational needs, including salaries for fighters and transport, fuel, food, weapons and explosives."[120] Payments received at the lowest organizational levels percolate through the leadership chain up to the highest levels of the organization.[121] In sum, the Taliban is estimated to receive nearly U.S.$250 million per year from internal and external sources.[122] This is balanced against an estimated operations expenditure of $70 million per year.[123] Income figures for other prominent insurgent organizations are neither readily available nor reliable, although they also likely generate quite handsome sums of revenue. The Haqqani network, for instance, is funded independently of the Taliban through highly diversified and resilient practices. Its tentacles reach into various transnational business interests supported by clans or with links to Arab finance, al Qaeda, and Pakistan's ISI.[124]

Afghanistan is the world's largest opium producer,[125] and the opium trade, by far, is the principal commodity driving Afghanistan's illicit economy.[126] Afghanistan's opium trade constitutes nearly half of Afghanistan's GDP,[127] or nearly U.S.$1.5 billion, and by 2008 opium was being grown and processed in twenty-eight of Afghanistan's thirty-four provinces.[128] Significantly, many of Afghanistan's farmers rely on opium farming as a source of revenue:[129] they have little incentive to quit production and even fewer viable agricultural alternatives to consider.[130] Opium is used as a means of bartering for goods and services,[131] and is in many dealings treated as a form of currency. The insurgency earns revenue from opium at all points in the production and distribution chain. It taxes farmers and refiners and earns additional revenue by providing safe passage and transport to smugglers and traffickers.[132] These opium exchange networks are governed by strategies, partnerships, codes of conduct, and "hierarchies of deference and power" and provide at least a semblance of stability and consistency in Afghanistan's war-torn society.[133]

Even the war economy serves as a significant source of funding for elements of the Afghan insurgency and its related factions. The maze of contracts and subcontracts that govern the shipment and passage of equipment and supplies for the Coalition and for the Afghan government are subject to payments, however indirect they might ultimately be, to the insurgency. Perversely, insurgents and militias are paid upward of millions of dollars to provide convoy security and safe passage within a corrupt system that also sees payments being made to warlords, politicians, and members of the police.[134] Similarly, development projects paid for and supported by the Coalition and international aid agencies provide substantial income to villages and tribes.[135] It is difficult to believe that a portion if not much of this money ends up funding the insurgency or its members in one way or another.

The insurgency has integrated itself into nearly all aspects of Afghanistan's formal and informal economy. Its larger organizations and groups have leveraged various social and market-based networks to thrive in the chaos of conflict. Through criminal and commercial entrepreneurship they derive not just a means of funding for their operations and ambitions but also a means of interacting with, monitoring, and supporting many villages and families throughout Afghanistan and even in neighboring Pakistan. In contrast to the Iraqi insurgency, the Afghan insurgency appears to have developed and managed a more coherent and controlled means of generating and sharing revenue—fewer internal or external actors seem to have the capacity to disrupt, significantly or permanently, their funding streams, and many organizations or agencies that could, because of the near ubiquity of corruption, would be undercutting their own means of survival by doing so. Additionally, applying pressure against and resources to combating one or even multiple lines of funding will only result in the insurgency adapting their practices, making short-term changes, or shifting emphasis to other streams of income.

Intelligence

The Afghan insurgency employs and maintains a thorough, if not very sophisticated,[136] intelligence network that helps its leadership control operations and better understand developments in Afghanistan and the outside world.[137] It also abets rapid organizational learning in support of organizational goals. Hierarchical chains, foreign agencies, embedded collectors, and social networks are all leveraged to support the insurgency's organizational intelligence needs. This intelligence architecture is more deliberate, enduring, hierarchical, and directed than the one used by the Iraqi insurgency—as is witnessed, for instance, in the Taliban's placement of dedicated intelligence collectors and analysts throughout its organization[138]—although its efficacy is probably comparable.

Insurgent leaders have developed relationships with their subordinates to help broaden their understanding of operational and on-the-ground conditions.[139] In combination with higher-order intelligence products generated within the Pakistani sanctuary provided to the Quetta Shura,[140] this understanding helps the leadership to tailor strategic messages, shift resources, and provide specialized support to areas of need. Contacts within the ISI have aided leader awareness directly by providing information regarding foreign troop locations and movements and indirectly by providing intelligence training to elements of the Afghan insurgency.[141] Additionally, the ISI has supplemented efforts to target and recruit insurgent foot soldiers and specialists from within Pakistan.[142]

The insurgency has also been effective in penetrating state security forces by either embedding organizational members within these forces, exploiting previous relationships with members of these forces, or by paying for information from corrupt elements of these forces.[143] These relationships allow the insurgency to gain sensitive information and to conduct counterintelligence: they provide access points for retrieving important, timely, and precise information and intelligence and allow the insurgency to plant discretionary information into its adversaries' collection networks. They also help to facilitate insider or "green on blue" attacks. Additionally, the insurgency has thoroughly infiltrated local police. This is a relationship it takes advantage of to gather information for use in targeting informants,[144] and to monitor, by proxy, the behavior of those that are employed by or might be sympathetic to the Karzai government or the Coalition. The insurgency also has connections, via guards and physicians, in Afghanistan's prisons that it uses to maintain contact with and receive analytical products from detained operatives.[145] There are few if any sectors of Afghanistan's government that have escaped penetration by the insurgency's intelligence apparatus.

Perhaps most significantly, the insurgency maintains a robust information and intelligence gathering capacity at the local level. The Taliban has put structures in place to develop intelligence networks where they did not exist before. It uses preachers to penetrate areas, mobilize locals, and to assess public sentiment.[146] It also sends out forward elements of the organization to infiltrate and influence what it considers to be towns and villages of strategic import.[147] The Taliban uses these and other local support networks to signal adversary behavior and activity,[148] to provide HUMINT and familiarity with local terrain,[149] and to ensure compliance with organizational edicts.[150] Having this capacity allows the insurgency to develop defenses in advance of adversary movements, to counter government efforts at nation building, and to inform the highest leadership of conditions across much of the country.[151] By maintaining a comprehensive and fairly coordinated intelligence system, from the highest to the lowest levels of the organization, the insurgency has expanded its capacity not only to adapt to its adversaries' activities but in many cases to preempt them. This gives the Afghan insurgency a strategic and tactical advantage that the Iraqi insurgency did not possess in the late stages of its conflict. The latter's intelligence apparatus was progressively disrupted by the incoherent activity of various insurgent groups, or was ultimately destroyed by the alienation of the local population.

ORGANIZATIONAL INPUTS—EXTERNAL ASSISTANCE

External assistance consists of practices of consultation, direct action, and cooperation.

Consultation

External consultation and support for the Afghan insurgency comes in the form of sanctuary, training and logistics, supplies, political and religious guidance, recruiting bases, and financial backing.[152] Foreign influence, via consultation, can also be seen in the tactics and techniques used by the insurgency, particularly in the construction and employment of IEDs.[153] Although the insurgency receives unofficial support and consultation from a variety of sources, to include the participation of jihadist volunteers from Arab states,[154] its two principal state-based benefactors are Iran and Pakistan.[155] While their initial levels of support following the 2001 invasion were tempered by historical enmity with the Taliban and pressure applied by the U.S. government and the Coalition, respectively, more recently, both have been much more active in facilitating the insurgency's operations.

For its part, the Iranian government's behavior has changed in step with the dynamics of the insurgency and with respect to the relative power of government in Kabul. Initially, Iran was friendly to the Karzai government and provided economic aid while maintaining its traditional hostility toward the Taliban.[156] But more recently, Iran has seen its strategic security interests align with the Taliban,[157] principally because of the latter's fight against the Coalition,[158] but also because the Iranian government is interested in retaining leverage over those who might form Afghanistan's future government. Beginning in about 2005, Iran started to provide medical and weapons support to individual

Taliban commanders in southern and western Afghanistan. And in 2008 it increased its support to include the provision of more advanced supplies and expertise to the Taliban.[159] The IRGC, through its Qods Force, has provided the Taliban with specialized training, surface-to-air missiles, and RPGs.[160]

Pakistan's relationship with the insurgency and the government in Afghanistan is much more complicated. After the 2001 invasion, Pakistan officially rejected supporting the Taliban but covertly supported it with refuge and the tacit acceptance of training camps within its boundaries.[161] It also turned a blind eye to the growing Afghan insurgent population in the FATA.[162] The refuge that Pakistan provided—and to a greater degree still provides—was critical to the survival of the Taliban's leadership and to the operations of such groups as HiG, al Qaeda, and the Haqqani network.[163] Sanctuary allowed these and other groups to consolidate after the invasion, avoid confrontation with the Coalition, and engage in recruitment.[164] Pakistan has also been instrumental in securing land trade routes between and among the Taliban and its partners and for the provisioning of supplies.[165] Its military and intelligence services have also been instrumental in providing logistical support.[166] Similarly, the Haqqani network and other organizations also enjoy comparable levels and types of support from the Pakistani military and the ISI.[167] Pakistan's military and the ISI provide medical support, training, and intelligence to insurgent factions.[168] Although Pakistan was at one point more of a silent partner to the Afghan insurgency it now is more open about its relationships and even admits to being able to influence the Taliban.[169]

To a greater degree than the Iraqi insurgency, the Afghan insurgency received and continues to receive substantial amounts of direct and indirect support and consultation from neighboring states.[170] Although the insurgency is not bound to any formal or official relationships with either Iran or Pakistan, it is and will be subject to their influence now and in the future.[171] This is significant in two ways: (1) if the insurgency ultimately "wins," both countries will try to enhance their leverage with the follow-on government; and (2) if either of these countries fails to achieve a future level of leverage that suits their interests, they might try to exploit relationships that have been further developed during this conflict to achieve their aims. In either case, the schisms that are likely to develop after the termination of the conflict might be exacerbated by either or both of these states. Pakistan, like Iran after the dissolution of the Iraqi insurgency, will likely wield the most influence is this regard.

Direct Action

Many individuals and groups engage in activity that either directly supports the insurgency, through collaborative practice, or aids the insurgency in parallel, by weakening the legitimacy of the Afghan government and expanding or supplementing the power and capability of insurgent organizations. Actors engaging in these activities include warlords, traffickers, smugglers,[172] criminal organizations,[173] manifold antigovernment factions,[174] and insurgents for hire.[175] Each might have multiple and overlapping connections to insurgent organizations—or to other parties engaged in insurgent activities—or they might operate independently among the chaos created by the conflict. Their activities, associations, and affiliations vary in accordance with the exigencies of the conflict, criminal market demands, and the capabilities that they can provide either on an individual or organizational basis.[176]

In respect to criminal groups and organizations, their activities help to funnel money and supplies to the insurgency and to maintain chains of corruption within the government. These groups operate for profit, and their activities help perpetuate the chaos within and surrounding Afghanistan. Criminal groups engage in protection activities,[177] narcotics transshipment, arms trading, extortion, theft, kidnapping, the smuggling of various licit and illicit goods, and the provision of otherwise unavailable services.[178] In some cases, they employ their own armed militias and can thus be hired out for protection services or attacks on Coalition forces.[179]

The linchpin of criminal enterprise, and indeed the Afghan insurgency,[180] is the manufacturing and transshipment of heroin. As noted earlier, heroin in Afghanistan is a huge business. The income of millions of Afghan citizens—as well as thousands of insurgents—is tied to its production and trade; its production is thoroughly ingrained into both the licit and illicit Afghan economies.[181] Traffickers traversing the Afghan-Pakistan border are complicit in operations supporting both licit and illicit trade and have helped spur a deepening of ties between the insurgency and the flow of narcotics.[182] Increasingly, the line is blurred between who is an insurgent and who is a drug trafficker.[183] Not helping matters is the fact that organizations designed to counter this kind of activity are notoriously corrupt. Thomas Johnson points out that U.S. drug enforcement officials stationed in Afghanistan estimated that 90 percent of police chiefs were "actively involved in or protecting the narcotics industry" in 2005.[184] There is no reason to believe that there has been significant change for the better since that period. Cooperation among law enforcement and criminal or insurgent organizations is not uncommon.[185] Whether or not this leads to a perverse order or further disorder depends on political conditions and the nature of the relationship between government officials, the Afghan people, and these criminal organizations.[186]

The insurgency is also supported by a host of regional and subregional organizations without or with very few tangible, or what might be called official, ties to professed insurgent organizations. Several Pakistani groups such as Tehreek-e Taliban (Pakistan) (TTP) and Lashkar-e Taiba (LeT) contribute to the activities of the Taliban, HiG, and the Haqqani network.[187] And subregional groups like the Mansur network contribute to the Taliban's activities "without organisationally being fully integrated" into the group.[188] Still others, such as the IMU, Tahir Yuldash's network, and the network led by Juma Naamangani, variously support HiG and the Taliban.[189]

The Taliban has also been instrumental in creating and operating organizations that are functionally aligned with the group but operate in support of broader Afghan society. These include a number of effective and comparatively legitimate shadow or parallel "provincial, district and even village" governance, justice, and security structures.[190] As Jeffrey Dressler and Carl Forsberg note, "[T]he Afghan government is being out-governed by the enemy."[191] The Taliban has appointed governors in each province to coordinate military efforts and to manage finances and the judiciary.[192] Its courts are supported by the Taliban's military elements and conduct various functions including the issuing of warrants, management of taxation, distribution of military supplies, and narcotics transportation.[193]

The patterns of direct action and the types of actors engaged in direct action in Afghanistan are not generally dissimilar to those of the Iraqi insurgency. As in Iraq, the actions and behaviors of these groups help to perpetuate the conflict in general, abet the insurgency, and weaken the perceived and actual legitimacy of the government. But there are two chief differences between the conflicts in Afghanistan and Iraq that have directly and indirectly increased the adaptive capacity of the Afghan insurgency: the creation of a shadow government and the perpetuation and ingraining of the heroin industry into the whole of Afghan society.

First, the shadow government has increased the insurgency's—principally the Taliban's—legitimacy and connection to the Afghan people. Providing alternative means of justice—through swift conflict resolution—and goods and services through a system that is not premised on corrupt practices and influence chains has been a boon to the insurgency and has dealt a serious blow to the legitimacy of the central and provincial governments. Second, the sheer scale of the heroin industry has allowed it to dominate the Afghan economy and therefore the lives and well-being of the majority of Afghans—even temporary impositions on the industry have led to backlashes or, worse yet, outright defections to the insurgency.[194] The funds generated by this industry serve to support the insurgency both directly and indirectly. For instance, these funds give the insurgency the capacity not only to pay for its operations but also to maintain various corruption schemes. One product of these schemes takes the form of locals and government agents providing tacit and sometimes overt support and information to the insurgency—a key to its adaptive practices.[195] Perhaps most damning, the government is bound to the heroin economy— anything affecting the industry affects the interests of not only the insurgency but also, paradoxically, the Afghan people and ultimately the government.

Cooperation

Many of the old power structures and means of cooperation attributable to older generations of Afghans have been destroyed through conflict and the development of Afghanistan's war economy. Relationships, the rule of law, and other structures that would once have dominated decision-making and interaction have either been weakened or sidelined by this new reality. This is not to say that they no longer exist in one form or another or that they will not again emerge at a future date, but that much of the power they once possessed has been diluted or redistributed to other actors and parties. These relationships have in many places given way to the cooperative and competitive undertakings of insurgent organizations.

Much of the cooperation between and among insurgent groups in Afghanistan is premised more on circumstantial but mutually held goals than any deeper interest in a perpetuated relationship.[196] Alliances, as they typically are within and between networks, are ephemeral or short-term, depending on the goals and needs of the organizations involved. In Afghanistan, historical enmity has been many times replaced by pragmatism.[197] Nonetheless, cooperation, if only represented by a lack of persistent infighting among insurgent groups and regardless of how tacit and short-term it might be, has strategically and, at times tactically, benefited the insurgency.

At the highest levels, many of the larger insurgent organizations have found ways to engage one another amicably. Or, they at least are not openly undermining one another on a consistent basis. It would be a stretch to say that any real truce has been reached, but in practice open conflict between organizations tends to be only temporary. Gulbuddin Hekmatyar, leader of HiG, has been quoted as saying, "We neither have organizational links with Al Qaida nor with the Afghan or Pakistani Taliban…We have asked our mujahidin to call every mujahid his brother, fight the enemies jointly [and] not to spare their help to any good mujahid."[198] And, as Major General Mike Flynn has noted, coordinated activity among insurgent groups "is the best I've seen it."[199]

The presence of cooperation does not obviate competition, though, particularly at the local level where organizational control and oversight are sometimes limited. Competition ensues over territory, power, prestige, and access to resources. But competitive urges are many times tempered by the need for or interest in cooperation. Elements of the Taliban in particular, because of its size and presence, frequently engage other organizations in both. It has competed and cooperated with the Tora Bora front, al Qaeda, HiG, the Haqqani network, and others.[200] Additionally, other functional organizations, such as criminal networks, frequently engage, collude, or compete with different elements of the insurgency when capability collides with either interest or necessity.[201] Tactical alliances of convenience are commonplace. These relationships generate a loose coordination of activities and spur interaction among the various participating groups, which can ultimately lead to the generation of more enduring partnerships, patterns of information sharing, and a better understanding of capabilities, resources, and mutual equities.

ORGANIZATIONAL OUTPUTS—CRITICAL GROUP PROCESSES

This section discusses the insurgency's adaptation of closely related critical group processes, including: the application of skills and knowledge; task performance competency; command, control, and communications; and cognition and behavior.

Application of Skills and Knowledge

Many of the insurgency's activities are political as much as military or combat-oriented and thus, they are more closely linked to longer-term organizational goals. This was not always the case, as the insurgency initially conducted a variety of attacks against the Coalition,[202] without necessarily tying these activities to broader organizational goals and without regard to their general efficacy or associated collateral damage.

The insurgency has learned that in order to effectively achieve its principal goal of defeating the Coalition and replacing the Karzi-led government, it must progressively coordinate its activities toward these ends. In this effort, indigenous organizations have become much more effective in crafting their messages, managing the population, engaging in military actions—mostly only when and where beneficial—and creating alternative means of order separate from the Afghan government. They have also recognized the utility and power of their networks. For instance, instead of trying to micromanage their organization, the Taliban's leadership has shifted its focus to shaping strategy and providing guidance;[203] direct control of the bulk of the organization has been delegated to trusted middle- and lower-level leaders that can take advantage of environmental conditions and better align or synchronize the organization's operations in respect to local circumstances and prevailing sentiments.[204]

For their part, external or foreign groups have acted as force multipliers. They have introduced advanced technologies, experiential knowledge from other conflicts, expertise, and particularized capabilities. This practical division of labor has allowed the Afghan elements of the insurgency to leverage the contributions of allied foreign fighters while not substantively subjecting themselves to their control or to the capriciousness and extreme violence that these same or similar groups perpetrated in Iraq.[205]

Al Qaeda's support, but not necessarily its actions, has been particularly beneficial to the insurgency. Its presence in Afghanistan is relatively small,[206] but, nonetheless, the organization is still capable of exploiting its international connections to obtain a range of resources. These resources include but are not limited to financial and religious support,[207] specialized personnel, and media and propaganda production expertise.[208] The indigenous elements of the insurgency have been able to incorporate this support into their organizations and have created systems that perpetuate the sharing of knowledge gleaned from organizations like al Qaeda. The Taliban in particular has used this knowledge to create specialized departments that pool resources and serve as a source of expertise for the whole of the organization.[209]

The utility of al Qaeda–imparted media and propaganda savvy has also been high.[210] Learning through experience, the insurgency rightly recognizes the importance of broad public support for its cause and for its ability to adapt. Accordingly, the insurgency has deftly used propaganda to control the narrative when civilian casualties occur. It has been adept at quickly responding to instances of civilian deaths and assigning blame for these deaths to other sources, thus redirecting much of the resulting backlash. This has been accomplished via interviews, online updates, email, and through print resources.[211] The insurgency supports these narratives through its operations as well. In some instances, the insurgency has leveraged high-mobility vehicles and its knowledge of local terrain to deliberately arrange ambushes that provoke airstrikes on villages and other civilian targets.[212] When this occurs, it quickly capitalizes on any direct or collateral damage with videos and online broadcasts designed to implicate Coalition forces.[213]

Over time, and unlike the Iraqi insurgency, which shifted from attacking military targets to attacking police and civilians, the Afghan insurgency has adapted its skills and knowledge to dodge direct and extemporaneous confrontations with Coalition forces, avoid unnecessary civilian casualties, and to engage targets with high-payoff potential.[214] For example, when conventional attacks were no longer successful, the Taliban switched to less costly and more effective ambushes, targeted killings, and roadside bombings.[215] Reflecting this shift, IED attacks rose substantially in number between 2003 and 2007. They proved effective in complicating or thwarting Coalition forces' movement and for causing substantial casualties, thus raising the political costs of foreign involvement in Afghanistan while simultaneously reducing insurgent casualties.[216]

In sum, the insurgency has adapted its skills and knowledge for progressively and more effectively aligning its activities with organizational goals. It has created a subtly sophisticated apparatus designed to coordinate operational conduct with strategic and tactical messaging in order to undermine the efforts of a much more sophisticated and better resourced foe.

Task Performance Competency

Although there are quite a few very capable individual insurgents and insurgent organizations operating in and near Afghanistan, the bulk of the insurgency has, at best, limited weapons skills or is capable of conducting only simple military tasks.[217] And although many Afghan insurgents have significant operational experience, the majority of the insurgency's fighters,[218] particularly the part-timers, lack the kind of formal training or regular experience that can be foundational for learning about or participating in more complicated combat-oriented tasks.[219] The Afghan insurgency is unlike the Iraqi insurgency in this respect. In Iraq, a large portion of the population had been trained either in the military, in support of the military, or in conflict, and over a long period.

In Afghanistan however, the most capable and competent members of the insurgency are likely the foreign fighters, who are relatively few in number, those who have had the opportunity to receive training in camps in Pakistan, or those who are frequent beneficiaries of the assistance provided by the insurgency's mobile training detachments. But this does not apply to most members of the insurgency. Conducting a significant or sophisticated military task thus usually requires substantial preparation and training in advance, if it is to be conducted effectively by rank-and-file insurgents.

But because the insurgency's goals are as much political as they are military and the fact that the insurgency deliberately tries to avoid chance contact with Coalition forces, its membership does not have to be nearly as militarily competent as it otherwise might need to be. It has been able to make up for what might be considered a defect by creatively and economically utilizing its resources and by maintaining robust information-gathering structures.

In short, the insurgency needs to be competent enough to accomplish those tasks that will support organizational goals, and for the most part, it is. Oftentimes this requires only an understanding of how to maintain covertness, an ability to support local and alternative governance efforts, a capacity for constructing and emplacing IEDs, and a basic capacity to support other more competent members in the conduct of an ambush or some other type of attack, when directed. Although, as it has evolved, the Taliban has directed larger and more sophisticated attacks against Coalition forces,[220] these attacks are more the exception than the rule and thus appropriately reflect what the insurgency can and, more important, needs to do to support its organizational goals.[221] In this regard, it has adapted its operations to reflect what the organization is capable of supporting (in terms of training and supplies) or conducting (in terms of sophistication) and has marshaled its resources accordingly.

Command, Control, and Communications

The insurgency manages command, control, and communications vertically through strategic guidance and messaging and horizontally through provincial,[222] or local, commanders acting upon this guidance but within the constraints of the local environment. The loose but layered hierarchy employed by the Taliban provides structure and defined chains of command for the organization but does not restrict leaders or their subordinates from operating independently.[223] This arrangement has resulted in localized resilience in line with strategic guidance and in support of overall organizational goals.

The Taliban provides guidance and sets organizational direction through edicts that are shared through publications, by word of mouth, or more formally through *layehas*. *Layehas*, among other things, provide rules that establish chains of command and the means or methods of interacting with those outside the organization.[224] Night letters, or *shabnamah*, are also used for conveying messages, usually covertly, with their content many times directed to media representatives for broadcast to wider audiences.[225] Because their means of conducting secure communication over long distances is limited,[226] the insurgency, particularly its leadership, uses more covert and traditional means of communicating messages and instructions. Operational and sensitive messages are often transmitted through couriers that leverage tribal linkages for speed and security.[227] The Taliban uses short-range radios for tactical communication and has developed intricate codes to disguise its messages and content.[228] Where this is not practical, its leadership issues more general instructions meant to convey intent and to put limits or emphasis on certain organizational behaviors.

Communications are used not only for organizational coordination but also for managing perceptions.[229] Communication is conducted through print and visual media, fax, email, the Internet, via cell or satellite phones, and even through a clandestine radio station called "Voice of Shariat."[230] Appointed spokespersons and others with contacts in the media are often responsible for rapid response messages and for broadcasting information of import to the insurgency to a broad audience.[231] The insurgency has also learned to leverage instant messaging and social media channels, like Twitter, for more immediate communications to larger audiences.[232]

Cognition and Behavior

The Afghan insurgency adjusts its behavior and operations based on a comprehensive and deep understanding of local conditions throughout the country. The insurgency is fully aware of how important the population's support is for information gathering, general cognition, and environmental understanding and therefore goes to great lengths to maintain these support structures. This requires a common understanding of not only how to behave—so as not to engender resentment—but also when behaviors must change.[233] It also necessitates an organizational structure that is less directive and thus more responsive to changes in different locations and at different times.

At the highest levels, and unlike the Iraqi insurgency, the Afghan insurgency takes deliberate steps to avoid actions that will cloud its claims of legitimacy whenever possible. It does this by denying involvement in attacks resulting in high numbers of civilian deaths,[234] by blaming the Coalition—rightly or wrongly—when these events occur, and by taking steps to control—via punishment and inducements—the behavior of peripheral groups and individuals whose actions might discredit the insurgency's message. Additionally, Taliban fighters often will inform allied populations of an impending operation, despite risks to security, so as to ensure their safety.[235]

The Taliban has also taken into account the capacities of its adversaries and has devolved a certain amount of control to lower-level commanders. It recognizes the need for and utility of local independence in decision-making. Local commanders, with the appropriate guidance, are much better disposed for this purpose and can adapt more rapidly and appropriately than can more distant and detached organizational elements.[236]

A better understanding of local conditions is also vital to the conduct of operations. Maintaining extensive and diverse networks within the insurgency, the population, and even the government, not only informs the planning of insurgent operations but also provides signals for when consolidation is possible and dispersal is necessary. Environmental understanding is requisite to individual and organizational cognition and to the effective conduct of operations. Maintaining the structures that support this understanding is thus critical to organizational adaptation and survival, a fact that the insurgency in general but the Taliban in particular understands quite well.

ORGANIZATIONAL LEARNING

This section examines insurgent knowledge collection, transfer, and integration.

Knowledge Collection

The insurgency's knowledge collection apparatus is large and diversified. Within the organization, the insurgency collects and transmits knowledge and information through technological means and through its trusted networks, which many times and in many areas are not new creations but are simply a revival of existing networks.[237] It does this locally through the indigenous population while leveraging its foreign elements for knowledge collection from other conflicts and regions. It also uses mobile detachments to collect knowledge in one area and to then transmit to another. Whether by design or merely circumstantially, these detachments act as knowledge repositories and serve to help collect and then share tacit knowledge that could not otherwise be transmitted throughout the organization.

While the insurgency itself has great reach and can collect vast sums of information, its external eyes and ears are ubiquitous. Like its counterparts in Iraq, the Afghan insurgency has operatives and associates embedded in Afghanistan's government, military, and police forces. To supplement these collection sources, or in instances where direct access or observation is not possible via these means, the insurgency employs an extensive system of bribery and other inducements to gain sensitive information from official sources. It also has supporters in villages throughout the country that passively collect information and then share it when the opportunity or need arises. These sources can also be cued as reconnaissance assets when the insurgency needs to develop information on specific targets or activities. It uses this knowledge to hone its operations, to modify its behavior, and to sharpen its counterintelligence capabilities.

Knowledge Transfer

Because the insurgency is structured as a decentralized and covert network, it is naturally limited in its capacity to transfer knowledge quickly between and among organizations and individuals without incurring significant risks to security. Furthermore, its capacity for centrally analyzing information and making judgments based upon this analysis is also limited.[238] If information cannot be shared easily and quickly within an organization, then analytic efforts will be incomplete or will fail to produce desired results in a timely fashion. This poses an operational problem to any organization with a large number of subparts that have to make decisions, either continually or rapidly, with bearing on the effectiveness or the survival of the organization as a whole.

One effective means of overcoming this organizational deficiency is to push responsibility for knowledge collection, analysis, and action based upon this analysis to the periphery of the organization. This solution requires organizational dexterity and individual competence and discipline at the lowest levels. It also requires fairly regular horizontal contact among peripheral organizations. Essentially, for this system to work, the core of the organization must issue general instructions to peripheral elements that then, based on their understanding of local environmental conditions, available resources, and knowledge gleaned from contact with similar or partner individuals or organizations, must take actions to support the missives of the organization's core. In this system, guidance and resources are pushed down and critical local information is pulled up through the organization. This results in local elements being supported in their efforts while the organization's leadership is apprised of local conditions, sentiment, and concerns, which can then be assessed and applied in the construction or modification of strategies and when obtaining, marshaling, or distributing organizational resources.

Knowledge transfer in this kind of organization is rarely both rapid and comprehensive and sometimes it is neither. But it is effective insofar as it allows the maintenance of covertness while supporting broad and general adaptation at the highest organizational levels and rapid and specific adaptation at the lowest organizational levels. To achieve this some vertical structure is necessary, frequent horizontal contact at the lowest organizational echelons is preferred, and maintaining an information collection apparatus is requisite.

Recently the Taliban has been, for the most part, effective in creating and managing the type of organization described above. In part this is circumstantial: it reflects the insurgency's need to maintain covertness and is thus a natural, or at least less deliberate, response to prevailing conditions. It is also likely due to the fact that, at this point, the organization cannot exercise stricter controls over its lowest levels without risking defection and serious degradation to its information collection apparatuses and operational reach. Regardless of the causes, the Taliban, with the support of other insurgent organizations, has created a knowledge transfer system that supplements the knowledge transfer capacity inherent to the insurgency's subnetworks (kinship, tribal, and so forth) existing or prefabricated networks that predate the current conflict. The insurgency's use of mobile specialists and associated operational techniques that require tactical mobility and frequent movement, support if not compel knowledge transfer. Experiential, tacit, explicit, specialized, and time-sensitive knowledge and information can be and is shared among individuals and organizations that come into contact with one another or are put into contact with one another when the need arises.

While the Afghan insurgency uses many of the same knowledge sharing techniques that the Iraqi insurgency employed, such as instructional manuals, the Internet, DVDs, and videos, it has been in the long term much more effective at creating fluid yet more permanent structures for frequently transferring knowledge and information throughout the organization. The system is by no means perfect.[239] And, because certain levels of covertness must be maintained, it rarely if ever facilitates rapid and comprehensive transfers of knowledge. But it is nonetheless adequate. It helps ensure that environmental and operational knowledge benefiting task performance and in tune with organizational objectives can be shared despite the organization's need to maintain covertness.

Knowledge Integration

As mentioned previously, the insurgency integrates knowledge into and through the organization and its operations via mobile detachments that assimilate themselves periodically into various fronts or smaller organizations specifically for the impartment of knowledge that could not otherwise be obtained, at least not without great cost. These detachments, or training teams, distribute specialized training and knowledge developed both within Afghanistan and from elsewhere. They use face-to-face communication and side-by-side instruction to share fundamental and more complex knowledge that would be difficult to obtain if not imparted through the conduct of an actual operation or through the intensive instruction provided by a professionally run and well resourced training camp. Given the organizational risks and costs of running and or sending a large number of insurgents to training camps, this means of integrating knowledge is particularly useful and practical.

In addition to in-person and on-the-job training, the insurgency takes advantage of technological means to collect, format, and then distribute knowledge to wider audiences. Films and photographs are used primarily for propaganda purposes, but they are also used for training and for conveying operational knowledge. Instructional manuals and other learning aids are placed in digital format or printed and then distributed. Like their Iraqi counterparts, the Afghan insurgency can also take advantage of military manuals and other publications available online and can share publications of their own making. These materials are used as a means of conveying training methodologies, techniques, and procedures of use in tactical operations.

The adaptive construction of IEDs is illustrative of the ways that collected knowledge is integrated into the insurgency's operations and general knowledge pool. Al Qaeda is instrumental in imparting and integrating this kind of knowledge into the broader insurgency. It runs training facilities and compounds that educate insurgents on how to construct IEDs and will on occasion assist in the emplacement and detonation of these explosives. And, because of its network and operational reach, al Qaeda is capable of quickly establishing contacts within and integrating lessons drawn from other theaters of operations. For instance, al Qaeda adopted, via in-person contact and through the Internet, general military and bomb-making tactics and techniques used in the Iraq War and elsewhere. The Taliban and other Afghan groups such as HiG have done the same and have used this knowledge to develop new equipment and capabilities specifically for operations in Afghanistan.[240]

COMPARING THE IRAQI AND AFGHAN INSURGENCIES' STRENGTHS AND WEAKNESSES

The Iraqi and Afghan insurgencies each leveraged the strengths and suffered from the weaknesses of the covert networked organizational form. For instance, both were able to take advantage of decentralization, while each had or has to contend with the limitations posed by the need to maintain covertness. But unlike the Iraqi insurgency, the Afghan insurgency has survived and has thus far been relatively successful in adapting toward achieving many of its principal organizational goals. This is the case because, comparatively, the Afghan insurgency has been more effective in comprehensively adapting its organizational inputs, outputs, and means of learning to achieve its organizational goals than was its Iraqi counterpart, despite being subject to the same, or at least very similar, organizational weaknesses. In order to better understand the Afghan insurgency's comparatively enhanced capacity for organizational adaptation, it is necessary to compare the two organizations. The following section will compare the Afghan insurgency's adaptive strengths and weaknesses against the findings presented at the end of Chapter 3.

Organizational Input Findings

This section will compare the organizational input findings of the two cases.

Organizational complexity led to differing and competing goals and rewards that detracted from shared goal achievement.

Unlike the Iraqi insurgency, the Afghan insurgency has not experienced significant levels of discord resulting in regular or widespread violent, internecine competition among its constituent organizations. Notably, the Afghan insurgency, although large and multifaceted, is not nearly as large or as diverse as the Iraqi insurgency and relies far less on the support provided by foreign fighters. And even though the insurgency has grown in both size and complexity over time, it is still largely dominated by only a handful of major groups. Most important, as the Afghan insurgency's composition has become more complex, it has still managed to suppress organizational differences for the achievement of commonly held goals. Whether or not this mutually beneficial arrangement will continue remains to be seen.

Organizational complexity enabled and disrupted information flows in consonance with levels of cooperation and competition.

Much like the Iraqi insurgency, the Afghan insurgency was and is required to maintain varying but certain levels of covertness, particularly in areas where the Coalition or the Karzai-led government might have greater levels of support. As such, overt cooperation or any practices of the sort that might come into view of the government or, more ominously, the Coalition—such as congregating or using open electronic channels of communication to share information—had to be studiously avoided until the insurgency gained a foothold in an area. But even when the insurgency did establish a foothold in an area it still had to be careful to avoid observation from a plethora of surveillance and reconnaissance platforms, whether technical or human in nature. Thus its complexity and decentralization, in combination with its need to maintain covertness, put significant pressures on information flows within and throughout the organization.

But because the Afghan insurgency has taken steps to promote the tacit cooperation of constituent organizations and to retain the passive—and to a far lesser degree, active—support of a portion of the civilian population by consistently promoting panorganizational goals, it has maintained or even grown a tenuous and geographically broad cohesiveness that the Iraqi insurgency might have attained only fleetingly, if it was attained at all. In addition, the Taliban's size (overwhelmingly the largest component of the insurgency), relative homogeneity, defined chains of leadership, and placement of dedicated intelligence analysts and collectors inside smaller affiliated organizations have all abetted vertical and horizontal information flows, even if these flows are stymied at times by setbacks, missteps, or interference from the Coalition or the Afghan government. By promoting cooperation and developing dedicated means of collecting and sharing information, the Afghan insurgency has been able leverage its complexity while concurrently being able to avoid, if not stave off, many of the competitive forces that disrupted information flows within the Iraqi insurgency.

Training was born of experimentation and shared experience but could not be conducted broadly for the achievement of more complex or panorganizational goals.

Training in Afghanistan was also born of experimentation and shared experience but *could* be and is conducted broadly for the achievement of organizational goals. Because the task performance competency required for successfully pursuing organizational goals has not changed substantially or frequently over time, the insurgency does not require either significant and complex initial training or regular retraining. And what training is required can generally be conducted fairly quickly and is rather easily imparted to and retained by new recruits. Furthermore, the Afghan insurgency is not trying to achieve its goals by regularly and directly confronting Coalition or government forces en masse, a task which, because of attrition and the need for complex maneuver, would require standardized and in-depth training for a large portion of insurgent forces. Instead, the insurgency is parsimoniously applying its limited combat power when and where it perceives advantage. Therefore, while many of the tasks the insurgency trains for might be simple, they are fundamental, and when combined with the direction and guidance provided by organizational leadership, are effective in supporting the organization's goals.

Additionally, it is important to note that the Afghan insurgency, particularly those elements originating from or located near Afghanistan's eastern border, is able to take advantage of training areas within Pakistan and, furthermore, receives substantial support from Pakistani agents and agencies on Afghan soil. Perhaps even more important, supplementary training for new techniques and procedures can be conducted in person and during the conduct of operations by a range of experienced and well-trained members of the insurgency operating as MTTs. These teams are deliberately constructed and are supported by a number of constituent insurgent organizations. They not only impart training and expertise but also, because of their mobility, they serve as a mechanism for knowledge transfer and integration. These training teams spread tactics and techniques developed during in-theater operations and adopted from out-of-theater experiences to local organizations that might not otherwise have the wherewithal to conduct or receive this kind of training.

While elements of the Iraqi insurgency also received external training support, leveraged sanctuary (in nearby Syria or Iran), and took advantage of MTT-like organizations, it did not experience nearly the same amount of either direct or indirect training support that has been provided to the Afghan insurgency—by Pakistan alone.[241] Additionally, because of the structures the Afghan insurgency has developed for integrating new techniques and procedures into its suborganizations on an as-needed basis, it is capable of ensuring that its training levels, skills, and organizational goals are better synchronized than those of the Iraqi insurgency.

Variable and loose constraints on organizational behavior led to organizational division and separation from supporters.

Although not foolproof—there are plenty of examples of atrocities that have been committed by the Afghan insurgency, to include in some respects, a number of mass-casualty suicide bombings—the Afghan insurgency has developed codes of conduct to constrain member behavior and has taken care to reinforce these codes of conduct both positively and negatively. Even minor offenses by organizational members are met with punishment, which can sometimes be severe. Comparatively, the Iraqi insurgency, particularly AQI, which regularly perpetrated mass-casualty attacks on broad swaths of Iraqi society and committed numerous barbarities (some of which were infamously captured on film by al Zarqawi and his associates), was far less constrained in its behavior than its Afghan counterparts.

Organizational diversity led to influxes of people, ideas, and resources but also led to goal divergence and uncooperative behavior.

The Afghan insurgency is arguably less complex than its Iraqi counterpart and is also likely less diverse. And despite the fact that the Taliban forms the preponderance of the insurgency and it is largely composed of Pashtuns, it still is supported by a range of organizations and individuals of varying ethnicity, tribal affiliation, and nationality. But the foreign and criminal elements of the Afghan insurgency are less core constituencies than they are enabling partners. While the Afghan insurgency is by no means a unified whole, it has maintained its coherence far better than did the Iraqi insurgency and has not (yet) suffered from significant goal divergence.

Norm variation led to discord and diminished levels of cooperation and support.

Norm variation within the insurgency has also been problematic in Afghanistan but not nearly to the degree that it was in Iraq. Perhaps the most significant variation occurred with the introduction of the tactic of suicide bombing. While not accepted broadly by the population or even portions of Taliban leadership, it was nonetheless, at least tacitly, permitted by the major insurgent groups, particularly because of its effectiveness.

Certainly the cooperative arrangements made by various insurgent groups and the rules imposed by the Taliban contributed to subduing significant norm variations, where they occurred. Perhaps the former more so than the latter has been important for reducing deleterious discord within the insurgency; in Afghanistan, and for now, cooptation and cooperation seem to be far more prevalent and preferred than open and violent conflict.

As the environment changed the insurgency was incapable of matching its tasks to its goals, particularly in the long term.

In Afghanistan, the insurgency has become *more* capable of matching its tasks to its goals over the long run. In the main, it has responded to the surge of Coalition forces by deliberately decreasing instantiations of direct and impromptu contact. Yet it still conducted and conducts high-profile attacks to try to weaken the resolve of the Coalition. Additionally, the insurgency has maintained its management of the illicit economy of Afghanistan and has continued to operate its shadow government. In the face of significant environmental change, the insurgency has been capable of making adjustments to its tasks and task performance to better account for this change.

Equipment was used parsimoniously and effectively in the achievement of organizational military goals.

Both the Iraqi and Afghan insurgencies showed great skill and economy in the use and procurement of equipment for the pursuit of organizational goals. But despite not having nearly as many military-grade supplies available to it, the Afghan insurgency has managed to supplement its equipment needs through state-based contacts and through criminal network partnerships.

Insurgent organizations created funding streams and adapted them to manage operations and organizational expansion.

The Afghan insurgency benefited from falling in on an already established "war economy" and a mature illicit drug manufacturing and trafficking industry. But it also managed to establish other funding streams through aligned insurgent and terrorist groups and via other international sources of finance. The funding received from these sources far outpaces the insurgency's operational costs, and the excess has been used for parallel governance efforts as well as for the cooptation and leveraging of corrupt members of the government, military, and police. Additionally, the pervasiveness of the heroin economy, and the drug trade in general, which is fully promoted and has been expanded by the insurgency, has either circumstantially or by design integrated the activities of the insurgency with almost all aspects of the Afghan economy and society.

Intelligence gathering and processes spanned organizations and provided invaluable information for adapting organizational inputs and outputs.

The depth and breadth of intelligence gathering and sharing by both the Iraqi and Afghan insurgencies is similar, although the Afghan insurgency has developed more permanent collection and analysis structures. The Taliban, in particular, has emplaced dedicated intelligence collectors and analysts in its suborganizations and maintains an analytical capability that is co-located with its leadership in Pakistan. Perhaps more important, it also maintains defined leadership chains that can push and pull information and intelligence through the organization—chains that were largely absent in the less deliberately structured apparatus employed by the Iraqi insurgency.

Limited external consulting resulted in greater independence but perhaps less coordination than could have been achieved otherwise.

The Afghan insurgency has received far more external consulting, principally from Pakistani sources, than did the Iraqi insurgency, and this has, to a degree, made the insurgency dependent on Pakistan's support. But this support is provided and accepted largely because Pakistan and the insurgency share similar goals. In this respect, the Afghan insurgency still retains a great degree of independence in its operations and behaviors—Pakistan does not have much cause or reason to significantly interfere with the Afghan insurgency, except in a supporting role.

While Pakistan's—and to a lesser degree Iran's—support has so far come without significant costs, this is not to say that costs will not be borne in the future. If the insurgency is ultimately successful in achieving its goals, it is likely that Pakistan (and Iran) will seek to exploit the relations it has either developed or cemented with various insurgent organizations over the course of the conflict. The divisions within the insurgency that have for the most part been suppressed can and likely will be exploited by these external actors, if the need or chance arises. The manifestation and significance of this interference, if it emerges, remains to be seen.

*The chaos manufactured by the insurgency increased exponentially
when other illicit organizations conducted direct action in support of
the insurgency or in parallel to its activities.*

Direct action conducted in support of or in parallel to the Afghan insurgency has not led to the levels of chaos experienced in Iraq, but it has nonetheless contributed to the insurgency's goals. In fact, direct action in Afghanistan has perhaps led to a perverse economic—via the heroin industry—and social—through shadow governance—stability that might not have otherwise been achieved. Criminal profiteers have indirectly weakened the power and legitimacy of the Afghan government by promoting the growth of the illicit economy and its integration into nearly all aspects of Afghan society. More directly, they have supported the insurgency through the generation of massive and various funding streams and by the provisioning of resources and services. The establishment of shadow governance structures has given Afghans an alternative to the corrupt bureaucracies of the official Afghan government. These structures have afforded the Taliban, in particular, a *relative* level of legitimacy that it might not otherwise have been able to obtain.

Cooperation was as likely as competition.

Cooperation between insurgent organizations in Afghanistan, thus far, seems to be more the norm than competition, even though organizations certainly compete and sometimes come into open conflict at the tactical or local level. It is likely, though not preordained, that competition will ensue after Coalition forces are drawn down. This remains to be seen.

Organizational Output Findings

This section will compare the organizational output findings of the two cases.

*Insurgent organizations quickly adapted skills and knowledge to the
effective completion of simple tasks.*

Although the Afghan insurgency does quickly adapt new skills and knowledge and has structures in place for sharing these adaptations, it has not had to adapt its skills and knowledge as often as the Iraqi insurgency, for two reasons: (1) training for the bulk of the Afghan insurgency is more standardized (and more readily available); and (2) the Afghan insurgency does not engage in conflict, particularly direct combat, nearly as often as did its Iraqi counterparts.

*Organizations, limited in size by a need for covertness, increased
task performance competency but with decreasing marginal returns
as the environment required more complex capabilities for goal
accomplishment.*

The Afghan insurgency has balanced its need for covertness with task performance requirements by taking a marginally lower profile while still engaging in high-payoff attacks, particularly during the so-called surge period. Additionally, by continuing to expand its means of shadow governance and by maintaining its control over the illicit economy—50 percent of Afghanistan's GDP—it has managed to pursue its organizational goals without necessarily having to expand its capacity for conducting complex military activities. This is not to say that the insurgency has not expanded its capacity for engaging in combat, but that it has not been compelled to do so in order to achieve its organizational goals.

*The Internet and other means of social networking and coordination
allowed for virtual command, control, and communications.*

The Internet and social networks are important means of facilitating virtual command, control, and communications in Afghanistan. But the one significant difference between Iraq and Afghanistan is the presence of defined leadership and organizational stratification in the latter. This, in combination with the Internet and other forms of networking, allows the Afghan insurgency to leverage both formal *and* informal chains of information dispersal, as needed.

*An ability to sense the environment and adapt accordingly shaped and
was shaped by cognition and behavior.*

The Afghan insurgency's cognition and behavior have not suffered the same breakdown as occurred in Iraq, principally because it has for the most part maintained behaviors and structures that promote cooperation and information sharing. Its efforts to avoid undue conflict with the population combined with its ability to tap local actors and to share information gathered at the periphery with the core have allowed it to adapt quickly and accurately to changes in its surrounding environment. Having dedicated intelligence collectors and analysts in place throughout these local organizations has served to strengthen and hasten this process.

Organizational Learning Findings

This section will compare the organizational learning findings of the two cases.

Knowledge collection enabled adaptation, but the insurgency's capacity
for collecting knowledge decreased as the network lost membership
through competition and defections.

Given that the Afghan insurgency has increased in size and breadth—and commensurately in its direct or indirect control over territory and the population—while maintaining tacit, and some explicit, cooperative relationships among its constituents, it has been able to avoid significant membership losses and an associated depletion of knowledge collection capabilities. But friction among groups—already occurring in some areas as the Taliban expands its territorial reach and has more frequent direct contact with marginally cooperative organizations—is likely to be on the rise and could be a source of significant discord when the Coalition reduces its presence. Whether or not the Taliban's information-sharing chains and intelligence collectors can still be effective with the weakening or absence of network ties in these areas remains to be seen.

Concealed and rapid knowledge transfer allowed disparate
organizations to share ideas and experiences without direct contact.

The Afghan insurgency has similarly leveraged discrete means and methods for rapid and concealed knowledge transfer. But it has also taken advantage of deliberately constructed MTTs for sharing tacit and explicit knowledge among smaller and larger insurgent groups in a way and to a degree that either was not possible or was not pursued by the Iraqi insurgency. This supplementary means of knowledge transfer has ensured the sharing of information and tactics in a more reliable and consistent fashion—a fashion that is, for practical purposes, nearly impossible to interdict.

Knowledge was integrated through experience and experimentation, but
levels of integration suffered from high personnel losses and turnover.

Knowledge integration in Afghanistan also occurs through experience and experimentation but is supported and indeed enabled by MTTs and the sharing of information through leadership chains and other cooperative practices. But in the aggregate and unlike its Iraqi counterpart, the Afghan insurgency over time has not been losing membership through significant defections, although there is a likelihood of splintering in advance of the upcoming elections.[242] Instead it has been increasing in size and breadth. Accordingly, it has not suffered from significant losses or turnover and therefore has been able to maintain levels and patterns of knowledge integration.

CONCLUSION

This chapter has evaluated the Afghan insurgency's adaptive cycle and then compared it with that of its Iraqi counterpart. As this comparison demonstrates, and as could be reasonably expected given their structure, the two insurgencies share many of the same organizational strengths and weaknesses. But despite similarities in structure, competitors, and even in size, the Afghan insurgency has been comparatively more adaptive. This is because it has taken steps to accentuate its organizational strengths while diminishing its weaknesses as it pursues organizational goals. A number of actions stand out in this regard: the development and maintenance of positive as opposed to merely obstructionist or nihilistic goals; meticulous attempts to cultivate and maintain the Afghan population's support; the imposition of defined leadership and information-sharing chains; the use of dedicated MTTs; and the integration of varied but substantial funding flows of value to both the insurgency and Afghanistan as a whole. These steps have allowed the Afghan insurgency to adapt cyclically and in a manner that was never quite achieved, at least not over a long period, by its counterpart in Iraq.

It is important to note that by no means does this analysis suggest that if the Afghan insurgency is successful in its efforts to remove the Coalition and replace the Karzai government that it will ultimately be "successful" in achieving its goals. In fact, it is just as likely, if not more so, that the insurgency's capacity for adaptation will suffer dramatically if this happens: principally, this will occur because organizational goals will change and competition will likely replace cooperation. It is also important to note that the findings presented in this and the previous chapter are not necessarily applicable to other insurgencies except as those insurgencies might be similarly composed as large, diverse, and complex covert networked organizations. The utility of these findings insofar as they relate to understanding, undermining, and/or efforts to defeat the adaptive capacities of similar organizations will be the subject of the following, concluding chapter.

5 It Takes More than a Network

INTRODUCTION

The Iraqi insurgency's key organizational strength was its ability to operate in small dispersed groups aided by a diversely capable and motivated membership that, for a time, was united by a common goal. Small group adaptations were frequent and widespread. Freed from many of the constrictive effects of norms, organizational culture, and bureaucratic inertia, the insurgency proceeded with mass experimentation in tactics and techniques and exploited the capabilities inherent to small, networked organizations. Over time, these experimentations, when combined with shared learning, enhanced individual and collective task performance competency. The insurgency accomplished all of this while dodging the incrementalist tendencies that plague more hidebound organizations.

Initially, the insurgency possessed a number of strengths: flexibility in structure and operations; an almost limitless supply of materiel and motivated personnel; strong environmental awareness; and few if any obstacles to the flow of information. As General Peter Chiarelli argues, "I have said for a long period of time that one of the reasons that this adversary has been so successful is that he doesn't have all the bureaucratic obstacles in place to stop the flow of information."[1] Accordingly, the insurgency was highly adept at marshaling the resources necessary for accomplishing its goals and adapting faster than its Coalition counterparts. But the insurgency's strengths were also its weaknesses. Latent capacity, which the insurgency had, did not ultimately translate into results. Adaptation, which is only effective if it is directed toward the achievement of organizational goals, suffered as unity of purpose was replaced by competition and divisiveness. Diversity of membership in this case meant diversity in goals: persistent friction among organizations eventually compelled the insurgency's dismemberment and progressively contributed to deleterious effects on its ability to adapt.

For example, organizational goals and the methods used for achieving these goals diverged so sharply in the later stages of the conflict as to precipitate a significant break among formerly cooperating organizations.[2] In 2007, polls showed that support for suicide bombings and other extremely violent attacks—both hallmarks of al Qaeda–affiliated organizations—was declining rapidly.[3] The brutal methods employed by AQI and other al Qaeda affiliates and franchises against the Iraqi population and later against their partner insurgent groups eventually backfired and ended up aiding the Coalition. In the late stages of the insurgency organizations began to adapt toward one another nearly as frequently as they adapted to environmental conditions and competitors.

Organizational coherence also broke down as some groups tried to attain more positive goals while other organizations merely sowed chaos: tasks no longer matched goals; inputs and outputs were adjusted inappropriately; and adaptability was impeded. The Iraqi insurgency demonstrated that being decentralized and networked is really effective only in the short term or if minimalist organizational goals are sought. As Ahmed Hashim argues, "I believe that journalists and observers used the term [decentralized and networked] because it sounded 'sexy' and because being 'decentralized and networked' seemed to be *de rigueur* for terrorist or insurgent groups. The reality is that you simply cannot be a wholly decentralized insurgent group and continue to exist for long or be able to carry out more than very limited operations in a limited geographical locale (e.g. one's neighborhood or tribal lands)."[4] Ultimately, the benefits that did accrue to independent but networked organizations did not accrue to the insurgency as a whole.

Waging a complex covert networked insurgency is no mean task. As both the Iraqi and Afghan cases demonstrate, coordination and cooperation must be endemic and nearly complete for the organization to be effective. Learning must occur continuously, or smaller constituent organizations will likely fall prey to their competitors. The use of force and violence must at some point be tempered by and then replaced with more positive methods and goals: engendering fear leads to loathing and resentment. The tactics of terrorism have a short half-life.[5] Despite claims to the contrary, the theoretical capabilities attributed to complex and diverse covert networked organizations do not necessarily obtain in practice. Organizational adaptation for long-term goal achievement, particularly if these goals include the vanquishing of a major military power, requires centralization of a kind familiar to more hierarchical organizations but wholly unfamiliar to diverse and disparate covert networked organizations.

If the primary objectives of the Iraqi insurgency were terror, chaos, and the disruption of Coalition operations, then the insurgency succeeded in spades for nearly five years. But outside of creating chaos and terror, the insurgency accomplished few, if any, positive goals. Sustaining organizational cooperation was impossible if the goal of this cooperation extended beyond anything other than sowing mass societal disruption. As Peter Mansoor argues, "Eventually, if a networked terrorist organization like the one we saw in Iraq wants to prevail, they have to coalesce into larger formations and actually do more than just fight but govern as well."[6] Almost all of the insurgency's adaptive qualities suffered or faded as the conflict progressed, and few positive goals were achieved. An ability to blend into the environment, membership recruitment and replacement, defensive and offensive capacities, and cohesiveness and cooperation were all weakened.[7] Correspondingly, organizational weaknesses were exacerbated as organizational differences increased in importance and as self-interest—which sparked an inability to establish cooperative mechanisms or led to a distinct lack of interest in cooperation—became supreme.[8] Ultimately it would have taken more than a network for the Iraqi insurgency to effectively adapt to achieve its organizational goals.

IMPLICATIONS

In the introduction to this book I argued that the Iraqi insurgency failed to achieve longer-term organizational goals because many of its organizational strengths were also its organizational weaknesses: these characteristics abetted and then corrupted the insurgency's ability to adapt. I have demonstrated how these strengths and weaknesses affected the insurgency's adaptation of organizational inputs, outputs, and learning across time. I have also compared and contrasted these findings against a similar analysis of the Afghan insurgency and have shown the measures it took to mitigate its organizational weaknesses, leverage its organizational strengths, and improve its capacity for adaptation. Although there is some risk in trying to generalize the findings of these two cases, however representative they might be of future insurgencies or complex covert networked organizations in general, and care must be taken with any conclusions drawn from them, I do argue that there are a number of important implications that flow from this study.

It Takes a Network to Defeat a Network

This oft repeated phrase suggests that an organization in competition with or combating a network must be able to act like a network. More to the point, it must be capable of conducting decentralized operations with rapidly adapting peripheral groups and units. It implies that the networked form of organization is necessarily predisposed to adaptation. But this overly simplified yet widely accepted view ignores the point of organizational adaptation: changing the organization based on experience and learning to achieve organizational goals. Being able to *act* like a network is generally useful, but it does not in and of itself guarantee success—being a network or acting like a network does not ensure that an organization can or will adapt appropriately to achieve its goals.

For instance, if an organization has goals (limited duration, small scale) that require it to structure itself or behave like a network, then a networked disposition probably makes the most sense for that organization. If a competing network has goals (long-term, large scale) that require greater centralization and control, then a more hierarchical or formal structure probably makes the most sense for that organization. Goals should dictate organizational form, not vice versa. Certainly, the Iraqi insurgency—a networked organization by most if not all accounts—would have benefited, despite the costs to covertness, from a greater degree of centralization and control as the conflict wore on, much the way that the Afghan insurgency benefited from its imposition of rules and its use of clearly defined leadership chains. Similarly, the Coalition in Iraq—a centralized and hierarchical organization by most if not all accounts—*did*, albeit not initially, benefit from an ability to conduct decentralized operations. The latter ultimately adapted; the former did not. Success requires that an organization is properly structured for adapting to achieve its organizational goals.[9]

An Insurgency Might Not Be an Insurgency

There is a rather significant assumption contained within in the common military definition of insurgency—*An organized movement aimed at the overthrow of a constituted government through the use of subversion and armed conflict*—and this is that its participants are interested in removing a government *and then* taking over the role of traditional governance. In the case of the Iraqi insurgency, this assumption is, at least, debatable. Certainly the broader and unifying aim of forcing the removal of Coalition forces from Iraq and delegitimizing, undermining, or overthrowing the fledgling Iraqi government fits the doctrinal definition of insurgency. But not all of the organizations, groups, or individuals constituting the Iraqi insurgency were necessarily interested in governance, even though their actions may have indirectly or tangentially contributed to the goals of the insurgency. Some groups, such as various criminal organizations and al Qaeda and its affiliates, likely had little to no interest in governing Iraq—at least not in the traditional sense of governing or through traditional means of governance—although they were interested in the subversion of its ruling authority. If the Iraqi insurgency is a harbinger of insurgencies to come, then how we define and think of insurgencies will have to change.[10]

This finding is important for a number of reasons, three of which are directly related to the topic of organizational adaptation: (1) a multiform insurgency might have a shared goal but might not have nor need a shared strategy to achieve its aims; (2) this shared goal might be negative rather than positive (overthrowing the government rather than constituting a new government); and (3) the adaptations occurring within a multiform insurgency can or perhaps will be highly fragmented and will appear chaotic rather than goal-directed. This type of nihilist "insurgency" defies prediction and disallows the application of standardized counterinsurgency techniques, even if it is operating within the same time period or same geographic locale.

If insurgencies are no longer insurgencies in the classical sense, as might be the case if the Iraqi insurgency is a harbinger of insurgencies to come, then their advent will have significant implications for military doctrine and for the design and application of military force.[11] Understanding organizational adaptation might end up being more important than trying to divine likely behavior from apparent or stated goals.

Networks Are Suited to Achieving Short-Term and Less Complex Goals

The Iraqi insurgency demonstrated that a mostly unsophisticated but complex networked force could adapt and progressively cause significant disruptions to the operations and goals of a massive and technologically advanced force. Over time, insurgent attacks became more complex (combined arms assaults and multimethod, sequenced attacks), catastrophic (number of deaths and injuries and amount of property damage), and exotic (use of chemical-laden explosives, EFPs, female suicide bombers). In reaction to the changing tactics of Coalition forces and in order to improve stand-off distances and survivability, the insurgency increased its use of IEDs, employed increased attacks on softer targets (police and civilians), and many times used less and less sophisticated weapons (small arms, simple bombs, Molotov cocktails) to avoid the detectable cues shed by more technologically advanced devices (either in their acquisition or use).

As useful as these adaptations were for outpacing the Coalition's adaptation and increasing short-term task performance competency, they did not benefit the insurgency in the long term. Because insurgent organizations could not or did not adapt in concert over long periods—they had to maintain a certain degree of anonymity, and organizations many times fell into competition—they failed to regularly mass their capabilities in the conduct of sustained and coordinated operations, whether military or political. The insurgency instead engaged in a campaign of "pinpricks" that saturated the environment with violence but was rarely decisive in the military sense of the term. Although the insurgency was relatively competent in its ability to coordinate efforts independently through spontaneously developed—and dissolved—networks, its disposition was more suited to limited duration attacks, however effective, than to the kinds of complex sustained military operations and governance activities typically required of a successful insurgency.

Inhibiting Insurgent Organizational Adaptation

Although the Iraqi and Afghan insurgencies were large, complex, and diverse, most of their constituent organizations and groups were or are lean: this is partly a function of their networked structure and partly due to a need to maintain varying levels of secrecy and covertness. Although lean, insurgent organizations can—for the most part and while personnel are available—add or remove members as needed or as compelled by operational losses. This adaptive capacity is useful for organizational protection and survival. But eliminating excess capacity and reducing the redundancy of organizational members while increasing the functions that an organization has to perform reduce the insurgency's capacity for adaptation.[12] In this respect, the Iraqi insurgency typified what Kathleen Carley terms maladaptive organizations: "[M]aladaptive organizations tend to spend excessive time bringing on and letting go...personnel have to spend excessive time learning who is still in the organization or learning what personnel know. Thus factors encouraging such personnel changes will also inhibit adaptivity."[13]

Structurally, the Iraqi insurgency had significant latent capacity for substantial cross-organizational interaction and cooperation. But many times inter-action among members in a networked organization, particularly in a covert networked organization operating in a violent, competitive environment, is re-duced because of secrecy protocols, membership attrition, competition, a lack of defined leadership, or because of frequent changes to the network's structure. Whether for competitive reasons or for the sake of maintaining covertness, the Iraqi insurgency did not fully or progressively take advantage of or realize the gains that could have been accrued from higher levels of collaboration. This has not been the case in Afghanistan, where collaboration has been achieved, however temporary this might be, through tacit agreements and efforts to maintain the cooperation of segments of the population. In Iraq, reduced lev-els of physical or virtual interaction among organizations and organizational members, either because of an inherent inability or deliberate unwillingness, reduced the chances of innovations being spread or expanded upon for use in the accomplishment of more complex goals. It also reduced the likelihood of organizations synchronizing their adaptations for mutually beneficial gains or for perhaps modifying their behavior toward more political and less combat-oriented goals.

Both the Iraqi and Afghan insurgencies' experience with organizational adaptation indicates that the adaptation of similarly composed and disposed organizations can be inhibited if not controlled by competing organizations. Indeed, two characteristics of complex covert networked organizations in par-ticular can be exploited to great advantage:

- Group and organizational cleavages can be exploited. If constituent orga-nizations are unwilling or unable to cooperate or coordinate their activi-ties, the insurgency as a whole will be much less effective. Steps can be taken to accentuate differences either through information campaigns (for example, highlighting and broadcasting unacceptable behaviors) or through organizational cooptation (choosing sides, even if only tempo-rarily).

- Decentralization can be compelled. The Iraqi insurgency's greatest strength was its *ability* to conduct decentralized operations: it demon-strated decentralized decision-making and small-group initiative; had an informed and imaginative organizational membership; permitted the freedom of operation in the achievement of organizational goals; and, for a period of time, maintained the capacity for and freedom to communicate pertinent information regarding organizational and individual operational effectiveness. But its *need* to be decentralized, especially without having some formal structures for cooperation and information sharing in place, was its greatest weakness. Unencumbered decentralization seriously compromised operational capability and prevented synchronous multigroup adaptations. Disrupting an insurgency's ability to centralize physically—by frequently disrupting meetings and engagements of multiple groups and by compromising leadership chains where they exist— or virtually, by controlling electronic means of information sharing, can significantly slow its ability to adapt.

Although these suggestions might seem counterintuitive—since exacerbating organizational cleavages and compelling decentralization will likely lead to more convoluted, less predictable, and probably more violent insurgencies— they can help ensure against the kind of collaboration and cooperation that have made the Afghan insurgency and would have made the Iraqi insurgency much more adaptive and therefore effective in the long term.

FOR FUTURE STUDY

This book has examined the adaptations of a large, complex, diverse, and covert networked organization in a conflict environment and compared it with a similarly composed and disposed contemporary organization operating in similar conditions and circumstances. It showed that while the Iraqi insurgency had many adaptive strengths, these strengths were also organizational liabilities. Organizational adaptation is a process born of circumstantially driven and structurally shaped but deliberate tradeoffs: speed for effectiveness; flexibility for durability; size for robustness and effect; and diverse skills for the coherence afforded by organizational homogeneity. Tradeoffs are important factors in the design of an organization. All organizations must make choices as to the initial commitment of resources and then to their adaptation over time. This is perhaps especially true for illicit organizations and for organizations that have limited material wealth and constrained employment or operational capabilities.

The framework used in this book's analysis could very well be applied to other instances of conflict and other similarly structured insurgencies. These findings would help us to understand not only how other martial organizations adapted but also how they adapted to one another across time, geography, and with different organizational inputs, outputs, and methods of learning. They would also have important implications for military force design and structure as well as for resource employment once a conflict has started. These findings would lend to a more comprehensive understanding of organizational adaptation in different types of conflict—where organizations had different goals—and by differently composed and disposed organizations requiring differing levels of covertness. A dataset of the adaptations made across a range of conflict types and as employed by a number of competitor organizations would not only abet a better understanding of organizational adaptation—a significant goal in its own right—but would also aid in the appreciation of how competition and conflict might unfold in the future. Undoubtedly, because of its successes and in spite of its failures, aspects of the Iraqi insurgency's adaptations will be imitated, if not adopted wholesale, by future adversaries. Although a contemporary case, Afghanistan might be prescriptive in this regard. A broader understanding of how different organizations might employ these adaptations is warranted.

Notes

1. I use the definition of insurgency provided by the U.S. military: "An organized movement aimed at the overthrow of a constituted government through the use of subversion and armed conflict." U.S. Department of the Army, *Counterinsurgency*, Glossary-5.

2. This according to data compiled by the National Counterterrorism Center (NCTC) Worldwide Incident Tracking System (witc.nctc.org), icasualties.org, and iraqbodycount.org.

3. The Iraqi insurgency, as well as the Afghan insurgency, will be treated as singular in this book's analysis. This is done for the purposes of: (1) analyzing these insurgencies, respectively, as large organizations networked for the accomplishment of commonly held goals; and (2) assessing each networked insurgency's capacity for and practice of adaptation. Although the differences between and among each insurgency's constituent organizations are significant for many reasons and during different periods, this book will not stress these differences individually in its analysis, except where and when these differences contributed to substantial organizational fractures and a correspondingly reduced capacity for adaptation. It will instead examine those organizational characteristics that were (1) held commonly across insurgent groups and within each insurgency as a whole, and that (2) contributed to each respective insurgency's capacity to adapt and actual practice of adaptation. For instance, organizations like the Mahdi Army (Mahdi Militia, Jaish al Mahdi [JAM]) or the Taliban will not be assessed individually and will be addressed only specifically, as or when noted.

4. This range of estimates of the size of the insurgency varied by the source of the report and the definition of who was an insurgent. See discussion in Herring and Rangwala, *Iraq in Fragments*, 164–67.

5. Molnar, Lybrand, Hahn, Kirkman, and Riddleberger, *Undergrounds*, 14–15.

6. Or, similarly, the insurgency in Afghanistan.

7. For the purpose of this book, variants of the term "covert" constitute a general and overarching reference to the employment of both covert and clandestine behaviors and activities insofar as the organizations examined employed or employ methods to maintain various levels of organizational secrecy and security in their formation and in the planning and conduct of their operations. Although, by definition, these terms do not readily apply to nongovernmental organizations, a distinction must be made nonetheless between the accepted Department of Defense (DOD) definitions of these terms and as they relate to insurgent, criminal, and other unofficial or illicit organizations and networks, which are sometimes referred to, variously, as "dark" organizations or networks. The DOD defines a clandestine operation as an "operation sponsored or conducted by governmental departments or agencies in such a way as to assure secrecy or concealment. A clandestine operation differs from a covert operation in that emphasis is placed on concealment of the operation rather than on the identity of the sponsor. In special operations, an activity may be both covert and clandestine and may focus equally on operational considerations and intelligence related activities." Joint Publication (JP) 1–02, 46. The DOD defines a covert operation as an "operation that is so planned and executed as to conceal the identity of or permit plausible denial by the sponsor." Ibid., 73.

In their Naval Postgraduate School thesis, Ian Davis, Carrie Worth, and Douglas Zimmerman offer an encompassing definition of dark networks and their use of covert and clandestine operations or tradecraft that is more appropriate for this book than derivations of the aforementioned DOD definitions. Dark networks are "interdependent entities that use formal and informal ties to conduct activities that may be perceived as illegal by an external entity and employ operational security measures and/or clandestine tradecraft techniques through varying degrees of overt, or more likely covert activity to achieve a purpose." Davis, Worth, and Zimmerman, "A Theory of Dark Network Design," 6. Dark networks' goals are often illegal within their prevailing environments; their activities may either be legal or illegal, but they regularly employ illegal means; and they take steps to conceal the identity of their membership. Ibid., 7. These distinctions are important given that, depending on changes in their operational environment and their organizational goals, these dark networks may vary their operations between covert, clandestine, or even overt.

8. See Fowler, *Amateur Soldiers*, 14.

9. Because the conflict in Iraq is for all intents and purposes over, I used it as the principal case in this book. Because the conflict in Afghanistan is not settled, I used it for comparative purposes. Although it can be risky to use findings from an incomplete case to compare with another settled case, I take care to make only conclusions that can be supported by the Afghan insurgency's organizational adaptations, in respect to organizational goals, as they have occurred so far.

10. For discussion, see Serena, *A Revolution in Military Adaptation*, 128–33; Rabasa

et al., *From Insurgency to Stability, Volume II*; Brimley, "Tentacles of Jihad," 34, 42; and Hosmer, *Why the Iraqi Resistance to the Coalition Invasion was So Weak*, 140–43.

11. Case studies are an appropriate methodology for studies that are exploratory or revelatory in nature. See Lee, *Using Qualitative Methods in Organizational Research*, 41. See also Yin, *Case Study Research*, 4–9; King, Keohane, and Verba, *Designing Social Inquiry*, 4; Marshall and Rossman, *Designing Qualitative Research*, 4–6, 9, 92; and George and Bennett, *Case Studies and Theory Development*, 18–20. Understanding change, and in this case adaptation, requires examining data over time. See Kiel, *Managing Chaos and Complexity in Government*, 22.

12. In an instrumental case study, "The case is of secondary interest, it plays a supportive role, and it facilitates our understanding of something else. The case is still looked at in depth, its contexts scrutinized, its ordinary activities detailed, but all because this helps the researcher to pursue the external interest. The case may be seen as typical of other cases or not.... Here the choice of case is made to advance understanding of that other interest." Stake, "Case Studies," 437. The external interest in this case is detailing and understanding how the insurgency adapted as a complex, covert, networked organization. See also the discussion of bounded systems in Stake, "The Case Study Method in Social Inquiry," 23–24.

13. As Robert Donmoyer argues, case study methods can be used "to expand and enrich the repertoire of social constructions available to practitioners and others; it may help, in other words, in the forming of questions rather than in the finding of answers." Donmoyer, "Generalizability and the Single-Case Study," 51–52.

14. Patterns of organizational behavior in general lend themselves to prediction. See Miles et al., "Organizational Strategy, Structure, and Process," 547.

15. This framework is explained in greater detail in Chapter 1.

16. This framework is adapted from Harrison's Action Model for Group Task Performance. See Harrison, *Diagnosing Organizations*, 61–63. The modified version of Harrison's model used in this book is presented and discussed in an analysis of U.S. Army organizational adaptation. See Serena, *A Revolution in Military Adaptation*, 11–18.

17. Serena, *A Revolution in Military Adaptation*, 17.

18. Specifically, I examined more than thirteen thousand attacks between the 2003 and 2008 period in: Al Tamin Province (Kirkuk); Anbar Province (Falluja, Ramadi); Baghdad Province (Baghdad); Basra Province (Basra); Diyala Province (Baquba, Muqdadiyah); Ninawa Province (Mosul, Tal Afar); Salah ad Din Province (Balad, Samarra, Tikrit).

19. Semistructured interviews allowed me to ask the same set of questions to a number of participants while retaining the freedom to probe particular revelations in greater detail. See May, *Social Research*, 123–24; and Flick, *An Introduction to Qualitative Research*, 74–81.

CHAPTER 1

1. Napolean D. Valeriano and Charles T. R. Bohannan argue that organization is the "first imperative" of a guerrilla movement and is essential for its success. Valeriano and Bohannan, *Counter-Guerrilla Operations*, 13.

2. See discussion in Rabasa et al., *From Insurgency to Stability, Volume I*, 2. See also discussion of competing organizational factors and goals within revolutionary movements in Spain and Ireland in Irvin, *Militant Nationalism*.

3. See discussion of organizational structuring in Singh and Mei, *Theory and Practice of Modern Guerrilla Warfare*, 33–34.

4. Metz and Millen, *Insurgency and Counterinsurgency in the 21st Century*, 25.

5. Adaptive speed was partly what kept coalition forces off balance in Iraq and Afghanistan. The Afghan insurgency's ability to adapt is discussed in Blank, *Rethinking Asymmetric Threats*.

6. See Serena, *A Revolution in Military Adaptation*, 23. Ben Connable and Martin Libicki, however, argue that unified hierarchies are better suited to conducting an insurgency than are fragmented networks. Connable and Libicki, *How Insurgencies End*, xvi.

7. Ben Connable and Martin Libicki argue that most insurgencies are hybrid in form (a mix of hierarchical forms and fragmented networks) but that urban insurgencies are more likely to be networked than their rural counterparts. See Connable and Libicki, *How Insurgencies End*, xvi.

8. Steve Metz contends that an organization that is a mix between a centralized hierarchical (for task effectiveness) and a decentralized networked form (for flexibility and adaptability) is best suited for effectiveness. Metz, *Rethinking Insurgency*, 12.

9. In particular, insurgent and terrorist groups that engaged in organized crime or used organized criminal networks for support. See discussion of organizations blending these methods in Oehme, "Terrorists, Insurgents, and Criminals—Growing Nexus?" See also Sanderson, "Transnational Terror and Organized Crime: Blurring the Lines"; Clarke, *Crime-Terror Nexus*; and Williams, *The Al Qaeda Connection*.

10. It is possible that other methods could have been applied at a later, less chaotic date. But at the time, force was seen as "the surest path to political advantage." Gompert, Kelly, and Watkins, *Security in Iraq*, 5.

11. Most illicit organizations have some requirement for covertness, even if only for certain types of activities. Networks, particularly those aided by technology, can mask their organizational form and activities. See Dombroski, Fischbeck, and Carley, "Estimating the Shape of Covert Networks."

12. All insurgencies require resources or an ability to replenish resources to conduct operations. Hamilton, *The Art of Insurgency*, 23. Resources can come from local populations, states, or even diaspora populations. See Byman et al., *Trends in Outside Support for Insurgent Movements*. One characteristic that distinguished the Iraqi insurgency was

that its complex and diverse linkages reduced the amount of overt support it needed from the Iraqi population. Metz, *Rethinking Insurgency*, 13–14.

13. One of the more spectacular divergences was between Sunni groups and AQI in al Anbar Province in 2006. See discussion in Long, "The Anbar Awakening." See also Ucko, "Militias, Tribes, and Insurgents," 103–4.

14. Muckian, "Structural Vulnerabilities of Networked Insurgencies: Adapting to the New Adversary," 16.

15. Record, *Beating Goliath*, 68.

16. This violated one of Mao's fundamental dictums for insurgent success. He argued that "proper guerrilla policy will provide for unified strategy and independent activity." Mao, *The Red Book of Guerrilla Warfare*, 67. The Iraqi insurgency did not have policies or strategies that led to regular and coordinated but independent activity. David Kilcullen argues that modern insurgencies, like the one in Iraq, may not have a coherent strategy and may not be interested in overthrowing the state and taking its place. See Kilcullen, "Counterinsurgency Redux," 4–6. This is problematic for organizations that are only loosely tied together by shared interests or goals and require a great degree of auto- or self-coordination to succeed.

17. When the term "network" is used in this book it is in reference to human networks and the organizations they form, unless otherwise indicated.

18. Kilduff and Tsai, *Social Networks and Organizations*, 5.

19. Anklam, *Net Work*, 5–6. Network effects are what occur when individuals are influenced by the behavior of the group when it is engaged in collective action. Takács, "Effects of Network Segregation in Intergroup Conflict," 59.

20. Zanini and Edwards, "The Networking of Terror in the Information Age," 31–32.

21. Borgatti and Halgin, "On Network Theory," 1169.

22. Ibid., 1174.

23. Ibid., 1169.

24. Zanini and Edwards, "The Networking of Terror in the Information Age," 31.

25. Wasserman and Faust, *Social Network Analysis*, 4–10.

26. See discussion in Williams, "Transnational Criminal Networks," 70.

27. McGrath and Krackhardt, "Network Conditions for Organizational Change."

28. Networks can be distinguished by their environments, operational needs, and the nature of organizational membership: Dark (high level of hostility in environment, high need for security, members know the nature of network); Light/Bright (low level of hostility in environment, security to harden network, members know the nature of network); Gray (fuzzy environment, elaborate security measures, deceptive and network nature is hidden or obfuscated). See Davis, Worth, and Zimmerman, *A Theory of Dark Network Design*, 5–12.

29. Jones, "Understanding the Form, Function, and Logic of Clandestine Cellular Networks," 5.

30. Ibid., 73–78.

31. Williams, "Transnational Criminal Networks," 72.

32. Jones, *Understanding the Form, Function, and Logic of Clandestine Cellular Networks*, 29.

33. Davis, Worth, and Zimmerman, *A Theory of Dark Network Design*, 15–16.

34. Krebs, "Mapping Networks of Terrorist Cells," 49.

35. This balance is achieved in various ways, depending on how much covertness any particular organization must maintain. Different covert organizations, whether in Iraq, Afghanistan, or elsewhere, engaged or engage in clandestine radio broadcasting and print publication. They also took or take advantage of protected and concealed trust networks to facilitate operations or recruitment needs. Or, when circumstances changed and the balance shifted allowing for more overt behaviors and activities, these organizations created shadow governance structures and organizations specifically tasked with media interaction. The capabilities afforded by the Internet and social media platforms have greatly changed this balance in favor of covert networked organizations. These groups can reach vast audiences quickly with vivid imagery and through media that are mobile, easily accessible, impart relative anonymity, and are nearly impossible to counteract on a long-term basis. Additionally, these media require few organizational resources to operate—in terms of money, time, print resources, or significant technical capabilities—and yet can create rapid and substantive tactical and strategic operational impact. See additional and specific discussion on this subject in Chapters 2, 3, and 4.

36. This is no different for most terrorist networks. See discussion in Mobley, *Terrorism and Counterintelligence*.

37. See discussion of criminal networks in Kenney, "The Challenge of Eradicating Transnational Criminal Networks," 16.

38. Arquilla, Ronfeldt, and Zanini, "Networks, Netwar, and Information-Age Terrorism," 48–52.

39. This was revealed in a study of terrorist organizational efforts to evade or overcome defensive technologies. See Jackson et al., *Breaching the Fortress Wall*, 116–17.

40. Williams, "Transnational Criminal Networks," 81.

41. Kilduff and Tsai, *Networks and Organizations*, 5.

42. See discussion of weak connections and loose coupling in Jackson, "Groups, Networks, or Movements," 248.

43. Williams, "The Nature of Drug-Trafficking Networks," 155.

44. Carley, Lee, and Krackhardt, "Destabilizing Networks," 88.

45. For a discussion of the relative efficacy of this tactic against different types of organizations and leaders, see Serena, "Dynamic Attenuation"; Price, "Targeting Top Terrorists"; Plaw, *Targeting Terrorists*; Jordan, "When Heads Roll"; and Johnston, "Does Decapitation Work?"

46. Williams, "The Nature of Drug-Trafficking Networks," 155.

47. See discussion of criminal networks in Lemieux, *Criminal Networks*, 12, 14, 18.

48. Tsvetovat and Carley, "Bouncing Back," 1.

49. See Lin and Carley, *Organizational Design and Adaptation in Response to Crises*, 24–25, 29.

50. Marc Sageman discusses "leaderless jihad" organizations that form organically and are shaped by strategies employed against them. Sageman, *Leaderless Jihad*, 125–46. These types of organizations are not organized and led in the traditional sense of an "organization" but instead form to accomplish shared goals and in response to their particular circumstances, environments, habitats, and competitors. The theory or concept of leaderless resistance can be traced back to Louis Beam's writings in the early 1980s. See Beam, "Leaderless Resistance."

51. While this at times can benefit the network in its ability to adapt rapidly and with less organizational friction, it can also be problematic insofar as what the organization knows of "what works" might be very limited. Additionally, procedures and doctrine can promote consistency and more competent behaviors depending on whether the behavior is repetitive or if members must know beforehand how other actors will behave in certain situations. Nonetheless, broad freedom of action is a characteristic that networks possess, whether helpful or not.

52. Cataldo, Carley, and Argote, *The Effect of Personnel Selection Schemes on Knowledge Transfer*, 29–30.

53. Granovetter, "The Strength of Weak Ties," 201–2.

54. Hansen, "The Search-Transfer Problem," 105. See also Krackhardt, "The Strength of Strong Ties," 234–37.

55. Organizational breakdowns in this respect sometimes result in the emergence of "splinter" or "spoiler" groups. These groups break off or away from another or parent group and conduct separate activities. Oftentimes this divergence or competition is caused by the splinters or spoilers having different goals, or by disagreements over how best to achieve organizational goals. For discussion of splinters and spoilers, see Boyle, "Explaining Strategic Violence after Wars"; Byman, "The Decision to Begin Talks"; and Nilsson and Kovacs, "Revisiting an Elusive Concept."

56. Gilchrist, *The Well-Connected Community*, 97.

57. Miller and Friesen, *Organizations*, 216–7.

58. Carley, "Stopping Adaptation."

59. When individuals do leave an organization, they tend to leave in groups (with similar interests or capabilities) and in patterned ways. See Raider and Krackhardt, "Intraorganizational Networks," 64.

60. Lempert and Popper, "High-Performance Government in an Uncertain World," 114.

61. March, Sproull, and Tamuz, "Learning from Samples of One or Fewer," 3.

62. When groups choose or are compelled to switch to cellular or dispersed network forms and away from more hierarchical forms, this can lead to varied and uneven learning within the dispersed groups and the organization as a whole. This can benefit the organization if the dispersed groups are capable of regularly sharing information and lessons, but it can also diminish organizational effectiveness if elements of the organization develop capacities and skills that are out of phase with the rest of the organization. Al Qaeda's capacity to share information and learn despite being a dispersed organization is an example of the former, while the problems that plagued the Provisional Irish Republican Army (PIRA), in respect to uneven learning and organizational and operational capacity, is an example of the latter. See discussion of the PIRA in Harnden, *"Bandit Country."*

63. Kochen and Deutsch, *Decentralization*, 248.

64. Cross, Borgatti, and Parker, "Making Invisible Work Visible," 26, 29, 31.

65. For a discussion of the inherent weaknesses and inefficiencies of covert and clandestine organizations, see Bell, "Aspects of the Dragonworld"; and McCormick and Owen, "Security and Coordination in a Clandestine Organization."

66. Axelrod, *The Evolution of Cooperation*, 129–31, 182.

67. Kaufman, *The Limits of Organizational Change*, 9.

68. Milward and Raab, "Dark Networks," 47.

69. Ibid., 50.

70. Carley, "Stopping Adaptation."

71. See Cherns, "Principles of Sociotechnical Design Revisited," 158.

72. See Hamel and Prahalad, *Competing for the Future*, 319.

73. Aldrich, *Organizations and Environments*, 95.

74. For instance, Abu Musab al-Zarqawi's behavior, and the behavior of AQI in general, led to substantial discord within the larger al Qaeda organization and with other affiliated groups in Iraq, particularly the tribes in al Anbar Province. This can also be seen in the metastasizing and waxing and waning of violence in Mexico and the North Caucasus. Criminal groups in the former and insurgent groups in the latter, despite having—at times—roughly similar goals, routinely experience significant and violent internal friction or engage in rampant violence against competitors (and bystanders that might get in the way). For discussion of patterns of violence within and by these groups, see Nichol, *Stability in Russia's Chechnya*; Kuchins, Malarkey, and Markendonov, *The North Caucasus*; and Grayson, *Mexico*.

75. Clayman, "Sequence and Solidarity," 248. See also Carlisle and McMillan, "Innovation in Organizations from a Complex Adaptive Systems Perspective," 5; and Cataldo, Carley, and Argote, *The Effect of Personnel Selection Schemes on Knowledge Transfer*, 49.

76. Miles et al., "Organizational Strategy, Structure, and Process," 561. See also Samoilenko, "Fitness Landscapes of Complex Systems," 38; Abrahamsson, *Why Organizations?*, 232; and Jackson, "Groups, Networks, or Movements," 248.

77. Although it can be beneficial if it produces innovation. Andrade, Plowman, and Duchon, "Getting Past Conflict Resolution," 24.

78. They are also more susceptible to long-term risks. Fukuyama and Shulsky, *The "Virtual Corporation" and Army Organization*, 19.

79. They are also more susceptible to short-term risks. Ibid.

80. Henry Mintzberg analyzes different organizational forms and configurations (simple structure, professional bureaucracy, machine bureaucracy, divisionalized form, and adhocracy) to demonstrate the strengths and weaknesses of each of these forms. He concludes that there are tradeoffs between organizational design and function or performance. For instance, an organization may sacrifice a capacity for adaptation to achieve efficiency, or vice versa. See Mintzberg, "Organization Design."

81. See Bell, "Aspects of the Dragonworld," 17–18. For a discussion of clandestine and covert behavior and how it is used to conceal individual and organizational involvement in insurgent organizations and movements, see Molnar, Tinker, and LeNoir, "Underground Organization within Insurgency," 17–35.

82. This framework is adapted from Harrison's Action Model for Group Task Performance. Harrison, *Diagnosing Organizations*, 61–63. The modified version of Harrison's model used in this book is presented in an analysis of U.S. Army organizational adaptation. See Serena, *A Revolution in Military Adaptation*, 11–18.

83. Serena, *A Revolution in Military Adaptation*, 17.

84. Ibid.

85. Brian Jackson and David Frelinger argue a similar point: terrorist organizations must match their capabilities and resources with the operational requirements of an attack. They must also benefit from a mismatch of security countermeasures and the terrorist organization's plans. See Jackson and Frelinger, *Understanding Why Terrorist Operations Succeed or Fail*, ix.

86. See Hutchins, "Organizing Work by Adaptation," 36–38. Kathleen Carley argues that the structure of an organization dictates its potential for adaptation. See Carley, "Stopping Adaptation."

87. This is especially true in unstable and uncertain environments. See Tushman and Nadler, "Information Processing as an Integrating Concept in Organizational Design," 617.

88. Jay Galbraith argues that an innovating organization requires an operational and innovative branch—a distinction is made between ideas and operational implementation. Galbraith, "Designing the Innovating Organization," 6. This capacity or differentiation is unlikely in smaller organizations, particularly insurgent organizations.

89. Arrow, McGrath, and Berdahl, *Small Groups as Complex Systems*, 234.

90. Carroll, Rudolph, and Hatakenaka, "Learning from Organizational Experience," 581.

91. Arrow, McGrath, and Berdahl, *Small Groups as Complex Systems*, 130.

92. Alberts, Garstka, and Stein, *Network Centric Warfare*, 37.

93. Carley, "Organizational Learning and Personnel Turnover."

94. Galbraith, "Organizational Design," 28.

95. See Ostrom, *Governing the Commons*, 23. See also the discussion of the effects of self-image and perceptions in group life in Bennis, *Changing Organizations*, 175–76.

96. Weinstein, *Inside Rebellion*, 264.

97. Wesensten, Belenky, and Balkin, "Cognitive Readiness in Network-Centric Operations," 95. See also Comfort, "Self-Organization in Complex Systems," 404; Daft and Lengel, "Organizational Information Requirements, Media Richness and Structural Design," 567–68.

98. Boisot, *Information Space*, 232.

99. Elsmore, *Organisational Culture*, 193.

100. See Cross and Parker, *The Hidden Power of Social Networks*, 126–27.

101. This is not to suggest that a newly formed network cannot have shared attitudes, values, and beliefs. Indeed, these characteristics are often the basis of organizational membership. What is instead argued is that if an organization forms to achieve particular goals, then preexisting normative beliefs and values might, at least in the short term, have less of an effect on the conduct of tasks than does a shared interest in goal achievement. Organizational culture is formed over time. While an organization may adopt the attitudes, values, and beliefs of other organizations, it is not necessarily, particularly initially, constrained by these factors.

102. This argument is made convincingly in Paul, Clarke, and Grill, *Victory has a Thousand Fathers*.

103. Herbert Kaufman argues that a lack of resources or the need to concentrate resources is a barrier to organizational change. See Kaufman, *The Limits of Organizational Change*, 45–61.

104. For an in-depth discussion of how assistance can be provided to underground organizations, see Grdovic, *A Leader's Handbook to Unconventional Warfare*.

105. Serena, *A Revolution in Military Adaptation*, 14.

106. Ibid.

107. Because clandestine organizations must expend organizational resources on maintaining their covertness, their ability to form temporary networks either to garner resources or for operational support can substantially improve their effectiveness.

108. Serena, *A Revolution in Military Adaptation*, 15.

109. See discussion in Cronin, "Cyber-Mobilization," 83–84. See also Long, *On "Other War,"* 17–18.

110. It is important to note that networked organizational effectiveness may also be improved by a "powerful doctrine or ideology" that influences group formation and behavior in the absence of hierarchical controls and directions. See Arquilla and Ron-

feldt, *The Advent of Netwar*, 10. This is particularly important for the types of networks discussed in this book.

111.   See discussion of organizational communication networks in Monge and Contractor, *Theories of Communication Networks*, 90–92.

112.   See discussion on the use of feedback for ordering behavior in Johnson, *Emergence*, 120–21.

113.   This is critical for illicit organizations. See Kostakos and Kostakos, "Criminal Group Behavior and Operational Environments," 7.

114.   Learning, change, and adaptation are not synonymous. See Fiol and Lyles, "Organizational Learning," 811.

115.   Tsoukas and Vladimirou, "What Is Organizational Knowledge?," 973, 978–79.

116.   Deevy, *Creating the Resilient Organization*, 214. See also Huber, "Organizational Learning"; and Jackson, "Application," 200.

117.   Marquardt, *Building the Learning Organization*, 38. Mark Easterby-Smith and Luis Araujo make a similar argument in that learning requires the adoption of new behaviors that may be outside the norm for the organization. Easterby-Smith and Araujo, "Organizational Learning," 5. See also Probst and Buchel, *Organizational Learning*, 33; and Argyris and Schon, *Organizational Learning II*, 20–21.

118.   Marquardt, *Building the Learning Organization*, 47.

119.   Garvin, "Building a Learning Organization," 90.

120.   See Garvin, "The Processes of Organization and Management," 37. See also Brown and Duguid, "Organizational Learning and Communities of Practice," 50. See also discussion of "metis" and "techne" in Kenney, *From Pablo to Osama*, 4–5.

121.   De Holan and Phillips, "Organizational Forgetting," 400.

122.   In some instances, organizations are dependent on environmental cues to ensure their survival. See Trice and Beyer, *The Cultures of Work Organizations*, 300.

123.   See Argyris, *On Organizational Learning*, 56, 58, 85. Addressing failures or errors is one of the ways that organizations can effectively decide on adaptive changes. See Sitkin, "Learning through Failure," 547–50, 568, 571. See also discussion of conservatism and defensive routines in Argyris, "Initiating Change That Perseveres," 303–4, *Strategy, Change, and Defensive Routines*, 353–54, and *Overcoming Organizational Defenses*, 43.

124.   Borgatti and Cross, "A Relational View of Information Seeking and Learning in Social Networks," 435.

125.   Fukuyama and Shulsky, "Military Organization in the Information Age," 342.

126.   See discussion of bureaucratic dysfunction in Nirenberg, *The Living Organization*, 21, 23; and Bosworth, "Inter-Firm Collaboration and Industrial Competitiveness," 120. It should be noted that decentralization can also lead to disagreement within organizations and among organizations. See Zaltman, Duncan, and Holbek, *Innovations and Organizations*, 145–46.

127. Nystrom and Starbuck, "To Avoid Organizational Crises, Unlearn."

128. Gilley and Hoekstra, "Creating a Climate for Learning Transfer," 272–73.

129. Daniel Levinthal notes that while learning contributes to inertia, these inertial forces are necessary for adaptation. There must be a balance between the collection and transfer of new knowledge and the retention of old knowledge. See Levinthal, "Organizational Adaptation and Environmental Selection," 140.

130. Boisot, *Knowledge Assets*, 38–39. See also Tsoukas, "Do we Really Understand Tacit Knowledge?," 425–26.

131. Existing skills and knowledge increase the absorptive capacity of individuals. See Szulanski and Cappetta, "Stickiness," 521.

132. Cragin et al., *Sharing the Dragon's Teeth*, 96. There is a distinct trade-off between exchanging knowledge "in-person" and at a distance. When knowledge is exchanged in person there exists the opportunity to share additional lessons, compound learning, and build weak organizational ties. But knowledge exchange at a distance can help protect the organization and individual by enabling the retention of anonymity. It can be conducted discretely on an almost as-needed basis and with little prior coordination. This is one of many trade-offs that must be assumed by covert networked organizations as they conduct their operations.

133. See discussion of organizational design, proximity, and collaboration in Cross et al., "Knowing What We Know," 105.

134. See discussion in Edmondson and Woolley, "Understanding Outcomes of Organizational Learning Interventions," 206.

CHAPTER 2

1. See, for instance, Paley, "Iraqis Joining Insurgency Less for Cause than Cash"; Looney "The Business of Insurgency," and "Economic Consequences of Conflict"; Siperco, "Subversive Markets"; and Beckett, *Insurgency in Iraq*, 4.

2. Steinberg, *The Iraqi Insurgency*, 14.

3. Hammes, *The Sling and the Stone*, 183–84; and Rabasa et al., *Beyond al-Qaeda, Part 2*, 52.

4. Hammes, "Countering Evolved Insurgent Networks," 18.

5. Rabasa et al., *Beyond al-Qaeda, Part 2*, 52.

6. Frank Hoffman argues that limited goals, such as destabilization, do not require popular support. See Hoffman, "Neo-Classical Counterinsurgency?," 81. For the most part, the insurgency spent little time or resources on forming "shadow governments" or developing serious political or economic agendas. See Andrade, "Three Lessons from Vietnam." See also Hashim, "Terrorism and Complex Warfare in Iraq."

7. This type of freedom is typical of insurgencies in their initial phases. See Darling, "A New Conceptual Scheme for Analyzing Counterinsurgency," 57–58.

8. Peter Mansoor and Mark Ulrich argue that insurgents, like counterinsurgent

forces, work in a premeditated fashion. See Mansoor and Ulrich, "Linking Doctrine to Action," 48.

9. This aid many times found its way to insurgent organizations. This phenomenon is much more pronounced in Afghanistan. See discussion in Chapter 4.

10. Steinberg, *The Iraqi Insurgency*, 25.

11. See discussion of profiteering in Parker and Moore, "The War Economy of Iraq."

12. Unemployment reached 67 percent after the invasion. Mockaitis, *The Iraq War*, 39. Walter Lacquer argues that there is a negative correlation between economic development and levels of insurgent or guerrilla activity. Laqueur, *Guerrilla Warfare*, 395. Certainly, in Iraq, as economic activity fell, insurgent and criminal activity rose.

13. Novikov, "Unmasking the Iraqi Insurgency," 6. Comparatively, this amount is high compared with the average Iraqi's salary, especially during this period of conflict. Interestingly, and perhaps because its organizational membership was not motivated nearly as much by financial as other rewards, AQI paid its members far less than what the average Iraqi earned. See Bahney et al., *An Economic Analysis*, 45–56.

14. Rabasa et al., *Beyond al Qaeda, Part 1*, xvii.

15. See Rosenau, "Waging the 'War of Ideas,'" 1141.

16. See Jenkins, "The Jihadists' Operational Code," 4; and Krepinevich, *The War in Iraq*, 2.

17. Steinberg, *The Iraqi Insurgency*, 16.

18. See Hashim, *Insurgency and Counter-Insurgency in Iraq*, 182.

19. See Jones, *The Report of the Independent Commission on the Security Forces of Iraq*, 127. Part of this savagery included indiscriminate murder, extremist tactics, and suicide bombings leading to the deaths of thousands of Iraqi civilians. See also Burns and Rubin, "U.S. Arming Sunnis in Iraq to Battle Old Qaeda Allies," *New York Times Late Edition*, June 11, 2007.

20. Blanche, "Splintering Iraq's Insurgency," 28.

21. Filkins, "U.S. Hands Off Pacified Anbar, Once Heart of Iraq Insurgency."

22. Ibid.

23. The identity that a group or organization creates or forms around can lead to group cohesion or to competition. See discussion of identity creation in Byman, *Understanding Proto-Insurgencies*, 11–12.

24. Hoffman, *The Use of the Internet by Islamic Extremists*, 14.

25. Ibid., 3.

26. Wright and Reese, *On Point II*, 287.

27. U.S. Agency for International Development, *Assistance for Iraq*. See also UNESCO, *Literacy in Iraq Fact Sheet*.

28. Although Arabic is Iraq's official language, Kurdish is widely used in the Kurdish regions of northern Iraq. AQI recognized a common language as an enabler and advantage early in the conflict in Iraq.

29. Hashim, *Insurgency and Counter-Insurgency in Iraq*, 167.

30. Methods for sharing information that took advantage of the networked structure of terrorist organizations were used extensively by al Qaeda and then by other organizations in Iraq. See Karzai and Mitchell, "Networked Power," 2.

31. Wright and Reese, *On Point II*, 288.

32. For instance, the discovery of the "Sinjar Records," recovered near the town of Sinjar, revealed in great detail information about how foreign fighters were brought into the insurgency.

33. Excessive casualties "and other damage" are some of the negative factors cited in a RAND study of public support for insurgency and terrorism. See Davis et al., *Understanding and Influencing Public Support for Insurgency and Terrorism*, xvii.

34. Soldier deployed to Mosul, Kirkuk, Diyala, and Baquba (July 2006–November 2007).

35. Major General Daniel Bolger, interview.

36. Christopher Harmon argues that most terrorist attacks are committed with low-tech devices such as automatic weapons, dynamite, or other explosives. Remotely detonated explosives are simply an advancement made to an old method. See Harmon, "What History Suggests about Terrorism and Its Future," 241. However, it is important to note that some IEDs, particularly those employing Explosively Formed Penetrators, or EFPs, can be much more sophisticated than others.

37. See Hashim, *Insurgency and Counter-Insurgency in Iraq*, 183–84.

38. A RAND study of five terrorist groups indicates that the "more tactics a group has in its repertoire—from bombings to firearms attacks to kidnappings to unconventional weapons—the greater its flexibility and operational freedom." Jackson et al., *Aptitude for Destruction, Volume 1*, 18. The training and specialized knowledge shared by former Iraqi military personnel with insurgent groups allowed these groups to better act in and respond to their operational environment, particularly when their operational needs were rather straightforward and when they had little previous training.

39. See Hashim, *Insurgency and Counter-Insurgency in Iraq*, 163.

40. Hanratty, "Can the United States Defeat Radical Islam?," 22.

41. See Chehab, *Inside the Resistance*, 7.

42. Much of the training that insurgents and insurgent organizations received, particularly contracted individuals and newly formed organizations, occurred on the job.

43. Felter and Fishman, *Iranian Strategy in Iraq*, 84. It must be noted that Iranian support applied to Shi'a groups but not the Sunni elements of the insurgency. Nonetheless, this did not prevent the knowledge and training imparted from diffusing throughout the insurgency as a whole.

44. Ibid.

45. Ibid. JAM and Special Group Criminals (SGC), specifically, received training in

Iran. See Cochrane, "Special Groups Regenerate," 2. Iran was particularly useful for instruction on the use of EFPs and similar devices.

46. See Kagan, "Iran's Proxy War against the United States and the Iraqi Government," 2.

47. Insurgents will typically operate at a lower level of technological sophistication than their opponents by circumstance. See Munck, "Deconstructing Terror," 1. But in Iraq, the insurgency operated at a lower level of sophistication by circumstance *and* by choice.

48. This is characteristic of modern insurgencies, or what has been called the "global insurgency" in general. See discussion in Hoehn et al., *A New Division of Labor*, 14.

49. These types of threats are much more challenging to manage with traditional means. See discussion of threats and intelligence in Steele, *The New Craft of Intelligence*.

50. Robb, *Brave New War*, 30.

51. How hidden or covert individuals and organizations must remain depends on the dangers posed by their operational environment.

52. See Tierney, *Chasing Ghosts*, 261.

53. See Kagan, "From 'New Way Forward' to New Commander," 6.

54. Hamilton, "The Fight for Mosul," 19.

55. This was further complicated by deliberate efforts, by mostly foreign insurgent groups, to attack Iraqi civilians, police, and leaders.

56. This kind of network is similar in nature to the "invitation-only" membership structures described by Anklam. See Anklam, *Net Work*, 71.

57. For discussion, see Watts, *Foreign Fighters*. See also Felter and Fishman, "The Demographics of Recruitment, Finances, and Suicide," 8–9.

58. Felter and Fishman, "The Demographics of Recruitment, Finances, and Suicide," 8. AQI was highly bureaucratized in recruitment and other matters. AQI required insurgents to sign entrance contracts and insisted that exiting fighters sign contracts stating that they would not join other Jihadi groups. See also Shapiro, "Bureaucratic Terrorists." The Combating Terrorism Center (CTC) at West Point has published a range of original language and translated documents indicative of the bureaucratic behavior of portions of the Iraqi insurgency to include oaths of allegiance; personnel databases; accounting receipts; martyrdom pledges; and separation pledges. See, for instance, Combating Terrorism Center, "Partial Muhammad Bin-Sabbar Muhammad al Khuwi Abu Yasir Martyrdom Pledge," "Abu Jasim Funds Distribution Report," "Mustafa Qudrah 'Adawi Request for Abroad Medical Treatment," "Personnel Database for 23 Individuals," "Khalid Sultan 'Abdallah Sultan Separation Pledge from AQI," "ISI Template for Suicide Operation Pledge," "Unsigned Oath of Allegiance to the ISI," "Personnel Database for 46 Individuals," "Flow Chart of the Organization Structure of an ISI Administrative," "ISI Accounting Receipt Template," and "Samara Attack Summary Report."

59. Active support consisted of collecting information on counterinsurgent forces and sharing this information with insurgents. It also included providing material support in the form of personnel, weapons, ammunition, and sustainment. Passive support refers to "turning a blind eye" to the activities of the insurgency.

60. For discussion of illicit network properties, see Williams, "The Nature of Drug-Trafficking Networks," 155.

61. Soldier deployed to Baghdad (early 2003; 2006–7).

62. Brigadier General David Perkins, interview.

63. See Steinberg, *The Iraqi Insurgency*, 18–19.

64. Ibid. Martin van Creveld argues that insurgent organizations rarely have a clear center of gravity. Creveld, *The Culture of War*, 299.

65. This was similar to the PIRA prior to its adopting a more cellular structure. Decentralization allowed the PIRA's Active Service Units (ASUs) to become semiautonomous, regionally oriented organizations that received guidance from a hierarchical national military headquarters.

66. Hashim, *Insurgency and Counter-Insurgency in Iraq*, 155.

67. This is similar to other networks constructed in this fashion. See the discussion of criminal network characteristics in Lemieux, *Criminal Networks*.

68. Merari, "Terrorism as a Strategy of Insurgency," 247.

69. Steinberg, *The Iraqi Insurgency*, 17–18.

70. Ibid.

71. While these groups held joint planning sessions, their coordination efforts had little practical effect.

72. Marsh, "The Ever-Mutating Iraq Insurgency," 5.

73. Ibid.

74. Nance, *The Terrorists of Iraq*, 281.

75. Ibid., 283.

76. Ibid., 284. See also Felter and Fishman, *Al-Qa'ida's Foreign Fighters in Iraq*, 4.

77. Hanratty, "Can the United States Defeat Radical Islam?," 24.

78. Hashim, "Foreign Involvement in the Iraqi Insurgency," 2.

79. Napoleoni, *Insurgent Iraq*, 99–100.

80. McFate, "Iraq," 39.

81. Schwarz, "Iraq's Militias," 55.

82. For instance, a simple but typical IED cell can consist of "six to eight people, including a financier, bomb maker, emplacer, triggerman, spotter, and often a cameraman." Wilson, *Improvised Explosive Devices (IEDs) in Iraq and Afghanistan*, 2.

83. O'Neill, *Insurgency & Terrorism*, 91.

84. Hashim, *Insurgency and Counter-Insurgency in Iraq*, 170.

85. Anonymous, "Smuggling, Syria, and Spending." It is important to note that these criminal networks acted sometimes as witting and other times unwitting support mech-

anisms for the insurgency. Although possibly motivated by religious or political ideology, they were principally interested in financial gain. These organizations provided invaluable support to insurgent organizations, particularly since they tended to operate under the radar of counterinsurgent forces.

86. For an extensive discussion and analysis of organized crime in Iraq, see Williams, *Criminals, Militias, and Insurgents.* For a discussion of the capacity of these groups in "ungoverned" areas, see Serena, "Dynamic Attenuation."

87. Hashim, *Insurgency and Counter-Insurgency in Iraq,* 169–70.

88. O'Neill, *Insurgency & Terrorism,* 61.

89. See Khalil, "Anbar Revenge Brigade Makes Progress in the Fight against al-Qaeda," 1–2.

90. Hashim, *Insurgency and Counter-Insurgency in Iraq,* 329.

91. Abu Musab al Zarqawi's organization had substantial disagreements with al Qaeda's foreign leadership on norms and behavior, with the latter realizing that the brutality of AQI was disrupting the achievement of broader organizational goals.

92. See Fishman, "After Zarqawi," 20.

93. Silverman and Jackson, "Terror in Insurgency Warfare," 63–64.

94. Hashim, *Insurgency and Counter-Insurgency in Iraq,* 166.

95. See International Crisis Group, *In Their Own Words,* 12.

96. Soldier deployed on initial invasion (September 2002–August 2003) and then to Baghdad (January 2005–January 2006).

97. Shultz and Dew, *Insurgents, Terrorists, and Militias,* 251.

98. White, *An Adaptive Insurgency,* 4.

99. Hashim, *Insurgency and Counter-Insurgency in Iraq,* 132.

100. International Crisis Group, *In Their Own Words,* 9–10.

101. Nine Eleven Finding Answers Foundation (NEFA), "Hamas in Iraq," 2.

102. Kagan. "The Anbar Awakening," 11.

103. See International Crisis Group, "Iraq after the Surge I," 12.

104. Smith and MacFarland. "Anbar Awakens," 47, 51.

105. Rosen, "The Many Faces of Abu Musab al Zarqawi."

106. Soldier deployed to Irbil, Kirkuk, and Mosul (March–June 2003) and then to Baghdad and Ramadi (November 2005–November 2006).

107. Eisenstadt, "U.S. Post-Surge Operations in Iraq," 2.

108. Knights and White, "Iraqi Resistance Proves Resilient," 21.

109. Ibid., 22.

110. This calculation is typical for organizations employing terrorism as a tactic. See Rubin, "Asymmetrical Threat Concept and Its Reflections on International Security." See also Merari, "Terrorism as a Strategy of Insurgency," 245.

111. Cordesman, *The Iraq War and Lessons for Counterinsurgency,* 9.

112. Eisenstadt and White, *Assessing Iraq's Sunni Arab Insurgency,* 19.

113.   AQI's bombing of the al-Askari Mosque in 2006 and 2007 is perhaps emblematic of these divisions.

114.   Soldier deployed on initial invasion and then to Samawah.

115.   See White and Schmidmayr, "Resistance in Iraq," 3.

116.   See McFate, "Iraq," 38–39.

117.   And, in some cases, by direct and indirect support from Iranian agents working with the Iraqi insurgency.

118.   In fact, the insurgency became, in many respects, less sophisticated in its methods over time. This is not to discount the complexity of some insurgent organizations' attacks or the sophistication of their equipment, in particular the use of EFPs. But as time passed, simple small arms attacks against softer targets—particularly civilian targets—increased. Thus requirements for advanced technology and equipment for the conduct of attacks decreased over time.

119.   Major General Daniel Bolger, interview.

120.   U.S. weaknesses in this regard were a relic of its intelligence community's structure. See Moll, "U.S. Army Special Forces Training for the Global War on Terror."

121.   See discussion of weapons acquisition in Bonomo et al., *Stealing the Sword*, 104, 111.

122.   See discussion in Kagan, "The Battle for Diyala," 12.

123.   For a detailed discussion of how terrorist organizations exchange information and resources, see Cragin et al., *Sharing the Dragon's Teeth*. There are risks even to this kind of interaction, but they are significantly lower than those posed by in-person meetings, particularly where a large number of people are involved, or where a number of members are traveling long distances and from different locations. Movements and the coordination made for these movements raise the risk of exposure.

124.   Kilcullen, "Counterinsurgency Redux," 7.

125.   The insurgency passively benefited from patronage by foreign individuals, charities, religious organizations, and terrorist groups. Actively, the insurgency engaged in fee collection for safe passage, kidnapping for ransom, extortion of legitimate services and government contracts, oil smuggling, racketeering, and robbery. See Burns and Semple, "Iraq Insurgency Has Funds to Sustain Itself, U.S. Finds." See also Oppel, "Iraq Insurgency Runs on Stolen Oil Profits"; Paley, "Iraqis Joining Insurgency Less for Cause than Cash"; and Guidere and Harling, "Withdraw, Move On and Rampage."

126.   For discussion, see RAND, *U.S. Counterterrorism Strategy Must Address Ideological and Political Factors at the Global and Local Levels*. This is similar to many more recent insurgencies—see in particular the discussion of insurgent funds in Afghanistan in Chapter 4 in this book.

127.   Largely because crime was uncontrollable and perceived as being rewarded. See Baker and Hamilton. *The Iraq Study Group Report*, 21.

128.   This process appears common to a number of modern insurgencies. Vanda

Felbab-Brown describes a process whereby insurgents and other belligerents not only gain financially from illicit activities but also develop freedom of action and political capital from their enterprise. Each of these benefits is fungible in providing the resources to support organizational objectives. Felbab-Brown, *Shooting Up*, 14–20.

129. This does not imply that monetary gain was their sole motivation. Certainly, grievances, nationalism, and religious fervor all combined to fuel the Iraqi insurgency. Nonetheless, economic opportunity was another and sometimes principal motivator for average Iraqis joining the insurgency.

130. Kilcullen, "Counterinsurgency Redux," 7.

131. Hashim, *Insurgency and Counter-Insurgency in Iraq*, 159. Combat Darwinism refers to the quick capture and/or death of many poorly trained or inexperienced fighters at the beginning of the insurgency.

132. Ibid. Figures for payments for conducting attacks vary but notably increased as the conflict wore on: "It used to cost just $50 to hire an Iraqi youth to fire a rocket-propelled grenade at American troops; it now costs $100 to $200 [in 2004]." Oppel, "In Northern Iraq, the Insurgency Has Two Faces, Secular and Jihad, but a Common Goal." The costs for insurgent organizations to conduct external hiring rose over the next four years.

133. Metz, *Rethinking Insurgency*, 44.

134. Looney, "The Mirage of Terrorist Financing."

135. See discussion of organized crime in Steliga, "Why They Hate Us," 73–74.

136. Burns and Semple, "Iraq Insurgency Has Funds to Sustain Itself, U.S. Finds," 1.

137. Cordesman, *Iraqi Security Forces*, 45.

138. In this respect, they operated as a network within a network.

139. In the waning stages of the insurgency, foreign insurgent groups, particularly al Qaeda, lost local favor, protection, and intelligence privileges and their capacity to engage in operations and to manipulate the operational and informational environments diminished significantly.

140. Soldier deployed to Baghdad (March 2004–March 2005).

141. Soldier deployed on initial invasion and then to Samawah.

142. Soldier deployed to Irbil, Kirkuk, and Mosul (March–June 2003) and then to Baghdad and Ramadi (November 2005–November 2006).

143. Ibid.

144. Cordesman, *Iraqi Security Forces*, 16.

145. Soldier deployed to Irbil, Kirkuk, and Mosul (March–June 2003) and then to Baghdad and Ramadi (November 2005–November 2006).

146. See Hashim, *Insurgency and Counter-Insurgency in Iraq*, 164.

147. Abu-Tariq, *Daily Diary of al-Qaeda Sector Leader Called Abu-Tariq*. For a broader discussion of the value of subversion to insurgent movements, see Rosenau, *Subversion and Insurgency*.

148. Insurgent organizations were not created by foreign states nor did they exist solely because of foreign sponsorship. Linkages and ties existed prior to the evolution of the insurgency or were developed by members that had multiple organizational bonds. Multiorganizational membership—based on shared experiences, kinship, ethnicity, and so forth—inherently expanded the scope of the network without the ties always being active or apparent.

149. For discussion, see Nasr, "When the Shiites Rise."

150. Particularly from official or state-based agents. Although, the value of consultation from states or state-sponsored agents or organizations can be quite high given the resources that they generally have available to them.

151. Farrell, "The Challenge of Providing Security in the Post-Combat Phase Urban Environment," 183.

152. Cordesman, *Iraqi Security Forces*, 287.

153. Novikov, "Unmasking the Iraqi Insurgency," 5.

154. Hashim, *Insurgency and Counter-Insurgency in Iraq*, 139.

155. Ibid., 139–40.

156. The Sinjar Records show that the mean reported birth year of fighters was 1982, and the median was 1984. Felter and Fishman, *Al-Qa'ida's Foreign Fighters in Iraq*, 16.

157. Major General Daniel Bolger, interview.

158. Williams, "Matrix Warfare," 3.

159. Ibid.

160. See discussion of the formation of these kinds of networks in Milward and Raab, "Dark Networks," 47.

161. Hammes, "Countering Evolved Insurgent Networks," 20.

162. Hassan, *Iraq*, 2.

163. Ibid., 3.

164. And, indeed, were the critical component of the al Anbar Awakening.

165. Hashim, "Iraq's Chaos."

166. Hashim, *Insurgency and Counter-Insurgency in Iraq*, 187.

167. Kilcullen, "Countering Global Insurgency, Version 2.2," 9.

168. Levitt, "Untangling the Terror Web," 42.

169. See Fishel and Manwaring, *Uncomfortable Wars Revisited*, 262.

170. Colonel H. R. McMaster, interview.

171. See discussion of Zarqawi's relationship with al Qaeda in Byman, *The Five Front War*, 227.

172. Beehner, "Iraq's Insurgency after Zarqawi."

173. Kohlmann, "State of the Sunni Insurgency in Iraq," 9.

174. Rabasa et al., *Counterterrorism Strategy Must Address Ideological and Political Factors at the Global and Local Levels*.

175. Felter and Fishman, *Al-Qa'ida's Foreign Fighters in Iraq*, 6.

176. Al Qaeda forced one of the 1920 Revolution Brigades (Jaffar al-Tayyar Brigade) to officially join its ranks. It also conspicuously formed the Mujahideen Shura Council (MSC) to consolidate like-minded groups. Nine Eleven Finding Answers Foundation, "Statement from the 1920 Revolution Brigades." For an in-depth discussion of the formation of the MSC and al Qaeda's proclamations surrounding it, see Abedin, "Mujahideen Shura Council in Iraq." See also Zambelis, "Iraqi Insurgent Media Campaign Targets American Audiences."

177. Bakier, "Al-Qaeda Adapts Its Methods in Iraq as Part of a Global Strategy," 6.

178. Ibid. See also Robinson, "The Battle for Iraq," 272.

179. Kohlmann, "State of the Sunni Insurgency in Iraq," 4.

180. See Petraeus, *Report to Congress on the Situation in Iraq*, 5.

181. Steliga, "Why They Hate Us," 68.

CHAPTER 3

1. Elements of organizational inputs might in some circumstances be relatively fixed, depending on the organization's structure, its need to maintain covertness, and its relationship to its operational environment. Organizational outputs are more fluid and less subject to rigidity. For instance, if an organization's inputs—say, its materiel and technical resources and levels of training—cannot be expanded or improved without significant effort, the organization might still be able to modify its behaviors and task performance as long as its means of and capacity for learning stay the same.

2. The insurgency expanded its knowledge and skills by referring to printed materials from other conflicts, military manuals, and through experimentation. This expansion included a number of innovations derived from multiple sources. For instance, insurgents began using "sticky" or magnetic IEDs for targeted assassinations in late 2004 and early 2005. These were likely derived from a combination of Limpet mines from World War II and magnetic booby traps used in Northern Ireland. For discussion, see Londono, "Iraq Militants Turning to Use of 'Sticky' Bombs." See also Zoepf and Al-Husaini, "Militants Turn to Small Bombs in Iraq Attacks."

3. Soldier deployed to Mosul (November 2004–October 2005).

4. Soldier deployed to Mosul, Kirkuk, Diyala, and Baquba (July 2006–November 2007).

5. Lieutenant Colonel James Crider, e-mail interview.

6. Colonel (Ret.) Peter Mansoor, telephone interview. AQI was perhaps the most dogmatic of organizations operating in Iraq.

7. Hashim, *Insurgency and Counter-Insurgency in Iraq*, 193.

8. Hashim, "Iraq's Chaos." The continuous process of increasing competency was reflected in the competitive evolution that surrounded the IED contest: wire-triggered IEDs were countered by eliminating the triggermen; and radio controlled IEDs were jammed.

9. Soldier deployed to Irbil, Kirkuk, and Mosul (March–June 2003) and then to Baghdad and Ramadi (November 2005–November 2006).

10. Avoiding hierarchical structures or minimizing the appearance of hierarchical lines of control was critical to organizational security; a fact well understood by insurgent organizations in Iraq and elsewhere. Abu Musab al-Suri's "The Global Islamic Resistance Call" specifically warned against creating hierarchical organizational structures and recommended instead decentralized groups of individuals "linked only by ideology." See The Economist, "The Brains Behind the Bombs."

11. Holohan, *Networks of Democracy*, 52–53.

12. This is true for illicit organizations in general. See Jackson et al., *Aptitude for Destruction, Volume 1*, 26.

13. See Santora and Cave, "Banned Station Beams Voice of Iraq Insurgency."

14. For instance, cellular phones, when activated and even when using encryption software, emit signals that can be detected and located. See Van Meter, "Terrorists/Liberators," 72.

15. For discussion of how insurgencies leverage the Internet, see Metz, "The Internet, New Media, and the Evolution of Insurgency."

16. See Weimann, *www.teror.net*, 9–11. Insurgent organizations benefited from the establishment of various websites including alneda.com, assam.com, almuhrajiroun. com, qassam.net, and jihadunspun.net.

17. For discussion of insurgent fragmentation, see Stoker, "Six Reasons Insurgencies Lose," 5.

18. Bogart, *One Valley at a Time*, 8. See also Steinberg, *The Iraqi Insurgency*, 6, 19–20. Al Qaeda is unique insofar as it can be described as an insurgency in waiting: it maintains structures capable of provoking, supporting, or expanding an existing insurgency in an unstable environment.

19. See International Crisis Group, *In Their Own Words*, 1. See also Zambelis, "Iraqi Insurgent Media Campaign Targets American Audiences," 2–3.

20. In this respect, command and control has two components: the organization and the guiding ideology or basis for the movement, broadly defined. The former allows for the development and transmission of guidance and the latter allows for ad hoc or spontaneous organizational generation or action based upon shared goals. See discussion of al Qaeda and Salafi ideology in Sageman, *Understanding Terror Networks*, 1–24.

21. There were costs and benefits in this regard: insurgent use of the Internet also opened up other avenues of exposure given that Internet transmissions were surely monitored by the Coalition for the purposes of gathering intelligence.

22. Colonel H. R. McMaster, telephone interview.

23. This is not to say that individuals were not affected or influenced by the culture of pre-existing organizations, groups, tribes, and so forth, that they belonged to but that

insurgent organizations had few entrenched martial characteristics or much of a historical legacy beyond that developed after the 2003 invasion.

24. See RAND, *Heads We Win*, 1.

25. White, *An Adaptive Insurgency*, 7.

26. Ibid., 9.

27. Ibid.

28. Soldier deployed to Mosul (November 2004–October 2005).

29. International Crisis Group, *In Their Own Words*, 20.

30. Soldier deployed to Irbil, Kirkuk, and Mosul (March–June 2003) and then to Baghdad and Ramadi (November 2005–November 2006).

31. Kimmage and Ridolfo, *Iraqi Insurgent Media*, 7–31.

32. Hashim, *Insurgency and Counter-Insurgency in Iraq*, 161.

33. Robb, *Epidemic Insurgency (Part 1)*.

34. Ibid.

35. Eisenstadt and White, *Assessing Iraq's Sunni Arab Insurgency*, 22.

36. Kimmage and Ridolfo, *Iraqi Insurgent Media*, 43.

37. International Crisis Group, *In Their Own Words*, 8.

38. Ibid., 7, 15. See also Economist, "A World Wide Web of Terror."

39. International Crisis Group, *In Their Own Words*, 15.

40. Kilcullen, "Countering Global Insurgency, Version 2.2," 12.

41. Soldier deployed to Irbil, Kirkuk, and Mosul (March–June 2003) and then to Baghdad and Ramadi (November 2005–November 2006).

42. International Crisis Group, *Iraq after the Surge I*, 2–3.

CHAPTER 4

1. Barfield argues that the post-1992 period is best described as a civil war or, worse, "chaos." Barfield, *Afghanistan*, 322.

2. See discussion in Rashid, *Taliban*, 21.

3. As a state or otherwise.

4. See discussion in Sullivan, "Tinder, Spark, Oxygen, and Fuel."

5. See Jones, "The State of the Afghan Insurgency," 2; and Golovnina, "FACTBOX."

6. NATO estimates put the number of insurgents at near thirty-five thousand. Jarvenpaa, *Making Peace in Afghanistan*, 2.

7. It is important to clarify, for the purposes of this analysis, how I conceive of "support" at least in light of the commonly used term "popular support." An insurgency can receive a population's support without being popular. It is probably safe to say that the Afghan insurgency is not popular, as the term "popular support" is commonly understood. But it does receive significant support from the population. This is the case for a number of reasons, two of which I will highlight. First, if a population neither actively

nor passively supports a government, it is at least tacitly supporting the insurgency. This is because an insurgency's operational and organizational strengths and weaknesses are tied more closely to a population's support—the benefits of having an unengaged population will most times accrue to the insurgency. Secondly, a combination of a population's dissatisfaction with a government and a fear of or concurrence with the goals of an insurgency will lead the population not to support either side, support both sides variously, passively support the insurgency, or actively support the insurgency. In Afghanistan, the combination of disaffection with the government, concurrence with the insurgency, and fear of the insurgency leads to significant levels of "population support" despite the fact that the insurgency, by many claims, is not popular.

8. As Anthony Cordesman notes, the insurgency can emerge from this conflict victorious without winning in the conventional military sense. Instead, the insurgency can win through "political attrition" or "if the regime loses sufficient popular support, if it fails to govern properly and control space—particularly in heavily populated areas. They can win if major factions desert the regime without joining the insurgents, if the government cannot afford to sustain the conflict, or if it loses a critical source of outside support." Cordesman, *The War in Afghanistan at the End of 2012*, 2. Indeed, while the insurgency is often, and correctly, painted as something less than united, the same case could be made for Afghanistan's government, particularly in advance of the country's upcoming elections. See International Crisis Group, *Afghanistan*.

9. Nonetheless, it appears as if the Afghan insurgency is progressively moving toward achieving its shared goals.

10. Even though it is not even itself a unified organization.

11. See Sanin and Giustozzi, "Networks and Armies," 842.

12. But similar to the evaluation in the preceding two chapters, the Afghan insurgency will be treated singularly. Again, this evaluation will not stress the individual differences between groups, except as warranted or notable, but instead will examine organizational characteristics held commonly across constituent groups and within the insurgency as a whole.

13. See discussion in Stenersen, *The Taliban Insurgency in Afghanistan*, 22–23, 35, 48, 51. For a lengthy discussion of goals and motivations, see Waldman, *Dangerous Liaisons with the Afghan Taliban*, 3–6. See also Thruelsen, "The Taliban in Southern Afghanistan," 262–68; Bajoria, "The Taliban in Afghanistan"; Kilcullen, "Taliban and Counter-Insurgency in Kunar," 240; Lister, "Accounting for the Resilience of the Taliban"; Metz and Millen, *Insurgency in Iraq and Afghanistan*, 14; Ruttig, "The Other Side," 2; Broschk, "Inciting the Believers to Fight," 7; Barfield, *Afghanistan*, 305; and Brahimi, "The Taliban's Evolving Ideology," 17.

14. International Crisis Group, *Taliban Propaganda*, 32.

15. Indeed, although new power structures in Afghanistan have not completely replaced older clan and tribal relationships, they certainly have weakened their power.

These new structures are at least partly premised on ideological or, perhaps more important, financial and economic incentives. See Thruelsen, "The Taliban in Southern Afghanistan," 262–63.

16. See Naylor, "Afghanistan Insurgency Has Grown 10-Fold." See also Acharya et al., "Making Money in the Mayhem," 103.

17. And because of its international scope, presence, capability, and goals, al Qaeda has attracted substantial attention despite presently numbering in the low triple digits in Afghanistan. See Giustozzi, *Negotiating with the Taliban*, 15.

18. See Lister, "Accounting for the Resilience of the Taliban." See also Giustozzi and Reuter, "The Northern Front," 5.

19. Sultan Barakat and Steven Zyck contend that the goals of the bulk of the insurgency do not extend beyond the district or local level. See Barakat and Zyck, "Afghanistan's Insurgency and the Viability of a Political Settlement," 198.

20. The Taliban deliberately portrays itself as a popular movement in order to enhance its legitimacy to and with a broader audience. Stenersen, *The Taliban Insurgency in Afghanistan*, 57. This is not to say that the Taliban abandoned these goals altogether but that it has made a deliberate effort to emphasize other goals so as to broaden its appeal.

21. See Giustozzi and Reuter, "The Northern Front," 5.

22. See discussion of *layeha* in Johnson and DuPee, "Analysing the New Taliban Code of Conduct (*Layeha*)."

23. Giustozzi, *Negotiating with the Taliban*, 10; Lister, "Accounting for the Resilience of the Taliban." Madrassas and refugee camps provide a steady stream of recruits for the Taliban. Johnson and Mason, "Understanding the Taliban and Insurgency in Afghanistan," 87. The Haqqani network also recruits heavily from madrassas in Pakistan, chiefly Waziristan. See Stenersen, *The Taliban Insurgency in Afghanistan*, 19.

24. The pace of recruitment increased in 2003. Stenersen, *The Taliban Insurgency in Afghanistan*, 30.

25. Ibid.

26. See Giustozzi, *Negotiating with the Taliban*, 11. See also Afsar, Samples, and Wood, "The Taliban," 67. Afghanistan and Pakistan have also seen recruitment drives for women through such organizations as the Revolutionary Association of the Women of Afghanistan. See discussion in Wahidi, "Female Taliban?! A Group Called RAWA."

27. Low-level friction is present and infighting is not uncommon within and among the insurgency's constituent organizations and groups. See Peters, *Crime and Insurgency in the Tribal Areas of Afghanistan and Pakistan*, 13; and Rosenberg and Nordland, "Second Afghan Insurgent Group Suspends Peace Talks." See also the discussion of the potential for conflict in Waldman, *Dangerous Liaisons with the Afghan Taliban*, 8; and the differences between the Pakistani and Afghan Taliban in Acharya et al., "Making Money in the Mayhem," 97. Particularly violent conflict broke out between HiG and the Taliban

in early 2010. See Gopal and DuPee, "Tensions Rise between Hizb-i-Islami and the Taliban in Afghanistan." Even within organizations and populations, like the Pashtuns, there are historical patterns of fragmentation. See Barfield, *Afghanistan*, 283. David Kilcullen describes the insurgency as a fragmented series of alliances of convenience. Leadership, composition, and goals vary among these groups: the Taliban, Lashkar-i-Tayba (LeT), HiG, the Haqqani network, and Tehreek-e-Nafaz-e-Shariat-e-Mohammadi (TNSM) are distributed geographically and have overlapping and sometimes opposing aims, depending on environmental circumstances. For discussion, see Kilcullen, "Taliban and Counter-Insurgency in Kunar," 231–32. But while these divisions present an internal challenge to the organization's capacity to adapt, these divisions and the diversity they spawn also make the organization particularly difficult to counter coherently. And much of this internal discord has been suppressed in the pursuit of commonly held goals and mutually shared equities.

28. The unifying presence of foreign or even internal threats to Afghanistan probably cannot be overstated insofar as they serve as a cause for difference reconciliation among and within insurgent groups. Even within the Pashtun tribes, divisions are at times subordinated when responding to an external threat. See Kilcullen, "Taliban and Counter-Insurgency in Kunar," 235. It is notable that there has recently been an increase in internecine conflict and jockeying in Afghanistan in anticipation of the upcoming elections both within the insurgency and among political leaders.

29. Alia Brahimi argues that the uncompromising views of foreign fighters will likely lead to future friction. Brahimi, "The Taliban's Evolving Ideology," 18.

30. Unlike the Taliban, the Haqqani network is "neither interested in nor capable of governing" Afghanistan, and its relationship with al Qaeda makes future cooperation less likely. Dressler, "The Afghan Insurgent Group That Will Not Negotiate."

31. For instance, as Linschoten and Kuehn point out, none of the leadership of al-Qaeda is Afghan. Linschoten and Kuehn, "Separating the Taliban from al-Qaeda," 2.

32. For a detailed discussion of reasons and rationales for potential uprisings against the Taliban, see Young, "The Anatomy of an anti-Taliban Uprising."

33. Linschoten and Kuehn, "Separating the Taliban from al-Qaeda," 6.

34. For discussion, see Stanekzai, *Thwarting Afghanistan's Insurgency*, 7. For an examination of grievances and differences among clans, warlords, and other groups, see Galli, "The Narcotics Counterinsurgency Dilemma," 23–26. For discussion of potential discord in the Kunar Province, see Kilcullen, "Taliban and Counter-Insurgency in Kunar," 237.

35. See Afsar, Samples, and Wood, "The Taliban," 67. For a discussion on swarming, see Arquilla and Ronfeldt, *Swarming & the Future of Conflict*.

36. See International Crisis Group, *Taliban Propaganda*, 1–2.

37. See Nathan, "Reading the Taliban," 36–37.

38. Ibid., 27, 32.

39. International Crisis Group, *Taliban Propaganda*, 29–30.

40. Daraghi, "Afghan Taliban Intelligence Network Embraces the New."

41. Stenersen, *The Taliban Insurgency in Afghanistan*, 19.

42. See International Crisis Group, *Taliban Propaganda*, 1.

43. As Afsar, Samples, and Wood note, "Because almost everyone in Pashtun tribal society is armed, recruits usually possess basic military skills. They receive significant on-the-job training and must prove their military ability in a peer-review system similar to those routinely employed in Pashtun tribes." Afsar, Samples, and Wood, "The Taliban," 68. This is significant since Pashtun tribes provide the bulk of the insurgency's recruits. It should be noted that, more recently, Iran has provided training support to elements of the insurgency. See Giustozzi, *Negotiating with the Taliban*, 15–16.

44. These actions have helped to overcome the inefficiencies inherent to insurgencies and other "rebel" organizations. See discussion of the rebel ecosystem in Bell, "Aspects of the Dragonworld."

45. See Kilcullen, "Taliban and Counter-Insurgency in Kunar," 239; Naylor, "Afghanistan Insurgency Has Grown 10-Fold"; and Stenersen, *The Taliban Insurgency in Afghanistan*, 38. Groups such as Pakistan's Lashkar-e Taiba also provide training to fighters in eastern and southern Afghanistan. Giustozzi, *Negotiating with the Taliban*, 15. This is not to ignore the role played by Iran, the IRGC, or the Quds force. Although significant, the training support received from Iranian sources pales in comparison to that provided by Pakistani sources.

46. See Kilcullen, "Taliban and Counter-Insurgency in Kunar," 240.

47. See Stenersen, *The Taliban Insurgency in Afghanistan*, 21–22. Many of these operatives were introduced to the Taliban through its links to Jaish-e Mohammed, Harakat-al-Mujahideen, and the Haqqani network. Lister, "Accounting for the Resilience of the Taliban."

48. Kilcullen, "Taliban and Counter-Insurgency in Kunar," 239. Larger engagements are generally avoided. U.S. Department of Defense, *Report on Progress toward Security and Stability in Afghanistan*, 18.

49. For instance, in 2001 the Taliban's leadership instructed its members not to fight with members of HiG. Ruttig, "The Haqqani Network," 59.

50. Thruelsen, "The Taliban in Southern Afghanistan," 260.

51. For instance, the Haqqani network has its own independent command and control structure and its own recruitment and funding mechanisms separate from those of the Taliban. Dressler, "The Afghan Insurgent Group That Will Not Negotiate."

52. Thruelsen, "The Taliban in Southern Afghanistan," 263. Thruelsen divides the organization into three tiers that roughly correspond to overall leadership, local leadership, and local supporters. The Taliban also employs four regional military *shuras*

(Quetta, Peshawar, Miramshah, and Gerdi Jangal) and a number of functional committees (finance, culture, education, and so forth). See Roggio, "The Afghan Taliban's Top Leaders."

53. Thruelsen, "The Taliban in Southern Afghanistan," 263.

54. Ibid., 263–64.

55. Ibid., 264.

56. Even among its majority Pashtun supporters. See Shinn and Dobbins, *Afghan Peace Talks*, 8.

57. This was a by-product of expansion in the 2006–7 period. Giustozzi, *Negotiating with the Taliban*, 16.

58. See Barakat and Zyck, "Afghanistan's Insurgency and the Viability of a Political Settlement," 196. See also International Crisis Group, *Taliban Propaganda*, 27. Historical divisions, like those that helped the Taliban come to power in the 1990s, will also likely reemerge and act to undermine future attempts at governance. See discussion of divisions among the mujahideen in Brahimi, "The Taliban's Evolving Ideology," 16–17.

59. See Barfield, *Afghanistan*, 326; and Ruttig, "The Haqqani Network," 59.

60. See the discussion in Barfield, *Afghanistan*, 326; and Ruttig, "The Haqqani Network," 59.

61. For discussion of these networks, see Trives, "The Haqqani Network as an Autonomous Entity," 89–93.

62. According to a recent UN Office on Drugs and Crime report, approximately 50 percent of the population of Afghanistan reported having to pay a bribe to public officials when requesting services in 2012. UNODC, *Corruption in Afghanistan*, 5.

63. See Lister, "Accounting for the Resilience of the Taliban"; Giustozzi, *Negotiating with the Taliban*, 6; and Irwin, *Disjointed Ways, Disunified Means*, 40.

64. Ruttig, "The Other Side," 10.

65. See Stenersen, *The Taliban Insurgency in Afghanistan*, 22–23.

66. Ibid., 18.

67. Ibid. See also Golovnina, "FACTBOX." The Pashtun population is large—roughly in the tens of millions—on both sides of Afghanistan's border with Pakistan. Tanner, *Afghanistan*, 336. See also Johnson, "On the Edge of the Big Muddy," 122; Johnson and Mason, "Understanding the Taliban and Insurgency in Afghanistan," 74; Jones, "The Rise of Afghanistan's Insurgency," 10; and Afsar, Samples, and Wood, "The Taliban," 59.

68. Thruelsen, "The Taliban in Southern Afghanistan," 263. These are still common goals, although the latter is subordinated and deemphasized in favor of the more broadly acceptable theme of removing the Coalition from Afghanistan and replacing the Karzai-led government.

69. See Giustozzi, *Koran, Kalashnikov, and Laptop*, 11.

70. See Barakat and Zyck, "Afghanistan's Insurgency and the Viability of a Political Settlement," 197.

71. For a discussion of the size of the Taliban, see Giustozzi, *Negotiating with the Taliban*, 4–5. See also Naylor, "Afghanistan Insurgency Has Grown 10-Fold"; Stenersen, *The Taliban Insurgency in Afghanistan*, 18–19; Barakat and Zyck, "Afghanistan's Insurgency and the Viability of a Political Settlement," 197; and Lister, "Accounting for the Resilience of the Taliban."

72. Ruttig, "How Tribal Are the Taleban?," 22–23.

73. Dressler argues that the Taliban was never cohesive or unitary. See Dressler and Forsberg, "The Quetta Shura Taliban," 1. Ruttig defines the organization as "heterogeneous and homogenous, unified and segmented at the same time." Ruttig, "The Other Side," 10. Differing characterizations probably reflect different interpretations and conceptions of the ambiguous notion of "decentralization."

74. For instance, see Giustozzi, *Negotiating with the Taliban*, 5; Sanin and Giustozzi, "Networks and Armies," 842; Brandt, "The Taliban's Conduct of Intelligence and Counterintelligence," 21; Stenersen, *The Taliban Insurgency in Afghanistan*, 44; and Afsar, Samples, and Wood, "The Taliban," 67.

75. Barakat and Zyck, "Afghanistan's Insurgency and the Viability of a Political Settlement," 197.

76. Giustozzi, *Negotiating with the Taliban*, 3. See also Afsar, Samples, and Wood, "The Taliban," 65.

77. Giustozzi, *Negotiating with the Taliban*, 3.

78. See Stenersen, *The Taliban Insurgency in Afghanistan*, 9.

79. See Thruelsen, "The Taliban in Southern Afghanistan," 266.

80. Ibid., 267.

81. Giustozzi, *Negotiating with the Taliban*, 8.

82. Sanin and Giustozzi, "Networks and Armies," 842.

83. Ibid. Fronts are not limited in size, but they are not supported by the central organization if they grow too large (more than three hundred men). Ibid.

84. Giustozzi, *Negotiating with the Taliban*, 5. See also Afsar, Samples, and Wood, "The Taliban," 67.

85. Afsar, Samples, and Wood, "The Taliban," 65–66.

86. See Kilcullen, "Taliban and Counter-Insurgency in Kunar," 240.

87. Ibid.

88. Lister, "Accounting for the Resilience of the Taliban."

89. Ibid. It also tries to appeal to various external audiences.

90. Substantial resources are dedicated to finding defectors. Sanin and Giustozzi, "Networks and Armies," 844.

91. Afsar, Samples, and Wood, "The Taliban," 68.

92. Giustozzi explains that looting was commonplace after the 2008 expansion and that many of its members were disciplined or executed as a result. Giustozzi, *Negotiating with the Taliban*, 16–17.

93. Peters, "The Taliban and the Opium Trade," 9.

94. Daraghi, "Afghan Taliban Intelligence Network Embraces the New."

95. See Brahimi, "The Taliban's Evolving Ideology," 16.

96. Afsar, Samples, and Wood, "The Taliban," 68; and Thruelsen, "The Taliban in Southern Afghanistan," 272.

97. Johnson and DuPee, "Analysing the New Taliban Code of Conduct (*Layeha*)." See also Combating Terrorism Center, "The Rules of Jihad Established for Mujahideen by the Leadership of Afghanistan Islamic Emirates."

98. The tactic became more prevalent in the 2005–6 period but had never been used in Afghanistan prior to 2003. Barfield, *Afghanistan*, 319; and Brahimi, "The Taliban's Evolving Ideology," 11–12. See also Jones, "The Rise of Afghanistan's Insurgency," 7.

99. Ruttig argues that this tactic, because of the bloodshed caused to Afghans, is abhorred by older and more pious members of the Taliban. Ruttig, "The Haqqani Network," 74.

100. Brahimi, "The Taliban's Evolving Ideology," 11–12.

101. Stenersen, *The Taliban Insurgency in Afghanistan*, 27.

102. Rhetorically and in a broad sense, the Taliban has led the charge in this respect. After the invasion, it reconstituted itself as an independence movement dedicated to defending the Afghan people. Brahimi, "The Taliban's Evolving Ideology," 4.

103. See Stenersen, *The Taliban Insurgency in Afghanistan*, 27; and Brahimi, "The Taliban's Evolving Ideology," 14.

104. International Crisis Group, *Taliban Propaganda*, 32.

105. See Afsar, Samples, and Wood, "The Taliban," 67.

106. Goodhand and Mansfield, "Drugs and (Dis)order," 6.

107. See Afsar, Samples, and Wood, "The Taliban," 63. See also Jones, "The Rise of Afghanistan's Insurgency," 32.

108. Lister, "Accounting for the Resilience of the Taliban."

109. See Daraghi, "Afghan Taliban Intelligence Network Embraces the New." See also Staniland, "Organizing Insurgency," 171–72.

110. See Giustozzi, *Negotiating with the Taliban*, 9. Although, more covert Internet communications, which are much more difficult to trace, are routinely used to broadcast messages to larger audiences. See International Crisis Group, *Taliban Propaganda*, 9, 33.

111. Kilcullen, "Taliban and Counter-Insurgency in Kunar," 239.

112. Afsar, Samples, and Wood, "The Taliban," 63.

113. Brahimi, "The Taliban's Evolving Ideology," 14.

114. Sanin and Giustozzi, "Networks and Armies," 843.

115. Ibid. According to figures from 2007. This figure would be in addition to the other money that is made conducting "freelance" operations such as kidnapping or supporting the drug trade.

116. Brahimi, "The Taliban's Evolving Ideology," 2.

117. Lister, "Accounting for the Resilience of the Taliban."

118. See Jones, "The State of the Afghan Insurgency," 14; Staniland, "Organizing Insurgency," 171; Afsar, Samples, and Wood, "The Taliban," 64; Stenersen, *The Taliban Insurgency in Afghanistan,* 39–40; Collins and Ali, "Financing the Taliban," 4–9; Goodhand, "Frontiers and Wars," 210; Thruelsen, "The Taliban in Southern Afghanistan," 271; Jarvenpaa, *Making Peace in Afghanistan,* 3; and Basile "Going to the Source." See also the discussion of the Taliban's sources of financing in Johnson, "Financing Afghan Terrorism," 93–114.

119. Peters, "The Taliban and the Opium Trade," 8–9, 11. See also Barfield, *Afghanistan,* 326–27; Bowley, "Potential for a Mining Boom Splits Factions in Afghanistan"; and Barakat and Zyck, "Afghanistan's Insurgency and the Viability of a Political Settlement," 198. Similarly, the Haqqani network is supported by connections on the Arabian Peninsula and within Pakistan. See Ruttig, "The Haqqani Network," 77, 83. Al Qaeda also supplies significant material and monetary funding drawn from its global network of supporters. See Barakat and Zyck, "Afghanistan's Insurgency and the Viability of a Political Settlement," 198.

120. Peters, "The Taliban and the Opium Trade," 9.

121. Ibid., 9, 14.

122. Giustozzi, *Negotiating with the Taliban,* 12.

123. Ruttig, "The Other Side," 20.

124. See Peters, *Haqqani Network Financing,* 62; and Ruttig, "The Other Side," 11. See discussion of Pakistan's relationship to the insurgency and narcotics production in Maloney, "On a Pale Horse?"

125. In 2007, Afghanistan produced more than 90 percent of the world's opium. Merz, "Coercion, Cash-Crops and Culture," 20.

126. See U.S. Senate Committee on Foreign Relations, *Afghanistan's Narco War;* and Goodhand, "From Holy War to Opium War?," 267.

127. Johnson, "On the Edge of the Big Muddy," 100–101; Peters, "The Taliban and the Opium Trade," 17–18; Blanchard, *Afghanistan,* 3, 30; and Anderson, "The Taliban's Opium War."

128. Barakat and Zyck, "Afghanistan's Insurgency and the Viability of a Political Settlement," 195.

129. Goodhand, "Frontiers and Wars," 208.

130. See Chouvy, "Afghanistan's Opium Production in Perspective," 23. Farmers are known to stockpile opium in order to maintain an income flow. See Taylor, "The Nexus of Terrorism and Drug Trafficking in the Golden Crescent," 4. By 2000, much of Afghanistan was dependent on the production of opium. McCoy, "The Costs of Covert Warfare," 233.

131. Peters, "The Taliban and the Opium Trade, 17. Using a system of informal bar-

tering makes it very difficult to track transactions or money flows and contributes to the actors' ability to maintain covertness.

132. Acharya et al., "Making Money in the Mayhem," 98.

133. Goodhand, "Frontiers and Wars," 209.

134. See DeYoung, "U.S. Trucking Funds Reach Taliban, Military-led Investigation Concludes"; and Roston, "How the US Funds the Taliban."

135. Jarvenpaa, *Making Peace in Afghanistan*, 3.

136. Similar to the Iraqi insurgency but probably to a greater degree, the Afghan insurgency is limited in its technical collection means and analytical capabilities. For instance, the Taliban does not have the capacity to eavesdrop on Coalition communications and has little to no comprehension of encryption technologies. See Daraghi, "Afghan Taliban Intelligence Network Embraces the New." Accordingly, it has had to adapt its means of collection to take advantage of social networks and embedded spies. Brandt, "The Taliban's Conduct of Intelligence and Counterintelligence," 21.

137. The Taliban, for one, follows the Twitter feeds of certain U.S. military personnel and monitors Afghan media, foreign news media, and Non-Governmental Organization (NGO) publications. Brandt, "The Taliban's Conduct of Intelligence and Counterintelligence," 22. See also Nathan, "Reading the Taliban," 25.

138. These officers also help facilitate information sharing among the organization's subordinate elements. Brandt, "The Taliban's Conduct of Intelligence and Counterintelligence," 21.

139. Giustozzi, *Negotiating with the Taliban*, 6.

140. Brandt, "The Taliban's Conduct of Intelligence and Counterintelligence," 21.

141. Ibid.

142. See Jones, "The Rise of Afghanistan's Insurgency," 32.

143. It is believed that both the Taliban and Haqqani network have penetrated Afghanistan's security services. See Brandt, "The Taliban's Conduct of Intelligence and Counterintelligence," 21. See also Ruttig, "The Other Side," 20; and discussion in Nasuti, "Taliban's Secret Weapon in Afghanistan—Intelligence 'Moles'?"

144. Chivers, "In Eastern Afghanistan, at War with the Taliban's Shadowy Rule."

145. Daraghi, "Afghan Taliban Intelligence Network Embraces the New."

146. Giustozzi, *Negotiating with the Taliban*, 11.

147. Lister, "Accounting for the Resilience of the Taliban."

148. Chivers, "In Eastern Afghanistan, at War with the Taliban's Shadowy Rule."

149. Lister, "Accounting for the Resilience of the Taliban."

150. Brandt, "The Taliban's Conduct of Intelligence and Counterintelligence," 21. At the village level, informants are paid as much as U.S.$10 for useful information. Peters, "The Taliban and the Opium Trade," 9.

151. See Daraghi, "Afghan Taliban Intelligence Network Embraces the New."

152. Kilcullen, "Taliban and Counter-Insurgency in Kunar," 241.

153. Chivers, "In Eastern Afghanistan, at War with the Taliban's Shadowy Rule." Although more difficult to qualify, it is certainly the case that those who defect from the Afghan security forces to the insurgency take with them the skills they gleaned from training, as well as the knowledge they gained from being on the "inside" of these organizations. In this respect, consultation also comes from adversaries and although indirect is a very effective means of gaining advanced situational awareness. Paradoxically, the drive to train Afghan security forces in support of an exit strategy might also be contributing to the training and tactical effectiveness of the insurgency.

154. Haqqani welcomed Arab volunteers into his group as early as 1987. Ruttig, "The Haqqani Network," 75.

155. See discussion in Naylor, "Afghanistan Insurgency Has Grown 10-Fold."

156. Barfield, *Afghanistan*, 323.

157. See Bajoria, "The Taliban in Afghanistan."

158. See Nader and Laha, *Iran's Balancing Act*, 1, 7.

159. Giustozzi, *Negotiating with the Taliban*, 15–16. Iran's Quds force has also been reportedly providing training within Afghanistan proper. See Naylor, "Afghanistan Insurgency Has Grown 10-Fold."

160. Gohel, "Iran's Ambiguous Role in Afghanistan," 14–15.

161. For discussion of how organizations can exploit refuge and havens, see Kittner, "The Role of Safe Havens in Islamist Terrorism."

162. Barfield, *Afghanistan*, 327. See also Cruickshank, "The Militant Pipeline"; and Lister, "Accounting for the Resilience of the Taliban."

163. Jones, "The Rise of Afghanistan's Insurgency," 30–31. See also Brandt, "The Taliban's Conduct of Intelligence and Counterintelligence," 20–21. Although many insurgent organizations enjoy the support of Pakistan's security structures and parts of the Pakistani population, it is the Haqqani network that has the closest relationship with Pakistan. Giustozzi, *Negotiating with the Taliban*, 15. See also Dressler, "The Haqqani Network," 5.

164. Jones, "The Rise of Afghanistan's Insurgency," 31. Estimates suggest that up to 40 percent of the insurgency's recruits come from Pakistan. Stenersen, *The Taliban Insurgency in Afghanistan*, 30. See also Lafraie, "Resurgence of the Taliban Insurgency in Afghanistan," 106–7.

165. Brahimi, "The Taliban's Evolving Ideology," 3.

166. Tanner, *Afghanistan*, 335. See also Jones, "The Rise of Afghanistan's Insurgency," 31–32; and Nathan, "Reading the Taliban," 23.

167. Ruttig, "The Haqqani Network," 75. See also Barakat and Zyck, "Afghanistan's Insurgency and the Viability of a Political Settlement," 197.

168. Barakat and Zyck, "Afghanistan's Insurgency and the Viability of a Political Settlement," 198.

169. Ruttig, "The Battle for Afghanistan," 2.

170. This is particularly true for the Sunni components of the Iraqi insurgency, although the support Iran provided to Shi'a elements of the Iraqi insurgency should by no means be discounted. Nonetheless, in terms of augmenting each respective insurgency's capacity to adapt, external state support has been more consequential in Afghanistan than it was in Iraq.

171. This is less of a concern now, since the insurgency's goals roughly parallel the interests of these states.

172. Peters argues that smugglers form the link between the insurgency and corrupt Afghan officials. Peters, "The Taliban and the Opium Trade," 17.

173. See Giustozzi, *Negotiating with the Taliban*, 6; and Lister, "Accounting for the Resilience of the Taliban."

174. Barakat and Zyck, "Afghanistan's Insurgency and the Viability of a Political Settlement," 196–97.

175. Some of these fighters could be paid as little as one meal per day. See Goodhand, "Frontiers and Wars," 203.

176. See discussion in Ruttig, "The Other Side," 16. See also Stenersen, *The Taliban Insurgency in Afghanistan*, 37; and Stanekzai, *Thwarting Afghanistan's Insurgency*, 2.

177. Stanekzai, *Thwarting Afghanistan's Insurgency*, 8–9.

178. Stenersen, *The Taliban Insurgency in Afghanistan*, 38.

179. Ibid. The presence of these militias weakens the perceived and actual legitimacy of government forces. Many of these militias are funded by drug money and thus are part of a cycle of related criminal activities that, although not deliberately, indirectly abet the achievement of the insurgency's goals. See Goodhand, "Frontiers and Wars," 203.

180. See Peters, *Crime and Insurgency in the Tribal Areas of Afghanistan and Pakistan*, 90.

181. Goodhand, "Frontiers and Wars," 207, 211.

182. One organization, led by Haji Juma Khan, specialized in smuggling arms and heroin in and out of Afghanistan in support of the insurgency. Stenersen, *The Taliban Insurgency in Afghanistan*, 38.

183. See Peters, *How Opium Profits the Taliban*, 33, and *Crime and Insurgency in the Tribal Areas of Afghanistan and Pakistan*, 90.

184. Johnson, "On the Edge of the Big Muddy," 101.

185. Giustozzi notes that police units in southern and western Afghanistan have made deals with the insurgency or have in some cases even defected wholesale to the Taliban. Giustozzi, *Negotiating with the Taliban*, 6.

186. For discussion, see Goodhand, "Corrupting or Consolidating the Peace?," 406, 410. See also Peters, *Crime and Insurgency in the Tribal Areas of Afghanistan and Pakistan*, 90.

187. Barakat and Zyck, "Afghanistan's Insurgency and the Viability of a Political Settlement," 197; and Lahoud et al., *Letters from Abbottabad*, 35.

188. Ruttig, "The Haqqani Network," 78.

189. Mohammad, "Taliban Expand Insurgency to Northern Afghanistan." See discussion of relationships in International Crisis Group, *Taliban Propaganda*, 29.

190. Ruttig, "The Other Side," 16. See also Bajoria, "The Taliban in Afghanistan." See also discussion in Rubin, "Saving Afghanistan," 60.

191. Dressler and Forsberg, "The Quetta Shura Taliban," 7.

192. Ibid., 7–8.

193. Ibid., 8.

194. Because the population has a much more difficult time adapting its income streams than do insurgent organizations, the effects of various eradication policies disproportionately fall upon producers or farmers. Consequently, farmers, whose *only* source of income might be that generated by opium or other drug production, will either actively or passively support those who can help secure this income and/or will oppose those who take actions to disrupt it. This does not necessarily reflect a preference for one side or the other in the conflict but is instead a practical survival response. It is also important to note that the Taliban has provided guidance on the subject of drug production and has indicated that since the income generated by drug production contributes to defeating infidels, it is not prohibited by *sharia*. This equivalency conveniently overlooks the growing drug abuse problems inside Afghanistan and among other majority Muslim populations nearby.

195. This is not necessarily an expensive arrangement either, given that the official income tied to these positions is low. Like many drug crop farmers, a number of corrupt officials are pragmatic—they collaborate for money and/or to establish relationships that will prove beneficial to their survival when foreign troops do finally leave.

196. Although some organizations have maintained their relationships for quite some time and to mutual benefit, including the Haqqani network and the Taliban and elements of al Qaeda. See Dressler, "The Afghan Insurgent Group That Will Not Negotiate"; Ruttig, "The Haqqani Network," 88; and Stanekzai, *Thwarting Afghanistan's Insurgency*, 9. See also Wormer, "The Networks of Kunduz," 45.

197. Stenersen, *The Taliban Insurgency in Afghanistan*, 20.

198. As quoted in Nathan, "Reading the Taliban," 32.

199. Major General Mike Flynn, as quoted in Naylor, "Afghanistan Insurgency Has Grown 10-Fold."

200. See discussion in Stenersen, *The Taliban Insurgency in Afghanistan*, 20; and Ruttig, "The Other Side," 12.

201. See Peters, *Crime and Insurgency in the Tribal Areas of Afghanistan and Pakistan*, 90–91.

202. See discussion in Barfield, *Afghanistan*, 319.

203. The Taliban's posturing toward politics is evident in its pre-election negotiations and its opening of an official office in Qatar. See Rosenberg, "Taliban Opening Qatar Office, and Maybe Door to Talks"; and Nissenbaum, Totakhil, and Barnes, "Taliban Agree to Open Office."

204. See Afsar, Samples, and Wood, "The Taliban," 66–67.

205. Nonetheless, extremists and terrorists from Arab countries, filtering out of Iraq, or affiliated with al Qaeda, have at times weakened the insurgency's pursuit of widespread legitimacy and support among Afghans. See Brahimi, "The Taliban's Evolving Ideology," 18.

206. See discussion of al Qaeda in Mueller, "How Dangerous Are the Taliban?"

207. Although, the utility of al Qaeda's financial support has withered over time.

208. Stenersen, *The Taliban Insurgency in Afghanistan*, 22. See also Nathan, "Reading the Taliban," 33.

209. See Afsar, Samples, and Wood, "The Taliban," 65.

210. Al-Sahab is al Qaeda's flagship media production enterprise.

211. See International Crisis Group, *Taliban Propaganda,* 23; Nathan, "Reading the Taliban," 35; and Lister, "Accounting for the Resistance of the Taliban."

212. See Lister, "Accounting for the Resilience of the Taliban."

213. The insurgency can almost always seize the initiative when reporting on civilian casualties because it is less constrained by accuracy or even whether or not the story it provides is true or false. In contrast, the Coalition *is* bound by these constraints and therefore cannot respond nearly as quickly.

214. See discussion of the Haqqani network's modus operandi in Ruttig, "The Haqqani Network," 74. Attacks on civilians still occur, but they are not typically or seemingly as random or catastrophic as those in Iraq. And, in any event, the Taliban does as much as possible to distance itself from these attacks. HiG has gone so far as to avoid attacking Afghan forces. Druzin, "Insurgent Group Wants All Foreign Troops Gone before Election."

215. This shift occurred around 2006. Barfield, *Afghanistan*, 329. See also discussion of violence in Bajoria, "The Taliban in Afghanistan"; and Rubin, "Taliban Causes Most Civilian Deaths in Afghanistan, U.N. Says."

216. See discussion in Trives, "The Haqqani Network as an Autonomous Entity," 93; and Barakat and Zyck, "Afghanistan's Insurgency and the Viability of a Political Settlement," 195–96.

217. See discussion of the Taliban in Chivers, "In Eastern Afghanistan, at War with the Taliban's Shadowy Rule."

218. See Kilcullen's discussion of flying and mobile columns in Kilcullen, "Taliban and Counter-Insurgency in Kunar," 239–40.

219. This challenge is compounded by high illiteracy rates—a lot of training must be conducted via hands-on means.

220. See Johnson, "On the Edge of the Big Muddy," 99.

221. These attacks are conducted as much for garnering the attention of the international press and for the purposes of recruitment and financial support as they are for accomplishing tactical goals. Individual commanders have an incentive to demonstrate success—it helps them attract support from external sponsors and from within the organization. See, for instance, the high-profile attack on Camp Bastion in September of 2012. See British Broadcasting Corporation, "Prince Harry at Camp Bastion during Taliban Attack."

222. Starting in 2003, the Taliban began to appoint and install governors, judges, and police across Afghanistan. See Giustozzi, *Negotiating with the Taliban*, 19–20.

223. Nor does it result in an inability to plan for and conduct operations. For instance, the planning conducted for the attack on Camp Bastion was very detailed and even reflected elements of the Military Decision Making Process (MDMP). See Live Leak, "Taliban Training Camp 'Prepares Camp Bastion Attack.'"

224. Brahimi, "The Taliban's Evolving Ideology," 14.

225. For instance, see Combating Terrorism Center, "Islamic Emirate of Afghanistan Urgent Warning."

226. See Stenersen, *The Taliban Insurgency in Afghanistan*, 44. See also Daraghi's discussion of the banning of cell phone use between 7:00 a.m. and 7:00 p.m. because of the raiding practices of Coalition forces. Daraghi, "Afghan Taliban Intelligence Network Embraces the New."

227. Afsar, Samples, and Wood, "The Taliban," 67. See also the discussion of communications security in Brandt, "The Taliban's Conduct of Intelligence and Counterintelligence," 22.

228. Afsar, Samples, and Wood, "The Taliban," 67.

229. Nathan, "Reading the Taliban," 24.

230. See discussion in Bajoria, "The Taliban in Afghanistan."

231. Thruelsen, "The Taliban in Southern Afghanistan," 272.

232. And because the Coalition is bound by various rules, laws, and regulations in respect to its media responses (not to mention a serious interest in ensuring the veracity of its stories or claims—if not a statutory requirement to do so), its public affairs and broadcast efforts almost always lag behind those of insurgent organizations.

233. See discussion in Broschk, "Inciting the Believers to Fight," 7.

234. See Nathan, "Reading the Taliban," 34.

235. Sanin and Giustozzi, "Networks and Armies," 847.

236. See Afsar, Samples, and Wood, "The Taliban," 64.

237. Barfield, *Afghanistan*, 325–26. See also discussion in Wormer, "The Networks of Kunduz," 45; and Goodhand, "Frontiers and Wars," 211.

238. See discussion of the Taliban's capacity for analysis in Brandt, "The Taliban's Conduct of Intelligence and Counterintelligence," 21.

239. Indeed, the value of different techniques or methods depends highly on the kind of knowledge being shared. See Kenney, "Organizational Learning and Islamic Militancy."

240. See discussion in Jones, "The Rise of Afghanistan's Insurgency," 35–36. See also Johnson, "On the Edge of the Big Muddy," 98.

241. The value of the provision of sanctuary to the survival of the Afghan insurgency cannot be overstated, particularly in the early years of its recrudescence.

242. As previously mentioned, and for instance, HiG and Taliban infighting is not uncommon, particularly as the latter impinges on the former's territory and power. HiG has also suffered defections insofar as factions of its organization have broken off to form political entities. Young, "Divide and Conquer Negotiations." Additionally, there have been significant maneuvering and posturing among numerous ethnic and political groups prior to the election. See Mashal, "The Question of Succession." These splintering conflicts are likely to become even more prevalent as the Taliban and other organizations seek to run candidates.

CHAPTER 5

1. General Peter Chiarelli, telephone interview.

2. See discussion of AQI and Sunni groups in al Anbar Province in Jones and Libicki, *How Terrorist Groups End*, 83–102.

3. See Echevarria, *Wars of Ideas and the War of Ideas*, 33. Hashim argues, "The insurgency's foreign element has had a greater impact than mere numbers would lead us to believe." This is true but for different reasons in the beginning and in the later stages of the insurgency. See Hashim, "Foreign Involvement in the Iraqi Insurgency," 1.

4. Hashim, *Insurgency and Counter-Insurgency in Iraq*, 154.

5. See Metz, *Learning from Iraq*, 19.

6. Colonel (Ret.) Peter Mansoor, telephone interview.

7. For a detailed discussion of the strengths of the Iraqi insurgency, see White, *An Adaptive Insurgency*, 12–13.

8. This is something which, very likely, might appear again in Afghanistan in the not too distant future.

9. Although not studied here, this is perhaps why various illicit networked organizations have struggled in other conflicts or in the conduct of their operations. Insurgencies and terrorist organizations have demonstrated that they can survive in various environments for long periods, even if they are ultimately unsuccessful in achieving their goals. This suggests that an organizational balance between merely existing and organizational success must be struck: a balance shaped by the organization's operational environment and its operational capacity. This further suggests that there is a tipping-

point at the nexus of organizational design and goals, competitors, and the operational milieux where an organization's goals and/or means of organization—toward greater centralization or political as opposed to violent methods of behavior, for instance— must change. This further implies that those charged with monitoring and combating these organizations must be capable of anticipating this change, forcing greater decentralization within the illicit organization when appropriate, or altering the operational environment to the illicit organization's adaptive disfavor.

10. David Kilcullen discusses the differences between modern as opposed to classical insurgencies and the implications of these differences in Kilcullen, "Counterinsurgency Redux," 2006.

11. See discussion of doctrine in Serena, "Combating a Combat Legacy," 55–57. Circumstantial social, political, and geographical nuances and considerations are particularly important when choosing approaches to monitor or combat various illicit organizations. See discussion in Simons and Tucker, "The Misleading Problem of Failed States."

12. Excess capacity and redundancy facilitate organizational adaptation. See Carley, "Stopping Adaptation."

13. Ibid.

References

INTERVIEWS

(Rank and affiliations shown are as of the date of the interview and may have subsequently changed.)

Bolger, Major General Daniel. Commander 1st Cavalry Division, Fort Hood, TX, September 13, 2008 (e-mail).

Chiarelli, General Peter W. Vice Chief of Staff of the U.S. Army, Washington, DC, October 27, 2008 (telephone).

Crider, Lieutenant Colonel James. Fellow, Center for a New American Security, Washington, DC, September 22, 2008 (e-mail).

Interview with soldier deployed on initial invasion (September 2002–August 2003) and then to Baghdad (January 2005–January 2006), October 8, 2008.

Interview with soldier deployed to Mosul (November 2004–October 2005), September 29, 2008.

Interview with soldier deployed to Mosul, Kirkuk, Diyala, and Baquba (July 2006–November 2007), September 23, 2008.

Interview with soldier deployed to Baghdad (March 2004–March 2005), September 22, 2008.

Interview with soldier deployed on initial invasion and then to Samawah, September 18, 2008.

Interview with soldier deployed to Baghdad (Early 2003; 2006–7), September 18, 2008.

Interview with soldier deployed to Irbil, Kirkuk, and Mosul (March–June 2003) and then to Baghdad and Ramadi (November 2005–November 2006), June 21, 2008.

Mansoor, Colonel Peter (ret.). U.S. Army, September 12, 2008 (telephone).

McMaster, Colonel H. R. Director, Army Capabilities Integration Center, Concepts Development and Experimentation Directorate, U.S. Army Training and Doctrine Command, Fort Monroe, VA, September 8, 2008 (telephone).

Perkins, Brigadier General David. Spokesman for Multi-National Force-Iraq, Baghdad, Iraq, September 21, 2008 (telephone).

WORKS CITED

Abedin, Mahan. "Mujahideen Shura Council in Iraq: Fact or Fiction?" *Terrorism Focus* 3, no. 12 (March 28, 2006). Available at www.jamestown.org/single/?no_cache=1&tx_ttnews%5Btt_news%5D=717.

Abrahamsson, Bengt. *Why Organizations? How and Why People Organize.* Newbury Park, CA: Sage Publications, 1993.

Abu-Tariq. *Daily Diary of al-Qaeda Sector Leader Called Abu-Tariq.* Available at www.foxnews.com/projects/pdf/021008_AbuTariqDiary.pdf.

Acharya, Arabinda, Syed Adnan, Ali Shah Bukhari, and Sadia Sulaiman. "Making Money in the Mayhem: Funding Taliban Insurrection in the Tribal Areas of Pakistan." *Studies in Conflict and Terrorism* 32, no. 2 (2009): 95–108.

Afsar, Shahid, Chris Samples, and Thomas Wood. "The Taliban: An Organizational Analysis." *Military Review* 87, no. 3 (May–June 2008): 58–73.

Alberts, David S., John J. Garstka, and Frederick P. Stein. *Network Centric Warfare: Developing and Leveraging Information Superiority.* Washington, DC: U.S. Department of Defense Command and Control Research Program, 1999.

Aldrich, Howard E. *Organizations and Environments.* Englewood Cliffs, NJ: Prentice Hall, 1979.

Anderson, Jon Lee. "The Taliban's Opium War: The Difficulties and Dangers of the Eradication Program." *New Yorker*, July 9, 2007, 60–71.

Andrade, Dale. "Three Lessons from Vietnam." *Washington Post*, December 12, 2005, A23.

Andrade, Leticia, Donde Ashmos Plowman, and Dennis Duchon. "Getting Past Conflict Resolution: A Complexity View of Conflict." *Emergence: Complexity and Organization* 10, no. 1 (January 2008): 23–38.

Anklam, Patti. *Net Work: A Practical Guide to Creating and Sustaining Networks at Work and in the World.* Burlington, MA: Elsevier, 2007.

Anonymous. "Smuggling, Syria, and Spending." In *Bombers, Bank Accounts & Bleedout: Al Qa'ida's Road in and out of Iraq*, edited by Brian Fishman, 81–97. West Point, NY: Combating Terrorism Center, 2008.

Argyris, Chris. "Initiating Change That Perseveres." *American Behavioral Scientist* 40, no. 3 (January 1997): 299–309.

———. *On Organizational Learning.* Malden, MA: Blackwell Business, 1993.

———. *Overcoming Organizational Defenses: Facilitating Organizational Learning.* Wellesley, MA: Allyn and Bacon, 1990.

———. *Strategy, Change, and Defensive Routines.* Boston: Pitman, 1985.

Argyris, Chris, and Donald A. Schon. *Organizational Learning II: Theory, Method, and Practice.* Reading, MA: Addison-Wesley Publishing Company, 1996.

Arquilla, John, and David Ronfeldt. *Swarming & the Future of Conflict*. Santa Monica, CA: RAND, 2000.

———. *The Advent of Netwar*. Santa Monica, CA: RAND, 1996.

Arquilla, John, David Ronfeldt, and Michele Zanini. "Networks, Netwar, and Information-Age Terrorism." In *Countering the New Terrorism*, edited by Ian O. Lesser, Bruce Hoffman, John Arquilla, David Ronfeldt, and Michele Zanini, 39–84. Santa Monica, CA: RAND, 1999.

Arrow, Holly, Joseph E. McGrath, and Jennifer L. Berdahl. *Small Groups as Complex Systems: Formation, Coordination, Development, and Adaptation*. Thousand Oaks, CA: Sage Publications, 2000.

Axelrod, Robert. *The Evolution of Cooperation*. New York: Basic Books, 1984.

Bahney, Benjamin, Howard J. Shatz, Carroll Ganier, Renny McPherson, Barbara Sude, Sara Beth Elson, and Ghassan Schbley. *An Economic Analysis of the Financial Records of al Qa-ida in Iraq*. Santa Monica, CA: RAND, 2010.

Bajoria, Jayshree. "The Taliban in Afghanistan." Available at www.cfr.org/afghanistan/taliban afghanistan/p10551.

Baker, James A., and Lee H. Hamilton. *The Iraq Study Group Report*. Washington, DC: Iraq Study Group, 2006.

Bakier, Abdul Hameed. "Al-Qaeda Adapts Its Methods in Iraq as Part of a Global Strategy." *Terrorism Monitor* 5, no. 24 (December 21, 2007): 6–8.

Barakat, Sultan, and Steven A. Zyck. "Afghanistan's Insurgency and the Viability of a Political Settlement." *Studies in Conflict and Terrorism* 33, no. 3 (2010): 193–210.

Barfield, Thomas. *Afghanistan: A Cultural and Political History*. Princeton: Princeton University Press, 2010.

Basile, Mark. "Going to the Source: Why Al Qaeda's Financial Network Is Likely to Withstand the Current War on Terrorist Financing." *Studies in Conflict and Terrorism* 27 (May–June 2004): 169–85.

Beam, Louis. "Leaderless Resistance." *Seditionist* 12 (February 1992). Available at www.louisbeam.com/leaderless.htm.

Beckett, Ian F. W. *Insurgency in Iraq: A Historical Perspective*. Carlisle, PA: U.S. Army War College, 2005.

Beehner, Lionel. "Iraq's Insurgency after Zarqawi." *Council on Foreign Relations*, June 9, 2006. Available at www.cfr.org/iraq/iraqs-insurgency-after-zarqawi/p10880.

Bell, J. Bowyer. "Aspects of the Dragonworld: Covert Communication and the Rebel Ecosystem." *Journal of Intelligence and Counterintelligence* 3, no. 1 (1989): 15–43.

Bennis, Warren G. *Changing Organizations*. New York: McGraw-Hill, 1966.

Blanchard, Christopher M. *Afghanistan: Narcotics and U.S. Policy*. New York: Nova Science Publishers, 2009.

Blanche, Ed. "Splintering Iraq's Insurgency." *Middle East* 379 (June 2007): 26–28.

Blank, Stephen J. *Rethinking Asymmetric Threats*. Carlisle, PA: Strategic Studies Institute, 2003.

Bogart, Adrian T., III. *One Valley at a Time*. Hurlburt Field, FL: Joint Special Operations University, 2006.

Boisot, Max H. *Knowledge Assets: Securing Competitive Advantage in the Information Economy*. New York: Oxford University Press, 1998.

————. *Information Space*. New York: Routledge, 1995.

Bonomo, James, Giacomo Bergamo, David R. Frelinger, John Gordon IV, and Brian A. Jackson. *Stealing the Sword: Limiting Terrorist Use of Advanced Conventional Weapons*. Santa Monica, CA: RAND, 2007.

Borgatti, Stephen P., and Rob Cross. "A Relational View of Information Seeking and Learning in Social Networks." *Management Science* 49, no. 4 (April 2003): 432–45.

Borgatti, Stephen P., and Daniel S. Halgin. "On Network Theory." *Organization Science* 22, no. 5 (September–October 2011): 1168–81.

Bosworth, Brian. "Inter-Firm Collaboration and Industrial Competitiveness." In *The Transition to Flexibility*, edited by Daniel C. Knudsen, 111–24. Norwell, MA: Kluwer Academic, 1996.

Bowley, Graham. "Potential for a Mining Boom Splits Factions in Afghanistan." *New York Times*, September 8, 2012. Available at www.nytimes.com/2012/09/09/world/asia/afghans-wary-as-efforts-pick-up-to-tap-mineral-riches.html?pagewanted=all&_r=1&.

Boyle, Michael J. "Explaining Strategic Violence after Wars." *Studies in Conflict and Terrorism* 32, no. 3 (2009): 209–36.

Brandt, Ben. "The Taliban's Conduct of Intelligence and Counterintelligence." *CTC Sentinel* 4, no. 6 (June 2011): 19–23.

Brahimi, Alia. "The Taliban's Evolving Ideology." *LSE Global Governance Working Paper 02/2010*, 2010. Available at eprints.lse/ac.uk/29970/1/WP022010_Brahimi.pdf.

Brimley, Shawn. "Tentacles of Jihad: Targeting Transnational Support Networks." *Parameters* 36 (Summer 2006): 30–46.

British Broadcasting Corporation. "Prince Harry at Camp Bastion during Taliban Attack." *BBC News*, September 15, 2012. Available at www.bbc.co.uk/news/uk-19608496.

Broschk, Florian. "Inciting the Believers to Fight: A Closer Look at the Rhetoric of the Afghan Jihad." *Afghanistan Analysts Network*. Available at aan-afghanistan.com/index.asp?id=1495.

Brown, John Seely, and Paul Duguid. "Organizational Learning and Communities of Practice: Toward a Unified View of Working, Learning, and Innovation." *Organization Science* 2, no. 1 (1991): 40–57.

Burns, John F., and Alissa J. Rubin. "U.S. Arming Sunnis in Iraq to Battle Old Qaeda Allies." *New York Times Late Edition*, June 11, 2007, A1.

Burns, John F., and Kirk Semple. "Iraq Insurgency Has Funds to Sustain Itself, U.S. Finds." *New York Times Late Edition*, November 26, 2006, 1.

Byman, Daniel. *The Five Front War: The Better Way to Fight Global Jihad*. Hoboken, NJ: John Wiley and Sons, 2008.

———. "The Decision to Begin Talks with Terrorists: Lessons for Policymakers." *Studies in Conflict and Terrorism* 29, no. 5 (2006): 403–14.

———. *Understanding Proto-Insurgencies*. Santa Monica, CA: RAND, 2007.

Byman, Daniel, Peter Chalk, Bruce Hoffman, William Rosenau, and David Brannan. *Trends in Outside Support for Insurgent Movements*. Santa Monica, CA: RAND, 2001.

Carley, Kathleen. "Organizational Learning and Personnel Turnover." *Organization Science* 3, no. 1 (February 1992): 20–46.

———. "Stopping Adaptation." Paper presented at the Center for Computational Analysis of Social and Organizational Systems (CASOS). Pittsburgh, PA: CASOS, June 2002. Available at www.casos.cs.cmu.edu/events/conferences/2002/pdf/day1.pdf.

Carley, Kathleen M., Ju-Sung Lee, and David Krackhardt. "Destabilizing Networks." *Connections* 24, no. 3 (2001): 79–92.

Carlisle, Ysanne, and Elizabeth McMillan. "Innovation in Organizations from a Complex Adaptive Systems Perspective." *Emergence: Complexity and Organization* 8, no. 1 (January 2006): 2–9.

Carroll, John, Jenny W. Rudolph, and Sachi Hatakenaka. "Learning from Organizational Experience." In *The Blackwell Handbook of Organizational Learning and Knowledge Management*, edited by Mark Easterby Smith and Marjorie A. Lyles, 575–600. Malden, MA: Blackwell Publishing, 2003.

Cataldo, Marcelo, Kathleen M. Carley, and Linda Argote. "The Effect of Personnel Selection Schemes on Knowledge Transfer." Pittsburgh, PA: Computational Analysis of Social and Organizational Systems (CASOS), Undated. Available at www.casos.cs.cmu.edu/publications/papers/marcelo_paper.pdf.

Chehab, Zaki. *Inside the Resistance: The Iraqi Insurgency and the Future of the Middle East*. New York: Nation Books, 2005.

Cherns, Albert. "Principles of Sociotechnical Design Revisited." *Human Relations* 40, no. 3 (March 1987): 153–62.

Chivers, C. J. "In Eastern Afghanistan, at War with the Taliban's Shadowy Rule." *New York Times*, February 6, 2011. Available at www.nytimes.com/2011/02/07/world/asia/07taliban.html?_r=1&pagewanted=all.

Chouvy, Pierre-Arnaud. "Afghanistan's Opium Production in Perspective." *China and Eurasia Forum Quarterly* 4, no. 1 (2006): 21–24.

Clarke, Ryan. *Crime-Terror Nexus in South Asia: States, Security and Non-State Actors*. New York: Routledge, 2011.

Clayman, Steven E. "Sequence and Solidarity." In *Group Cohesion, Trust and Solidarity*, edited by Shane R. Thye and Edward J. Lawler, 229–53. Oxford: Elsevier Science, 2002.

Clunan, Anne L., and Harold A. Trinkunas. *Ungoverned Spaces: Alternatives to State Authority in an Era of Softened Sovereignty*. Stanford: Stanford University Press, 2010.

Cochrane, Marisa. "Special Groups Regenerate." *Institute for the Study of War and the Weekly Standard* (Summer 2007–Summer 2008), August 29, 2008, 1–36.

Collins, Catherine, and Ashraf Ali. "Financing the Taliban: Tracing the Dollars behind the Insurgencies in Afghanistan and Pakistan." *New America Foundation*, 2010. Available at counterterrorism.newamerica.net/publications/policy/financing_the_taliban.

Combating Terrorism Center. "Abu Jasim Funds Distribution Report." West Point, NY: Combating Terrorism Center. Available at www.ctc.usma.edu/posts/abu-jasim-funds-distribution-report-english-language.

———. "Flow Chart of the Organization Structure of an ISI Administrative." West Point, NY: Combating Terrorism Center. Available at www.ctc.usma.edu/posts/flow-chart-of-the-organization-structure-of-an-isi-administrative-engligh-translation.

———. "ISI Accounting Receipt Template." West Point, NY: Combating Terrorism Center. Available at www.ctc.usma.edu/posts/isi-accounting-receipt-template-english-translation.

———. "ISI Template for Suicide Operation Pledge." West Point, NY: Combating Terrorism Center. Available at www.ctc.usma.edu/posts/isi-template-for-suicide-operation-pledge-english-translation.

———. "Islamic Emirate of Afghanistan Urgent Warning." West Point, NY: Combating Terrorism Center. Available at www.ctc.usma.edu/posts/islamic-emirate-of-afghanistan-urgent-warning-english-translation.

———. "Khalid Sultan 'Abdallah Sultan Separation Pledge from AQI." West Point, NY: Combating Terrorism Center. Available at www.ctc.usma.edu/posts/khalid-sultan-%e2%80%98abdallah-sultan-separation-pledge-from-aqi-english-language.

———. "Mustafa Qudrah 'Adawi Request for Abroad Medical Treatment." West Point, NY: Combating Terrorism Center. Available at www.ctc.usma.edu/posts/mustafa-qudrah-%e2%80%98adawi-request-for-abroad-medical-treatment-english-translation.

———. "Partial Muhammad Bin-Sabbar Muhammad al Khuwi Abu Yasir Martyrdom Pledge." West Point, NY: Combating Terrorism Center. Available at www.ctc.usma.edu/wp-content/uploads/2010/11/CTC-MuhammadBinSabbarMartyrdomPledge_Trans.pdf.

———. "Personnel Database for 23 Individuals." West Point, NY: Combating Terrorism Center. Available at www.ctc.usma.edu/posts/personnel-database-for-23-individuals-english-translation.

———. "Personnel Database for 46 Individuals." West Point, NY: Combating Terrorism Center. Available at www.ctc.usma.edu/posts/personnel-database-for-46-individuals-english-translation.

————. "The Rules of Jihad Established for Mujahideen by the Leadership of Afghanistan Islamic Emirates." West Point, NY: Combating Terrorism Center. Available at www.ctc.usma.edu/posts/the-rules-of-jihad-established-for-mujahideen-by-the-leadership-of-afghanistan-islamic-emirates-english-translation-2.

————. "Samara Attack Summary Report." West Point, NY: Combating Terrorism Center. Available at www.ctc.usma.edu/posts/samara-attack-sumary-report-english-language.

————. "Unsigned Oath of Allegiance to the ISI." West Point, NY: Combating Terrorism Center. Available at www.ctc.usma.edu/posts/unsigned-oath-of-allegiance-to-the-isi-english-translation.

Comfort, Louise. "Self-Organization in Complex Systems." *Journal of Public Administration Research and Theory* 4, no. 3 (July 1994): 393–410.

Connable, Ben, and Martin C. Libicki. *How Insurgencies End.* Santa Monica, CA: RAND, 2010.

Cordesman, Anthony H. *The Iraq War and Lessons for Counterinsurgency.* Washington, DC: Center for Strategic and International Studies, 2006.

————. *Iraqi Security Forces: A Strategy for Success.* Westport, CT: Praeger Security International, 2006.

————. *The War in Afghanistan at the End of 2012: The Uncertain Course of the War and Transition.* Washington, DC: Center for Strategic and International Studies, 2012.

Cragin, Kim, Peter Chalk, Sara A. Daly, and Brian A. Jackson. *Sharing the Dragon's Teeth: Terrorist Groups and the Exchange of New Technologies.* Santa Monica, CA: RAND, 2007.

Creveld, Martin van. *The Culture of War.* New York: Presidio Press, 2008.

Cronin, Audrey Kurth. "Cyber-Mobilization: The New Levee en Masse." *Parameters* 36 (Summer 2006): 77–87.

Cross, Rob, Stephen P. Borgatti, and Andrew Parker. "Making Invisible Work Visible: Using Social Network Analysis to Support Strategic Collaboration." *California Management Review* 44, no. 2 (Winter 2002): 25–46.

Cross, Rob, and Andrew Parker. *The Hidden Power of Social Networks: Understanding How Work Really Gets Done in Organizations.* Boston: Harvard Business School, 2004.

Cross, Rob, Andrew Parker, Laurence Prusak, and Stephen P. Borgatti. "Knowing What We Know: Supporting Knowledge Creation and Sharing in Social Networks." *Organizational Dynamics* 30, no. 2 (2001): 100–120.

Cruickshank, Paul. "The Militant Pipeline." *New American Foundation*, July 6, 2011. Available at counterterrorism.newamerica.net/publications/policy/the_militant_pipeline_0.

Daft, Richard L., and Robert H. Lengel. "Organizational Information Requirements,

Media Richness and Structural Design." *Management Science* 32, no. 5 (May 1986): 554–71.

Daraghi, Borzou. "Afghan Taliban Intelligence Network Embraces the New." *Los Angeles Times*, April 13, 2011. Available at articles.latimes.com/2011/apr/13/world/la-fg-taliban-intelligence-20110414.

Darling, Roger. "A New Conceptual Scheme for Analyzing Counterinsurgency." *Military Review* 54, no. 6 (June 1974): 54–86.

Davis, Ian S., Carrie L. Worth, and Douglas W. Zimmerman. "A Theory of Dark Network Design." Thesis. Monterey, CA: Naval Postgraduate School, 2010.

Davis, Paul K., Eric V. Larson, Zachary Haldeman, Mustafa Oguz, and Yashodhara Rana. *Understanding and Influencing Public Support for Insurgency and Terrorism.* Santa Monica, CA: RAND, 2012.

De Holan, Pablo Martin, and Nelson Phillips. "Organizational Forgetting." In *The Blackwell Handbook of Organizational Learning and Knowledge Management*, edited by Mark Easterby-Smith and Marjorie A. Lyles, 393–409. Malden, MA: Blackwell, 2003.

Deevy, Edward. *Creating the Resilient Organization: A Rapid Response Management Program.* Englewood Cliffs, NJ: Prentice Hall, 1995.

Dempsey, Martin E. *The Army Capstone Concept and Institutional Adaptation.* Arlington, VA: Institute of Land Warfare, March 2010.

DeYoung, Karen. "U.S. Trucking Funds Reach Taliban, Military-led Investigation Concludes." *Washington Post*, July 24, 2011. Available at www.washingtonpost.com/world/national-security/us-trucking-funds-reach-taliban-military-led-investigation-concludes/2011/07/22/gIQAmMDUXI_story.html.

Dombroski, Matthew, Paul Fischbeck, and Kathleen M. Carley. "Estimating the Shape of Covert Networks." Proceedings of the 8th International Command and Control Research and Technology Symposium. Washington, DC, June 2003.

Donmoyer, Robert. "Generalizability and the Single-Case Study." In *Case Study Method: Key Issues, Key Texts*, edited by Roger Gomm, Martyn Hammersley, and Peter Foster, 45–68. Thousand Oaks, CA: Sage Publications, 2000.

Dressler, Jeffrey. "The Afghan Insurgent Group That Will Not Negotiate." *Atlantic*, October 25, 2010. Available at www.theatlantic.com/international/archive/2010/10/the-afghan-insurgent-group-that-will-not-negotiate/65056/.

———. "The Haqqani Network: From Pakistan to Afghanistan." *Institute for the Study of War, Report 6*, March 2012. Available at www.understandingwar.org/sites/default/files/Haqqani_StrategicThreatweb_29 AR 0.pdf.

———. "Reconciliation with the Taliban: Fracturing the Insurgency." *Institute for the Study of War*, June 13, 2012. Available at www.understandingwar.org/backgrounder/reconciliation-taliban-fracturing-insurgency.

Dressler, Jeffrey, and Carl Forsberg. "The Quetta Shura Taliban in Southern Afghanistan: Organization, Operations, and Shadow Governance." *Institute for the Study of War*,

December 21, 2009. Available at www.understandingwar.org/report/quetta-shura-taliban-southern-afghanistan.

Druzin, Heath. "Insurgent Group Wants All Foreign Troops Gone before Election." *Stars and Stripes*, November 5, 2012. Available at www.stripes.com/news/middle-east/afghanistan/insurgent-group-wants-all-foreign-troops-gone-before-election 1.196029.

Easterby-Smith, Mark, and Luis Araujo. "Organizational Learning: Current Debates and Opportunities." In *Organizational Learning and the Learning Organization: Developments in Theory and Practice*, edited by Mark Easterby-Smith, John G. Burgoyne, and Luis Araujo, 1–22. London: Sage Publications, 1999.

Echevarria, Antulio J. *Wars of Ideas and the War of Ideas.* Carlisle, PA: Strategic Studies Institute, June 2008.

Economist. "A World Wide Web of Terror." *Economist,* July 12, 2007. Available at www.economist.com/node/9472498.

———. "The Brains Behind the Bombs." *The Economist,* November 1, 2007. Available at www.economist.com/node/10059748.

Edmondson, Amy C., and Anita Williams Woolley. "Understanding Outcomes of Organizational Learning Interventions." In *The Blackwell Handbook of Organizational Learning and Knowledge Management*, edited by Mark Easterby Smith and Marjorie A. Lyles, 185–211. Malden, MA: Blackwell, 2003.

Eisenstadt, Michael. "U.S. Post-Surge Operations in Iraq." Testimony before the House of Representatives, House Armed Services Committee, Subcommittee on Oversight and Investigations, Washington, DC: U.S. House of Representatives, January 23, 2008.

Eisenstadt, Michael, and Jeffrey White. *Assessing Iraq's Sunni Arab Insurgency*. Washington, DC: Washington Institute for Near East Policy, 2005.

Elsmore, Peter. *Organisational Culture: Organisational Change?* Burlington, VT: Gower, 2001.

Farrell, Kevin. "The Challenge of Providing Security in the Post-Combat Phase Urban Environment." In *Warfare in the Age of Non-State Actors: Implications for the US Army*, edited by Kendall D. Gott and Michael G. Brooks, 179–88. Proceedings of the Combat Studies Institute, 2007 Military History Symposium. Fort Leavenworth, KS: Combat Studies Institute Press, 2007.

Felbab-Brown, Vanda. *Shooting Up: Counterinsurgency and the War on Drugs*. Washington, DC: Brookings Institution Press, 2010.

Felter, Joseph, and Brian Fishman. *Al-Qa'ida's Foreign Fighters in Iraq: A First Look at the Sinjar Records.* West Point, NY: Combating Terrorism Center, 2008.

———. "The Demographics of Recruitment, Finances, and Suicide." In *Bombers, Bank Accounts, & Bleedout: Al Qa'Ida's Road in and out of Iraq*, edited by Brian Fishman, 32–65. West Point, NY: Combating Terrorism Center, 2008.

———. *Iranian Strategy in Iraq: Politics and "Other Means."* West Point, NY: Combating Terrorism Center, 2008.

Filkins, Dexter. "U.S. Hands Off Pacified Anbar, Once Heart of Iraq Insurgency." *New York Times*, September 2, 2008, A1.

Fiol, C. Marlene, and Marjorie A. Lyles. "Organizational Learning." *Academy of Management Review* 10, no. 4 (October 1985): 803–13.

Fishel, John T., and Max G. Manwaring. *Uncomfortable Wars Revisited*. Norman: University of Oklahoma Press, 2006.

Fishman, Brian. "After Zarqawi: The Dilemmas and Future of Al Qaeda in Iraq." *Washington Quarterly* 29, no. 4 (Autumn 2006): 19–32.

Flick, Uwe. *An Introduction to Qualitative Research*. London: Sage Publications, 2002.

Foreign Policy. *Failed States* (2012). Available at www.foreignpolicy.com/failed_states_index_2012_interactive.

Fowler, Michael. *Amateur Soldiers, Global Wars: Insurgency and Modern Conflict*. Westport, CT: Praeger Security International, 2005.

Fukuyama, Francis, and Abram N. Shulsky. "Military Organization in the Information Age: Lessons from the World of Business." In *Strategic Appraisal: The Changing Role of Information in Warfare*, edited by Zalmay Khalilzad, John White, and Andy W. Marshall, 327–60. Santa Monica, CA: RAND, 1999.

———. *The "Virtual Corporation" and Army Organization*. Santa Monica, CA: RAND, 1997.

Galbraith, Jay R. "Designing the Innovating Organization." *Organizational Dynamics* 10, no. 3 (Winter 1982): 5–25.

———. "Organizational Design: An Information Processing View." *Interfaces* 4, no. 3 (May 1974): 28–36.

Galli, Thomas I. "The Narcotics Counterinsurgency Dilemma." Monograph. Fort Leavenworth, KS: School of Advanced Military Studies, 2008.

Garvin, David A. "Building a Learning Organization." *Harvard Business Review* 71, no. 4 (July–August 1993): 78–91.

———. "The Processes of Organization and Management." *Sloan Management Review* 39, no. 4 (Summer 1998): 33–50.

George, Alexander L., and Andrew Bennett. *Case Studies and Theory Development in the Social Sciences*. Cambridge: MIT Press, 2005.

Gilchrist, Alison. *The Well-Connected Community: A Networking Approach to Community Development*. Bristol, Great Britain: Policy Press, 2009.

Gilley, Jerry W., and Erik Hoekstra. "Creating a Climate for Learning Transfer." In *Improving Learning Transfer in Organizations*, edited by Elwood F. Holton III and Timothy T. Baldwin, 271–306. San Francisco: Jossey Bass, 2003.

Giustozzi, Antonio. *Koran, Kalashnikov, and Laptop: The Neo-Taliban Insurgency in Afghanistan*. New York: Columbia University Press, 2008.

———. *Negotiating with the Taliban: Issues and Prospects*. New York: Century Foundation, 2010.

Giustozzi, Antonio, and Christoph Reuter. "The Northern Front: The Afghan Insurgency Spreading beyond the Pashtuns." *Afghanistan Analysts Network*. Available at aan-afghanistan.com/index.asp?id=848.

Gohel, Saijan M. "Iran's Ambiguous Role in Afghanistan." *CTC Sentinel* 3, no. 3 (March 2010): 13–16.

Golovnina, Maria. "FACTBOX: Insurgency in Afghanistan: Who Are They?" *Reuters*, September 25, 2009. Available at www.reuters.com/article/2009/09/25/us-afghanistan-insurgency-sb-idUSTRE5802F620090925.

Gompert, David C., Terrence K. Kelly, and Jessica Watkins. *Security in Iraq: A Framework for Analyzing Emerging Threats as U.S. Forces Leave*. Santa Monica, CA: RAND, 2010.

Goodhand, Jonathan. "Corrupting or Consolidating the Peace?: The Drugs Economy and Post-Conflict Peacebuilding in Afghanistan." *International Peacekeeping* 15, no. 3 (June 2008): 405–23.

———. "From Holy War to Opium War? A Case Study of the Opium Economy in North Eastern Afghanistan." *Central Asian Survey* 19, no. 2 (2000): 265–80.

———. "Frontiers and Wars. The Opium Economy in Afghanistan." *Journal of Agrarian Change* 5, no. 2 (April 2005): 191–216.

Goodhand, Jonathan, and David Mansfield. "Drugs and (Dis)order: A Study of the Opium Trade, Political Settlements and State-making in Afghanistan." *Crisis States Working Papers Series, No. 2*. London: London School of Economics, 2010.

Gopal, Anand, and Matthew DuPee. "Tensions Rise between Hizb-i-Islami and the Taliban in Afghanistan." *CTC Sentinel*, August 1, 2010. Available at www.ctc.usma.edu/posts/tensions-rise-between-hizb-i-islami-and-the-taliban-in-afghanistan.

Granovetter, Mark. "The Strength of Weak Ties: A Network Theory Revisited." *Sociological Theory* 1 (1983): 201–33.

Grayson, George W. *Mexico: Narco-Violence and a Failed State?* New Brunswick, NJ: Transaction Publishers, 2010.

Grdovic, Mark. *A Leader's Handbook to Unconventional Warfare*. Fort Bragg, NC: John F. Kennedy Special Warfare Center and School, November 2009.

Guidere, Mathieu, and Peter Harling. "'Withdraw, Move On and Rampage': Iraq's Resistance Evolves." *Le Monde Diplomatique*, May 2006. Available at mondediplo.com/2006/05/02irak.

Hamel, Gary, and C. K. Prahalad. *Competing for the Future*. Boston: Harvard Business School Press, 1994.

Hamilton, Donald W. *The Art of Insurgency: American Military Policy and the Failure of Strategy in Southeast Asia*. Westport, CT: Praeger Publishers, 1998.

Hamilton, Eric. "The Fight for Mosul." *Institute for the Study of War and the Weekly Standard*, March 2003–March 2008, 1–28.

Hammes, Thomas X. "Countering Evolved Insurgent Networks." *Military Review* 86, no. 4 (July–August 2006): 18–26.

————. *The Sling and the Stone: On War in the 21st Century*. St. Paul, MN: Zenith Press, 2004.

Hanratty, Martin E. "Can the United States Defeat Radical Islam?" Monograph. Fort Leavenworth, KS: School of Advanced Military Studies, 2008.

Hansen, Morten T. "The Search-Transfer Problem: The Role of Weak Ties in Sharing Knowledge across Organization Subunits." *Administrative Science Quarterly* 44, no. 1 (1999): 82–111.

Harmon, Christopher C. "What History Suggests about Terrorism and Its Future." In *The Past as Prologue: The Importance of History to the Military Profession*, edited by Williamson Murray and Richard Hart Sinnreich, 217–46. New York: Cambridge University Press, 2006.

Harnden, Toby. *"Bandit Country": The IRA & South Armagh*. London: Hodder and Stoughton, 1999.

Harrison, Michael I. *Diagnosing Organizations: Methods, Models, and Processes*. Thousand Oaks, CA: Sage Publications, 2005.

Hashim, Ahmed. "Foreign Involvement in the Iraqi Insurgency." *Terrorism Monitor* 2, no. 16 (August 2004). Available at www.jamestown.org/single/?no_cache=1&tx_ttnews%5Btt_news%5D=26749.

————. *Insurgency and Counter-Insurgency in Iraq*. Ithaca, NY: Cornell University Press, 2006.

————. "Iraq's Chaos: Why the Insurgency Won't Go Away." *Boston Review* (October/November 2004). Available at bostonreview.net/BR29.5/hashim.php.

————. "Terrorism and Complex Warfare in Iraq." *Jamestown Foundation Terrorism Monitor* 2, no. 12 (May 2005). Available at www.jamestown.org/single/?no_cache=1&tx_ttnews%5Btt_news%5D=385.

Hassan, Hussein D. *Iraq: Tribal Structure, Social, and Political Activities*. Washington, DC: Congressional Research Service, 2007.

Herring, Eric, and Glen Rangwala. *Iraq in Fragments: The Occupation and Its Legacy*. Ithaca, NY: Cornell University Press, 2006.

Hoehn, Andrew R., Adam Grissom, David A. Ochmanek, David A. Shlapak, and Alan J. Vick. *A New Division of Labor: Meeting America's Security Challenges beyond Iraq*. Santa Monica, CA: RAND, 2007.

Hoffman, Bruce. *The Use of the Internet by Islamic Extremists*. Testimony presented to the House Permanent Select Committee on Intelligence, Washington, DC: U.S. House of Representatives, May 4, 2006.

Hoffman, Frank G. "Neo-Classical Counterinsurgency?" *Parameters* 37 (Summer 2007): 71–87.

Holohan, Anne. *Networks of Democracy*. Stanford: Stanford University Press, 2005.

Hosmer, Stephen T. *Why the Iraqi Resistance to the Coalition Invasion was So Weak*. Santa Monica, CA: RAND, 2007.

Huber, George P. "Organizational Learning: The Contributing Processes and the Literatures." *Organization Science* 2, no. 1 (1991): 88–115.

Hutchins, Edwin. "Organizing Work by Adaptation." *Organization Science* 2, no. 1 (1991): 14–39.

International Crisis Group. *Afghanistan: The Long, Hard Road to the 2014 Transition.* Washington, DC: ICG, 2012.

———. *In Their Own Words: Reading the Iraqi Insurgency.* Washington, DC: ICG, 2006.

———. *Iraq after the Surge I: The New Sunni Landscape.* Washington, DC: ICG, 2008.

———. *Taliban Propaganda: Winning the War of Words?* Washington, DC: ICG, 2008.

Irvin, Cynthia L. *Militant Nationalism: Between Movement and Party in Ireland and the Basque Country.* Minneapolis: University of Minnesota Press, 1999.

Irwin, Lewis G. *Disjointed Ways, Disunified Means: Learning from America's Struggle to Build an Afghan Nation.* Carlisle, PA: Strategic Studies Institute, 2012.

Jackson, Brian A. "Application: The Four Components of Organizational Learning in the Case Study Groups." In *Aptitude for Destruction, Volume 2: Case Studies of Organizational Learning in Five Terrorist Groups,* edited by Brian A. Jackson, John C. Baker, Kim Cragin, John Parachini, Horacio R. Trujillo, and Peter Chalk, 191–98. Santa Monica, CA: RAND, 2005.

———. "Groups, Networks, or Movements: A Command-and-Control-Driven Approach to Classifying Terrorist Organizations and Its Application to Al Qaeda." *Studies in Conflict and Terrorism* 29, no. 3 (April–May 2006): 241–62.

Jackson, Brian, John C. Baker, Kim Cragin, John Parachini, Horacio R. Trujillo, and Peter Chalk. *Aptitude for Destruction, Volume 1: Organizational Learning in Terrorist Groups and Its Implications for Combating Terrorism.* Santa Monica, CA: RAND, 2005.

Jackson, Brian A., Peter Chalk, R. Kim Cragin, Bruce Newsome, John V. Parachini, William Rosenau, Erin M. Simpson, Melanie Sisson, and Donald Temple. *Breaching the Fortress Wall: Understanding Terrorist Efforts to Overcome Defensive Technologies.* Santa Monica, CA: RAND, 2007.

Jackson, Brian A., and David R. Frelinger. *Understanding Why Terrorist Operations Succeed or Fail.* Santa Monica, CA: RAND, 2009.

Jarvenpaa, Minna. *Making Peace in Afghanistan: The Missing Political Strategy.* Washington, DC: U.S. Institute of Peace, 2011.

Jenkins, Brian Michael. "The Jihadists' Operational Code." In *Three Years After: Next Steps in the War on Terror,* edited by David Aaron, 3–8. Santa Monica, CA: RAND, 2005.

Johnson, Steven. *Emergence: The Connected Lives of Ants, Brains, Cities, and Software.* New York: Touchstone, 2002.

Johnson, Thomas H. "Financing Afghan Terrorism: Thugs, Drugs, and Creative Movements of Money." In *Terrorism Financing and State Responses,* edited by Jeanne K.

Giraldo and Harold A. Trinkunas, 93–114. Stanford: Stanford University Press, 2007.

———. "On the Edge of the Big Muddy: The Taliban Resurgence in Afghanistan." *China and Eurasia Forum Quarterly* 5, no. 2 (2007): 93–129.

Johnson, Thomas H., and Matthew C. DuPee. "Analysing the New Taliban Code of Conduct (*Layeha*): An Assessment of Changing Perspectives and Strategies of the Afghan Taliban." *Central Asian Survey* 31, no. 1 (2012): 77–91.

Johnson, Thomas H., and M. Chris Mason. "Understanding the Taliban and Insurgency in Afghanistan." *Orbis* 51, no. 1 (January 2007): 71–89.

Johnston, Patrick B. "Does Decapitation Work? Assessing the Effectiveness of Leadership Targeting in Counterinsurgency Campaigns." *International Security* 36, no. 4 (Spring 2012): 47–79.

Joint and Coalition Operational Analysis. *Decade of War, Volume I: Enduring Lessons from the Past Decade of Operations.* Suffolk, VA: Joint and Coalition Operational Analysis, June 15, 2012.

Jones, Derek. "Understanding the Form, Function, and Logic of Clandestine Cellular Networks: The First Step in Effective Counternetwork Operations." Monograph. Fort Leavenworth, KS: School of Advanced Military Studies, 2009.

Jones, James L. *The Report of the Independent Commission on the Security Forces of Iraq.* Washington, DC: Independent Commission on the Security Forces of Iraq, 2007.

Jones, Seth. G. "The Rise of Afghanistan's Insurgency: State Failure and Jihad." *International Security* 32, no. 4 (Spring 2008): 7–40.

———. "The State of the Afghan Insurgency." *Testimony Presented before the Canadian Senate National Security and Defence Committee*, December 10, 2007.

Jones, Seth G., and Martin C. Libicki. *How Terrorist Groups End: Lessons for Countering al Qa'ida.* Santa Monica, CA: RAND, 2008.

Jordan, Jenna. "When Heads Roll: Assessing the Effectiveness of Leadership Decapitation." *Security Studies* 18, no. 4 (2009): 719–55.

Kagan, Kimberly. "The Anbar Awakening: Displacing al Qaeda from Its Stronghold in Western Iraq." *Institute for the Study of War and the Weekly Standard*, August 21, 2006–March 30, 2007, 1–18.

———. "The Battle for Diyala." *Institute for the Study of War and the Weekly Standard*, February 11–April 25, 2007, 1–30.

———. "From 'New Way Forward' to New Commander." *Institute for the Study of War and the Weekly Standard*, January 10–February 10, 2007, 1–21.

———. "Iran's Proxy War against the United States and the Iraqi Government." *Institute for the Study of War and the Weekly Standard*, May 2006–August 20, 2007, 1–32.

Karzai, Hekmat, and Paul T. Mitchell. "Networked Power: Insurgents versus 'Big Army.'" Singapore: Institute of Defense and Strategic Studies (IDSS), January 27, 2006.

Kaufman, Herbert. *The Limits of Organizational Change.* Tuscaloosa: University of Alabama Press, 1975.

Kenney, Michael. "The Challenge of Eradicating Transnational Criminal Networks: Lessons from the War on Drugs." Paper prepared for delivery at the 2002 Annual Meeting of the American Political Science Association, Boston, MA: August 28, 2002.

———. *From Pablo to Osama: Trafficking and Terrorist Networks, Government Bureaucracies, and Competitive Adaptation*. State College: Pennsylvania State University Press, 2007.

———. "Organizational Learning and Islamic Militancy." *National Institute of Justice* 265 (April 2010). Available at www.nij.gov/journals/265/militancy.htm.

Khalil, Lydia. "Anbar Revenge Brigade Makes Progress in the Fight against al-Qaeda." *Terrorism Focus* 3, no. 12 (March 2006). Available at www.jamestown.org/single/?no_cache=1&tx_ttnews%5Btt_news%5D=715.

Kiel, L. Douglas. *Managing Chaos and Complexity in Government: A New Paradigm for Managing Change, Innovation, and Organizational Renewal*. San Francisco: Jossey Bass, 1994.

Kilcullen, David. "Countering Global Insurgency, Version 2.2." *Small Wars Journal*, November 30, 2004. Available at smallwarsjournal.com/documents/kilcullen.pdf.

———. "Counterinsurgency Redux." *Small Wars Journal* (2006). Available at smallwarsjournal.com/documents/kilcullen1.pdf.

———. "Taliban and Counter-Insurgency in Kunar." In *Decoding the New Taliban*, edited by Antonio Giustozzi, 231–46. New York: Columbia University Press, 2009.

Kilduff, Martin, and Wenpin Tsai. *Social Networks and Organizations*. London: Sage Publications, 2003.

Kimmage, Daniel, and Kathleen Ridolfo. *Iraqi Insurgent Media: The War of Images and Ideas*. Washington, DC: Radio Free Europe, Radio Liberty, 2007.

King, Gary, Robert O. Keohane, and Sidney Verba. *Designing Social Inquiry*, Princeton: Princeton University Press, 1994.

Kittner, Cristiana C. Brafman. "The Role of Safe Havens in Islamist Terrorism." *Terrorism and Political Violence* 19, no. 3 (2007): 307–29.

Knights, Michael, and Jeffrey White. "Iraqi Resistance Proves Resilient." *Jane's Intelligence Review* (November 2003): 20–24.

Kochen, Manfred, and Karl W. Deutsch. *Decentralization: Sketches toward a Rational Theory*. Cambridge, MA: Oelgeschlager, Gunn and Hain Publishers, 1980.

Kohlmann, Evan F. "State of the Sunni Insurgency in Iraq: August 2007." New York: NEFA, August 2007.

Kostakos, Panos A., and Vassillis Kostakos. "Criminal Group Behavior and Operational Environments." *ECPR Standing Group on Organized Crime eNewsletter* 5, no. 2 (May 2006): 6–7. Available at www.ecprnet.eu/standinggroups/crime/documents/SGOC_Vol5_2.pdf.

Krackhardt, David. "The Strength of Strong Ties: The Importance of Philos in Organizations." In *Networks and Organizations: Structure, Form, and Action*, edited by Nitin

Nohria and Robert G. Eccles, 216–39. Boston: Harvard Business School Press, 1992.

Krebs, Valdis E. "Mapping Networks of Terrorist Cells." *Connections* 24, no. 3 (2001): 43–52.

Krepinevich, Andrew. *The War in Iraq: The Nature of Insurgency Warfare.* Washington, DC: CSBA, 2004.

Kuchins, Andrew C., Matthew Malarkey, and Sergey Markendonov. *The North Caucasus: Russia's Volatile Frontier.* Washington, DC: Center for Strategic and International Studies, 2011.

Lafraie, Najibullah. "Resurgence of the Taliban Insurgency in Afghanistan: How and Why?" *International Politics* 46, no. 1 (2009): 101–13.

Lahoud, Nelly, Stuart Caudill, Liam Collins, Gabriel Koehler-Derrick, Don Rassler, Muhammad al-'Ubaydi. *Letters from Abbottabad: Bin Ladin Sidelined?* West Point, NY: Combating Terrorism Center, 2012.

Lamb, Robert D. *Ungoverned Areas and Threats from Safe Havens.* Washington, DC: Office of the Under Secretary of Defense for Policy, 2008.

Laqueur, Walter. *Guerrilla Warfare: A Historical & Critical Study.* New Brunswick, NJ: Transaction Publishers, 1998.

Lee, Thomas W. *Using Qualitative Methods in Organizational Research.* Thousand Oaks, CA: Sage Publications, 1999.

Lemieux, Vincent. *Criminal Networks.* Ottawa, Canada: Royal Canadian Mounted Police Research and Evaluation Branch, 2003.

Lempert, Robert J., and Steven W. Popper. "High-Performance Government in an Uncertain World." In *High Performance Government: Structure, Leadership, Incentives,* edited by Robert Klitgaard and Paul C. Light, 113–38. Santa Monica, CA: RAND, 2005.

Levinthal, Daniel A. "Organizational Adaptation and Environmental Selection: Interrelated Processes of Change." *Organization Science* 2, no. 1 (March 1991): 140–45.

Levitt, Matthew. "Untangling the Terror Web: Identifying and Counteracting the Phenomenon of Crossover between Terrorist Groups." *SAIS Review* 24, no. 1 (Winter/ Spring 2004): 33–48.

Lin, Zhiang, and Kathleen M. Carley. "Organizational Design and Adaptation in Response to Crises: Theory and Practice." Pittsburgh, PA: Computational Analysis of Social and Organizational Systems (CASOS), July 2002. Available at www.casos. cs.cmu.edu/publications/papers/OrgCrisisResponse.pdf.

Linschoten, Alex Strick van, and Felix Kuehn. "Separating the Taliban from al-Qaeda: The Core of Success in Afghanistan." February 2011. Available at www.cic.nyu.edu/ afghanistan/docs/gregg_sep_tal_alqaeda.pdf.

Lister, Charles R. "Accounting for the Resilience of the Taliban." *e-International Relations,* March 30, 2011. Available at www.e-ir.info/2011/03/30/accounting-for-the-resilience-of-the-taliban.

Live Leak. "Taliban Training Camp 'Prepares Camp Bastion Attack.'" Available at www.liveleak.com/view?i=2bc_1348579573.

Londono, Ernesto. "Iraq Militants Turning to Use of 'Sticky' Bombs." *Washington Post*, October 9, 2008. Available at www.washingtonpost.com/wp-dyn/content/article/2008/10/08/AR2008100803568.html.

Long, Austin. "The Anbar Awakening." *Survival* 50 (April 2008): 67–94.

———. On *"Other War": Lessons from Five Decades of RAND Counterinsurgency Research*. Santa Monica, CA: RAND, 2006.

Looney, Robert. "The Business of Insurgency: The Expansion of Iraq's Shadow Economy." *National Interest* 81 (2005): 67–72.

———. "Economic Consequences of Conflict: The Rise of Iraq's Informal Economy." *Journal of Economic Issues* 40, no. 4 (December 2006): 991–1007.

———. "The Mirage of Terrorist Financing: The Case of Islamic Charities." *Strategic Insights* 5, no. 3 (March 2006). Available at www.nps.edu/Academics/centers/ccc/publications/OnlineJournal/2006/Mar/looneyMar06.pdf.

Maloney, Sean M. "On a Pale Horse? Conceptualizing Narcotics Production in Southern Afghanistan and Its Relationship to the Narcoterror Nexus." *Small Wars and Insurgencies* 20, no. 1 (March 2009): 203–14.

Mansoor, Peter R., and Mark S. Ulrich. "Linking Doctrine to Action: A New COIN Center-of-Gravity Analysis." *Military Review* 87, no. 5 (September–October 2007): 45–51.

March, James G., Lee S. Sproull, and Michael Tamuz. "Learning from Samples of One or Fewer." *Organization Science* 2, no. 1 (March 1991): 1–13.

Marquardt, Michael J. *Building the Learning Organization: A Systems Approach to Quantum Improvement and Global Success*. New York: McGraw Hill, 1996.

Marshall, Catherine, and Gretchen B. Rossman. *Designing Qualitative Research*. Thousand Oaks, CA: Sage Publications, 2006.

Mashal, Mujib. "The Question of Succession." *Afghanistan Analysts Network*, May 18, 2012. Available at aan-afghanistan.org/index.asp?id=2768.

May, Tim. *Social Research: Issues, Methods, and Research*. Philadelphia: Open University Press, 2001.

McCormick, G. H., and G. Owen. "Security and Coordination in a Clandestine Organization." *Mathematical and Computer Modeling* 31, no. 6 (March–April 2000): 175–92.

McCoy, Alfred W. "The Costs of Covert Warfare: Airpower, Drugs, and Warlords in the Conduct of U.S. Foreign Policy." *New England Journal of Public Policy* 19, no. 1 (2003): 223–41.

McFate, Montgomery. "Iraq: The Social Context of IEDs." *Military Review* 85, no. 3 (May–June 2005): 37–40.

McGrath, Cathleen, and David Krackhardt. "Network Conditions for Organizational Change." *Journal of Applied Behavioral Science* 39, no. 3 (September 2003): 324–36.

Merari, Ariel. "Terrorism as a Strategy of Insurgency." *Terrorism and Political Violence* 5, no. 4 (Winter 1993): 213–51.

Merz, Andrew A. "Coercion, Cash-Crops and Culture: From Insurgency to Proto-State in Asia's Opium Belt." Thesis. Monterey, CA: Naval Postgraduate School, 2008.

Metz, Steven. "The Internet, New Media, and the Evolution of Insurgency." *Parameters* 42, no. 3 (Autumn 2012): 80–90.

———. *Learning from Iraq: Counterinsurgency in American Strategy*. Carlisle, PA: Strategic Studies Institute, 2007.

———. *Rethinking Insurgency*. Carlisle, PA: Strategic Studies Institute, 2007.

Metz, Steven, and Raymond Millen. *Insurgency and Counterinsurgency in the 21st Century: Reconceptualizing Threat and Response*. Carlisle, PA: Strategic Studies Institute, 2004.

———. *Insurgency in Iraq and Afghanistan: Change and Continuity*. Carlisle, PA: Strategic Studies Institute, 2003.

Miles, Raymond E., Charles C. Snow, Alan D. Meyer, and Henry J. Coleman, Jr. "Organizational Strategy, Structure, and Process." *Academy of Management Review* 3, no. 3 (July 1978): 546–62.

Miller, Danny, and Peter Friesen. *Organizations: A Quantum View*. Englewood Cliffs, NJ: Prentice Hall, 1984.

Milward, H. Brinton, and Jorg Raab. "Dark Networks: The Structure, Operation, and Performance of International Drug, Terror, and Arms Trafficking Networks." Paper presented at the International Conference on the Empirical Study of Governance, Management, and Performance. Barcelona, Spain, October 4–5, 2002.

Mintzberg, Henry. "Organization Design: Fashion or Fit?" *Harvard Business Review* 59, no. 1 (January–February 1981): 103–16.

Mobley, Blake. *Terrorism and Counterintelligence: How Terrorist Groups Elude Detection*. New York: Columbia University Press, 2012.

Mockaitis, Thomas R. *The Iraq War: Learning from the Past, Adapting to the Present, and Planning for the Future*. Carlisle, PA: Strategic Studies Institute, 2007.

Mohammad, Wahidullah. "Taliban Expand Insurgency to Northern Afghanistan." *Terrorism Monitor* 2, no. 36 (November 25, 2009). Available at www.jamestown.org/programs/gta/single/?tx_ttnews%5Btt_news%5D=35774&t_ttnews%5BbackPid%5D=412&no_cache=1.

Moll, Daniel C. "U.S. Army Forces Training for the Global War on Terror." Monograph. Fort Leavenworth, KS: Command and General Staff College, 2003.

Molnar, Andrew R., William A. Lybrand, Lorna Hahn, James L. Kirkman, and Peter B. Riddleberger. *Undergrounds in Insurgent, Revolutionary, and Resistance Warfare*. Washington, DC: Special Operations Research Office, 1963.

Molnar, Andrew R., Jerry M. Tinker, and John D. LeNoir. "Underground Organization within Insurgency." In *Human Factors Considerations of Undergrounds in Insurgencies*. Washington, DC: Special Operations Research Office, 1965.

Monge, Peter R., and Noshir S. Contractor. *Theories of Communication Networks*. Oxford: Oxford University Press, 2003.

Muckian, Martin J. "Structural Vulnerabilities of Networked Insurgencies: Adapting to the New Adversary." *Parameters* 36 (Winter 2006–7): 15–25.

Mueller, John. "How Dangerous Are the Taliban?" *Foreign Affairs*. Available at www.foreignaffairs.com/articles/64932/john-mueller/how-dangerous-are-the-taliban.

Munck, Ronaldo. "Deconstructing Terror: Insurgency, Repression and Peace." In *Postmodern Insurgencies: Political Violence, Identity Formation and Peacemaking in Comparative Perspective*, edited by Ronaldo Munck and Purnaka L. de Silva, 1–13. New York: St. Martin's Press, 2000.

Nader, Alireza, and Joya Laha. *Iran's Balancing Act in Afghanistan*. Santa Monica, CA: RAND, 2011.

Nance, Malcolm W. *The Terrorists of Iraq: Inside the Strategy and Tactics of the Iraq Insurgency*. Booksurge, 2007.

Napoleoni, Loretta. *Insurgent Iraq: Al Zarqawi and the New Generation*. New York: Seven Stories Press, 2005.

Nasr, Vali. "When the Shiites Rise." *Foreign Affairs* 85, no. 4 (July/August 2006): 58–74.

Nasuti, Matthew J. "Taliban's Secret Weapon in Afghanistan—Intelligence 'Moles'?" *KabulPress.Org* (October 14, 2012). Available at kabulpress.org/my/spip.php?article128168.

Nathan, Joanna. "Reading the Taliban." In *Decoding the New Taliban*, edited by Antonio Giustozzi, 23–42. New York: Columbia University Press, 2009.

Naylor, Sean D. "Afghanistan Insurgency Has Grown 10-Fold." *Army Times*, October 31, 2009. Available at www.armytimes.com/news/2009/10/military_afghanistan_foreign_insurgents_103109/.

Nichol, Jim. *Stability in Russia's Chechnya and Other Regions of the North Caucasus: Recent Developments*. Washington, DC: Congressional Research Service, 2010.

Nilsson, Desiree, and Mimmi Soderberg Kovacs. "Revisiting an Elusive Concept: A Review of the Debate on Spoilers in Peace Processes." *International Studies Review* 13, no. 4 (December 2011): 606–26.

Nine Eleven Finding Answers Foundation (NEFA), trans. "Hamas in Iraq: An Interview with the Commander of the Diyala Sector." New York: NEFA, January 4, 2008.

———. "Statement from the 1920 Revolution Brigades." New York: NEFA, October 10, 2007.

Nirenberg, John. *The Living Organization: Transforming Teams into Workplace Communities*. Homewood, IL: Business One Irwin, 1993.

Nissenbaum, Dion, Habib Khan Totakhil, and Julian E. Barnes. "Taliban Agree to Open Office for Peace Talks." *Wall Street Journal*, January 4, 2012. Available at online.wsj.com/article/SB10001424052970203462304577138431516260746.html.

Novikov, Evgenii. "Unmasking the Iraqi Insurgency." *Jamestown Foundation Terrorism Monitor* 2, no. 12 (June 2004). Available at www.jamestown.org/single/?no_cache=1&tx_ttnews%5Btt_news%5D=29973.

Nystrom, Paul C., and William H. Starbuck. "To Avoid Organizational Crises, Unlearn." *Organizational Dynamics* 12, no. 4 (Spring 1984): 53–65.

Oehme, Chester G., III. "Terrorists, Insurgents, and Criminals—Growing Nexus?" *Studies in Conflict and Terrorism* 31, no. 1 (January 2008): 80–93.

O'Neill, Bard E. *Insurgency & Terrorism: Inside Modern Revolutionary Warfare*. Dulles, VA: Brassey's, 1990.

Oppel, Richard A., Jr. "In Northern Iraq, the Insurgency Has Two Faces, Secular and Jihad, but a Common Goal." *New York Times*, December 19, 2004. Available at www.nytimes.com/2004/12/international/19mosul.html?pagewanted=print&position=.

———. "Iraq Insurgency Runs on Stolen Oil Profits." *New York Times Late Edition*, March 16, 2008, A1.

Ostrom, Elinor. *Governing the Commons: The Evolution of Institutions for Collective Action*. Cambridge, UK: Cambridge University Press, 1990.

Paley, Amit. "Iraqis Joining Insurgency Less for Cause than Cash." *Washington Post Foreign Service*, November 20, 2007, A01.

Parker, Christopher, and Pete W. Moore. "The War Economy of Iraq." *Middle East Report* 243. Available at www.merip.org/mer/mer243.

Paul, Christopher, Colin P. Clarke, and Beth Grill. *Victory Has a Thousand Fathers: Sources of Success in Counterinsurgency*. Santa Monica, CA: RAND, 2010.

Peters, Gretchen. *Crime and Insurgency in the Tribal Areas of Afghanistan and Pakistan*. West Point, NY: Combating Terrorism Center, 2010.

———. *Haqqani Network Financing: The Evolution of an Industry*. West Point, NY: Combating Terrorism Center, 2012.

———. *How Opium Profits the Taliban*. Washington, DC: U.S. Institute of Peace, 2009.

———. "The Taliban and the Opium Trade." In *Decoding the New Taliban*, edited by Antonio Giustozzi, 7–22. New York: Columbia University Press, 2009.

Petraeus, David H. *Report to Congress on the Situation in Iraq*. Testimony to a Joint Hearing of the House Committee on Foreign Affairs and the House Committee on Armed Services. Washington, DC: U.S. House of Representatives, September 10, 2007.

Plaw, Avery. *Targeting Terrorists: A License to Kill?* Burlington, VT: Ashgate Publishing, 2008.

Price, Bryan C. "Targeting Top Terrorists: How Leadership Decapitation Contributes to Counterterrorism." *International Security* 36, no. 4 (Spring 2012): 9–46.

Probst, Gilbert J. B., and Bettina S. T. Buchel. *Organizational Learning: The Competitive Advantage of the Future*. London: Prentice Hall, 1997.

Rabasa, Angel, Peter Chalk, Kim Cragin, Sara A. Daly, Heather S. Gregg, Theodore W.

Karasik, Kevin A. O'Brien, and William Rosenau, *Beyond al Qaeda, Part 1: The Global Jihadist Movement*. Santa Monica, CA: RAND, 2006.

———. *Beyond al-Qaeda, Part 2: The Outer Rings of the Terrorist Universe*. Santa Monica, CA: RAND, 2006.

———. *U.S. Counterterrorism Strategy Must Address Ideological and Political Factors at the Global and Local Levels*. Santa Monica, CA: RAND, 2006.

Rabasa, Angel, John Gordon, IV, Peter Chalk, Christopher S. Chivvis, Audra K. Grant, K. Scott McMahon, Laurel E. Miller, Marco Overhaus, and Stephanie Pezard. *From Insurgency to Stability, Volume I: Key Capabilities and Practices*. Santa Monica, CA: RAND, 2011.

Rabasa, Angel, John Gordon, IV, Peter Chalk, Audra K. Grant, K. Scott McMahon, Stephanie Pezard, Caroline Reilly, David Ucko, and S. Rebecca Zimmerman. *From Insurgency to Stability, Volume II: Insights from Selected Case Studies*. Santa Monica, CA: RAND, 2011.

Raider, Holly, and David J. Krackhardt. "Intraorganizational Networks." In *Companion to Organizations*, edited by Joel A. C. Baum, 58–74. Oxford, UK: Blackwell Publishers, 2002.

RAND. *Heads We Win: Improving Cognitive Effectiveness in Counterinsurgency*. Santa Monica, CA: RAND, 2007.

———. *U.S. Counterterrorism Strategy Must Address Ideological and Political Factors at the Global and Local Levels*. Santa Monica, CA: RAND, 2006.

Rashid, Ahmed. *Taliban*. New Haven: Yale University Press, 2001.

Record, Jeffrey. *Beating Goliath: Why Insurgencies Win*. Dulles, VA: Potomac Books, 2007.

Robb, John. *Brave New War: The Next Stage of Terrorism and the End of Globalization*. Hoboken, NJ: John Wiley and Sons, 2007.

———. *Epidemic Insurgency (Part 1)*. 2004. Available at globalguerrillas.typead.com/globalguerrillas/2004/11/epidemic_insurg.html.

Robinson, Glenn E. "The Battle for Iraq: Islamic Insurgencies in Comparative Perspective," *Third World Quarterly* 28, no. 2 (2007): 261–73.

Roggio, Bill. "The Afghan Taliban's Top Leaders." *Long War Journal*, February 23, 2010. Available at www.longwarjournal.org/archives/2010/02/the_talibans_top_lea.php.

Rosen, Nir. "The Many Faces of Abu Musab al Zarqawi." Available at www.truthdig.com/dig/item/20060609_abu_musab_al_zarqawi/.

Rosenau, William. *Subversion and Insurgency*. Santa Monica, CA: RAND, 2007.

———. "Waging the 'War of Ideas.'" In *The McGraw-Hill Homeland Security Handbook*, edited by David G. Kamien, 1131–48. New York: McGraw-Hill, 2006.

Rosenberg, Matthew. "Taliban Opening Qatar Office, and Maybe Door to Talks." *New York Times*, January 3, 2012. Available at www.nytimes.com/2012/01/04/world/asia/taliban-to-open-qatar-office-in-step-toward-peace-talks.html?pagewanted=all.

Rosenberg, Matthew, and Rod Nordland. "Second Afghan Insurgent Group Suspends Peace Talks." *New York Times*, March 29, 2012. Available at www.nytimes.com/2012/03/30/world/asia/afghanistan-security.html.

Roston, Aram. "How the US Funds the Taliban." *Nation*, November 11, 2009. Available at www.thenation.com/article/how-us-funds-taliban?page=full.

Rubin, Alissa J. "Taliban Causes Most Civilian Deaths in Afghanistan, U.N. Says." *New York Times*, March 9, 2011. Available at www.nytimes.com/2011/03/10/world/asia/10afghanistan.html?_r=1.

Rubin, Barnett R. "Saving Afghanistan." *Foreign Affairs* 86, no. 1 (January–February 2007): 57–74, 76–78.

Rubin, Michael. "Asymmetrical Threat Concept and Its Reflections on International Security." Presentation to the Strategic Research and Study Center (SAREM) under the Turkish General Staff. Istanbul: May 2007.

Ruttig, Thomas. "The Battle for Afghanistan: Negotiations with the Taliban: History and Prospects for the Future." *New America Foundation*, May 23, 2011. Available at security.newamerica.net/publications/policy/negotiations _with_the_taliban.

———. "The Haqqani Network as an Autonomous Entity." In *Decoding the New Taliban*, edited by Antonio Giustozzi, 57–88. New York: Columbia University Press, 2009.

———. "How Tribal Are the Taleban? Afghanistan's Largest Insurgent Movement between Its Tribal Roots and Islamist Ideology." *Afghanistan Analysts Network*. Available at aan-afghanistan.com/index.asp?id=865.

———. "The Other Side: Dimensions of the Afghan Insurgency: Causes, Actors and Approach to 'Talks.'" *Afghanistan Analysts Network*. Available at aan-afghanistan.com/index.asp?id=114.

Sageman, Marc. *Leaderless Jihad: Terror Networks in the Twenty-First Century*. Philadelphia: University of Pennsylvania Press, 2008.

———. *Understanding Terror Networks*. Philadelphia: University of Pennsylvania Press, 2004.

Samoilenko, Sergey. "Fitness Landscapes of Complex Systems: Insights and Implications on Managing a Conflict Environment of Organizations." *Emergence: Complexity and Organization* 10, no. 4 (October 2008): 38–45.

Sanderson, Thomas M. "Transnational Terror and Organized Crime: Blurring the Lines." *SAIS Review* 24 (Winter/Spring 2004): 49–61.

Sanin, Francisco Guiterrez, and Antonio Giustozzi. "Networks and Armies: Structuring Rebellion in Colombia and Afghanistan." *Studies in Conflict and Terrorism* 33, no. 9 (September 2010): 836–53.

Santora, Marc, and Damien Cave. "Banned Station Beams Voice of Iraq Insurgency." *New York Times*, January 21, 2007. Available at query.nytimes.com/gst/fullpage.html?res=9F07E7DE1F30F932A15752C0A9619C8B6&pagewnted=all.

Schwarz, Anthony J. "Iraq's Militias: The True Threat to Coalition Success in Iraq." *Parameters* 37 (Spring 2007): 55–71.

Serena, Chad C. "Combating a Combat Legacy." *Parameters* 40 (Spring 2010): 47–59.

———. "Dynamic Attenuation: Terrorism, Transnational Crime and the Role of the US Army Special Forces." *Global Crime* 8, no. 4 (November 2007): 345–65.

———. *A Revolution in Military Adaptation: The U.S. Army in the Iraq War*. Washington, DC: Georgetown University Press, 2011.

Shapiro, Jacob. "Bureaucratic Terrorists: Al-Qa'ida in Iraq's Management and Finances." In *Bombers, Bank Accounts & Bleedout: Al-Qa'ida's Road in and out of Iraq*, edited by Brian Fishman, 66–80. West Point, NY: Combating Terrorism Center, 2008.

Shinn, James, and James Dobbins. *Afghan Peace Talks: A Primer*. Santa Monica, CA: RAND, 2011.

Shultz, Richard H., Jr., and Andrea J. Dew. *Insurgents, Terrorists, and Militias: The Warriors of Contemporary Combat*. New York: Columbia University Press, 2006.

Silverman, Jerry M., and Peter M. Jackson. "Terror in Insurgency Warfare." *Military Review* 50, no. 10 (October 1970): 61–67.

Simons, Anna, and David Tucker. "The Misleading Problem of Failed States: A 'Socio-Geography' of Terrorism in the Post-9/11 Era." *Third World Quarterly* 28, no. 2 (2007): 387–401.

Singh, Baljit, and Ko-Wang Mei. *Theory and Practice of Modern Guerrilla Warfare*. New York: Asia Publishing House, 1971.

Siperco, Ian. "Subversive Markets: The Economic Roots of the Iraq Insurgency." N.d. Available at rusi.org/downloads/assets/Subversive_Markets.pdf.

Sitkin, Sim B. "Learning through Failure: The Strategy of Small Losses." In *Organizational Learning*, edited by Michael D. Cohen and Lee S. Sproull, 541–78. Thousand Oaks, CA: Sage Publications, 1996.

Smith, Niel, and Sean MacFarland. "Anbar Awakens: The Tipping Point." *Military Review* 88, no. 2 (March–April 2008): 41–52.

Stake, Robert E. "Case Studies." In *Handbook of Qualitative Research*, edited by Norman K. Denzin and Yvonna S. Lincoln, 435–54. Thousand Oaks, CA: Sage Publications, 2000.

———. "The Case Study Method in Social Inquiry." In *Case Study Method: Key Issues, Key Texts*, edited by Roger Gomm, Martyn Hammersley, and Peter Foster, 19–26. Thousand Oaks, CA: Sage Publications, 2000.

Stanekzai, Mohammad Masoom. *Thwarting Afghanistan's Insurgency: A Pragmatic Approach toward Peace and Reconciliation*. Washington, DC: U.S. Institute of Peace, 2008.

Staniland, Paul. "Organizing Insurgency: Networks, Resources, and Rebellion in South Asia." *International Security* 37, no. 1 (Summer 2012): 142–77.

Steele, Robert D. *The New Craft of Intelligence: Achieving Asymmetric Advantage in the Face of Nontraditional Threats.* Carlisle, PA: Strategic Studies Institute, 2002.

Steinberg, Guido. *The Iraqi Insurgency: Actors, Strategies, and Structures.* Berlin: German Institute for International and Security Affairs, 2006.

Steliga, Mark A. "Why They Hate Us: Disaggregating the Iraqi Insurgency." Thesis. Monterrey, CA: Naval Post Graduate School, 2005.

Stenersen, Anne. *The Taliban Insurgency in Afghanistan—Organization, Leadership and Worldview.* Norway: Norwegian Defence Research Establishment (FFI), 2010.

Stoker, Donald. "Six Reasons Insurgencies Lose: A Contrarian View." *Small Wars Journal* (2009): 1–11. Available at smallwarsjournal.com/blog/journal/docs-temp/268-stoker.pdf.

Sullivan, Daniel P. "Tinder, Spark, Oxygen, and Fuel: The Mysterious Rise of the Taliban." *Journal of Peace Research* 44, no. 1 (January 2007): 93–108.

Szulanski, Gabriel, and Rossella Cappetta. "Stickiness: Conceptualizing, Measuring, and Predicting Difficulties in the Transfer of Knowledge within Organizations." In *The Blackwell Handbook of Organizational Learning and Knowledge Management*, edited by Mark Easterby-Smith and Marjorie A. Lyles, 513–34. Malden, MA: Blackwell Publishing, 2003.

Takács, Károly. "Effects of Network Segregation in Intergroup Conflict: An Experimental Analysis." *Connections* 27, no. 2 (2007): 59–76.

Tanner, Stephen. *Afghanistan: A Military History from Alexander the Great to the War against the Taliban.* Philadelphia: Da Capo Press, 2009.

Taylor, Lowry. "The Nexus of Terrorism and Drug Trafficking in the Golden Crescent: Afghanistan." Strategy Research Project. Carlisle, PA: U.S. Army War College, 2006.

Thruelsen, Peter Dahl. "The Taliban in Southern Afghanistan: A Localised Insurgency with a Local Objective." *Small Wars and Insurgencies* 21, no. 2 (June 2010): 259–76.

Tierney, John J., Jr. *Chasing Ghosts: Unconventional Warfare in American History.* Dulles, VA: Potomac Books, 2006.

Trice, Harrison M., and Janice M. Beyer. *The Cultures of Work Organizations.* Englewood Cliffs, NJ: Prentice Hall, 1993.

Trives, Sébastien. "The Haqqani Network as an Autonomous Entity." In *Decoding the New Taliban*, edited by Antonio Giustozzi, 89–100. New York: Columbia University Press, 2009.

Tsoukas, Haridimos. "Do We Really Understand Tacit Knowledge?" In *The Blackwell Handbook of Organizational Learning and Knowledge Management*, edited by Mark Easterby-Smith and Marjorie A. Lyles, 410–27. Malden, MA: Blackwell Publishing, 2003.

Tsoukas, Haridimos, and Efi Vladimirou. "What Is Organizational Knowledge?" *Journal of Management Studies* 38, no. 7 (November 2001): 973–93.

Tsvetovat, Maksim, and Kathleen M. Carley. "Bouncing Back: Recovery Mechanisms of

Covert Networks." NAACSOS Conference Proceedings, Pittsburgh, PA, 2003. Available at www.casos.cs.cmu.edu/publications/working_papers/tsvetovat_2003_recovery.pdf.

Tushman, Michael L., and David A. Nadler. "Information Processing as an Integrating Concept in Organizational Design." *Academy of Management Review* 3, no. 3 (July 1978): 613–24.

Ucko, David H. "Militias, Tribes, and Insurgents: The Challenge of Political Reintegration in Iraq." In *Reintegrating Armed Groups after Conflict: Politics, Violence, and Transition*, edited by Mats Berdal and David H. Ucko, 89–118. New York: Routledge, 2009.

UNESCO. *Literacy in Iraq Fact Sheet.* Available at iauiraq.org/documents/1050/Literacy%20Day%20Factsheet_Sep8.pdf.

UNODC. *Corruption in Afghanistan: Recent Patterns and Trends.* Vienna, Austria: UN Office on Drugs and Crime, 2012.

U.S. Agency for International Development. *Assistance for Iraq.* Available at www.usaid.gov/iraq/accomplishments/education.html.

U.S. Army Training and Doctrine Command. TRADOC Pamphlet 525–3-1. *The United States Army Operating Concept, 2016–2028.* Fort Monroe, VA: TRADOC, 2010.

U.S. Department of the Army. Army Doctrinal Publication (ADP) 3–0. *Unified Land Operations.* Washington, DC: U.S. Army, 2011.

———. Field Manual (FM) 3–24. *Counterinsurgency.* Washington, DC: U.S. Army, 2006.

U.S. Department of Defense. Joint Publication (JP) 1–02. *Department of Defense Dictionary of Military and Associated Terms.* Washington, DC: U.S. DOD, November 8, 2010 (as amended through April 15, 2012).

———. *Report on Progress toward Security and Stability in Afghanistan.* Washington, DC: U.S. DOD, December 2012.

U.S. Senate Committee on Foreign Relations. *Afghanistan's Narco War: Breaking the Link between Drug Traffickers and Insurgents.* Washington, DC: U.S. Government Printing Office, 2009.

Valeriano, Napolean D., and Charles T. R. Bohannan. *Counter-Guerrilla Operations: The Philippine Experience.* Westport, CT: Praeger Security International, 2006.

Van Meter, Karl M. "Terrorists/Liberators: Researching and Dealing with Adversary Social Networks." *Connections* 24, no. 3 (2001): 66–78.

Wahidi, Mohammad Amin. "Female Taliban?! A Group Called RAWA." *KabulPress.Org* (March 17, 2012). Available at kabulpress.org/my/spip.php?article102543.

Waldman, Matt. *Dangerous Liaisons with the Afghan Taliban: The Feasibility and Risks of Negotiations.* Washington, DC: U.S. Institute of Peace, 2010.

Wasserman, Stanley, and Katherine Faust. *Social Network Analysis: Methods and Applications.* New York: Cambridge University Press, 2005.

Watts, Clinton. *Foreign Fighters: How Are They Being Recruited? Two Imperfect Recruit-*

ment Models. Available at smallwarsjournal.com/blog/journal/docs-temp/69-watts. pdf?q=mag/docs-temp/69-watts.pdf.

Weimann, Gabriel. *www.terror.net: How Modern Terrorism Uses the Internet.* Washington, DC: U.S. Institute of Peace, 2004.

Weinstein, Jeremy M. *Inside Rebellion: The Politics of Insurgent Violence.* New York: Cambridge University Press, 2007.

Wesensten, Nancy J., Gregory Belenky, and Thomas J. Balkin. "Cognitive Readiness in Network-Centric Operations." *Parameters* 35 (Spring 2005): 94–105.

White, Jeffrey. *An Adaptive Insurgency: Confronting Adversary Networks in Iraq.* Washington, DC: Washington Institute for Near East Policy, 2006.

White, Jeffrey, and Michael Schmidmayr. "Resistance in Iraq." *Middle East Quarterly* 10, no. 3 (Fall 2003): 17–32.

Williams, J. Noel. "Matrix Warfare: The New Face of Competition and Conflict in the 21st Century." *Small Wars Journal* (August 2005). Available at smallwarsjournal.com/documents/williams2.pdf.

Williams, Paul L. *The Al Qaeda Connection: International Terrorism, Organized Crime, and the Coming Apocalypse.* Amherst, NY: Prometheus Books, 2005.

Williams, Phil. *Criminals, Militias, and Insurgents: Organized Crime in Iraq.* Carlisle, PA: Strategic Studies Institute, 2009.

———. "The Nature of Drug-Trafficking Networks." *Current History* 97 (April 1998): 154–59.

———. "Transnational Criminal Networks." In *Networks and Netwars: The Future of Terror, Crime, and Militancy,* edited by John Arquilla and David Ronfeldt, 61–98. Santa Monica, CA: RAND, 2001.

Wilson, Clay. *Improvised Explosive Devices (IEDs) in Iraq and Afghanistan: Effects and Countermeasures.* Washington, DC: Congressional Research Service, 2006.

Wormer, Nils. "The Networks of Kunduz: A History of Conflict and Their Actors, from 1992 to 2001." *Afghanistan Analysts Network.* Available at aan-afghanistan.com/index.asp?id=2901.

Wright, Donald P., and Timothy R. Reese. *On Point II, Transition to the New Campaign: The United States Army in Operation IRAQI FREEDOM May 2003—January 2005.* Fort Leavenworth, KS: Combat Studies Institute Press, 2008.

Yin, Robert K. *Case Study Research: Design and Methods.* Thousand Oaks, CA: Sage Publications, 2003.

Young, David H. "The Anatomy of an anti-Taliban Uprising." *ForeignPolicy.com,* September 12, 2012. Available at afpak.foreignpolicy.com/posts/2012/09/12/the_anatomy_of_an_anti_taliban_uprising.

———. "Divide and Conquer Negotiations." *ForeignPolicy.com,* February 14, 2012. Available at afpak.foreignpolicy.com/posts/2012/02/14/divide_and_conquer_negotiations.

Zaltman, Gerald, Robert Duncan, and Jonny Holbek. *Innovations and Organizations.* New York: John Wiley and Sons, 1973.

Zambelis, Chris. "Iraqi Insurgent Media Campaign Targets American Audiences." *Terrorism Focus* 4, no. 33 (October 16, 2007). Available at www.jamestown.org/ single/?no_cache=1&tx_ttnews%5Btt_news%5D=4479.

Zanini, Michele, and Sean J. A. Edwards. "The Networking of Terror in the Information Age." In *Networks and Netwars: The Future of Terror, Crime, and Militancy,* edited by John Arquilla and David Ronfeldt, 29–60. Santa Monica, CA: RAND, 2001.

Zedong, Mao. *The Red Book of Guerrilla Warfare.* El Paso, TX: El Paso Norte Press, 2010.

Zoepf, Katherine, and Mudhafer Al-Husaini. "Militants Turn to Small Bombs in Iraq Attacks." *New York Times,* November 14, 2008, A1.

Index

AARs, *see* After action reviews

Adaptation, *see* Afghan insurgency, adaptation by; Iraqi insurgency, adaptation by; Organizational adaptation

Afghan insurgency: civilian casualties, 109, 121–22, 125, 132, 184n214; command, control, and communications, 101–2, 123–24, 125, 136; complexity, 106, 129–30; composition, 97, 98, 106–8, 129–30; constraints, 104–6, 108–9, 132; contract employees, 111, 117; cooperation within, 104, 119–20, 130, 132, 135, 145; divisions within, 98, 100–101, 105, 173–74n27, 186n242; external assistance, 115–20, 121, 134–35, 179n119; foreign fighters, 99, 103, 115, 121, 123, 181n154, 184n205; funds, 111–13, 119, 133–34; future of, 101, 137, 138, 172n8; goals, 99–101, 110, 121, 176n68; group design and culture, 106–10; information flows, 101–2, 130; intelligence gathering, 113–15, 125–26, 134, 180nn136–37; knowledge transfer, 121, 126–28, 137; leadership, 103, 105, 107–8, 121; lessons for Iraqis, 74; materiel and technical resources, 110–15, 133–34; norms, 108–9, 132–33;

organizational inputs, 99–120, 129–35; organizational learning, 125–29, 136–37; organizational outputs, 120–25, 135–36; organizational structure, 104–5, 123; public support, 97–98, 100, 105, 109, 121–22, 130, 171–72n7; recruitment, 100, 107, 116, 173n26, 175n47; rewards, 108; size, 97, 107, 171n6; skills and knowledge, 120–22, 135, 175n43; strengths, 129, 138; tactics, 103–4, 106, 109, 122, 123, 133, 185n221; task performance competency, 122–23, 136; tasks, 103, 109–10, 133; training, 102–4, 123, 128, 131–32, 135, 175n43, 185n219; tribal groups, 97. *See also* Taliban

Afghan insurgency, adaptation by: capacity, 118–19; compared to Iraqi insurgency, 98, 118, 129–38, 142; successful, 98, 129, 136, 138; tactical, 103–4, 122, 123, 133; by Taliban, 99–100

Afghanistan: corruption, 106, 113, 117–18, 119, 176n62, 182n172, 183n195; criminal activity, 99, 117–18, 135, 182n172, 182n182; development projects, 113; ethnic groups, 99, 101; history of conflict, 97, 110; Karzai government, 99, 100, 106, 119, 126; opium trade, 112, 117–18, 119, 134, 179n125, 179n130, 183n194; police, 113, 114, 117, 126, 134,